The Winky-Eyed Jesus and Other Undescribables

Scott M. Wayland

High Adventure Publishers
Tehachapi, California

ISBN-10: 1463645368
ISBN-13: 978-1463645366

Cover design by John Schuler, Prospect Design Studio

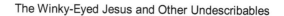

To my father, for giving me a love of adventure. To my mother, for giving me a love of books. To my wife, Jodi, for giving me the love, support and companionship to ride this wild and crazy life.

"The world is a book, and those who do not travel read only one page."

St. Augustine of Hippo

"I don't know how I'd get through this without alcohol."

A road-weary trans-continental
bicyclist on the Colorado/
Kansas frontier

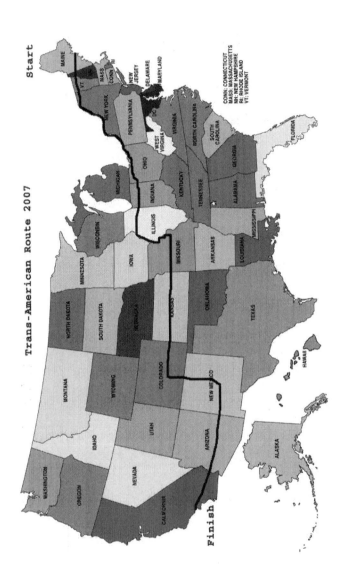

Trans-American Route 2007

Start

Finish

MAINE
VT
MASS
CONN RI
NEW YORK
NEW JERSEY
DELAWARE
MARYLAND
PENNSYLVANIA
OHIO
WEST VIRGINIA
VIRGINIA
NORTH CAROLINA
SOUTH CAROLINA
GEORGIA
FLORIDA
MICHIGAN
INDIANA
KENTUCKY
TENNESSEE
ALABAMA
MISSISSIPPI
ILLINOIS
WISCONSIN
IOWA
MISSOURI
ARKANSAS
LOUISIANA
MINNESOTA
NORTH DAKOTA
SOUTH DAKOTA
NEBRASKA
KANSAS
OKLAHOMA
TEXAS
MONTANA
WYOMING
COLORADO
NEW MEXICO
IDAHO
UTAH
ARIZONA
WASHINGTON
OREGON
NEVADA
CALIFORNIA
HAWAII
ALASKA

CONN: CONNECTICUT
MASS: MASSACHUSETTS
NH: NEW HAMPSHIRE
RI: RHODE ISLAND
VT: VERMONT

6

Contents

Prologue: Making Life Difficult

Part I: The Northeast

Part II: The Midwest

Part III: The West

The Sweet Ache of Desire

I am bitumen's bitch, a slave to the pavement, an addict with a blacktop monkey on his back. The North American plate hangs in all its incomprehensible mass from my rear wheel. Atlas shrugs; I pedal with the reach of a continent trailing from my slowly rotating spokes. A November sky of painful clarity glows like a radiant jewel over my sweating head. "Mojo," my German recumbent bicycle, supports my straining carcass with steady confidence. We're old friends at this point, man and bike joined through the work of days and weeks and months of riding from the Atlantic coast in Maine to this, my penultimate pull towards a mountain pass on the far western edge of the United States. Out of sight, some painful distance above, I will cross the last significant obstacle on my quest to ride from ocean to ocean, to see my home from the seat of a bicycle, always traveling under my own power. I've been pounded by the wind, made ill by flying debris, ravaged by insects, oppressed by the hot, soggy fists of a humid Midwestern summer, climbed in a screaming rage up mountain grades that took every ounce of strength I had and more...over 4,600 miles, over 136,000 feet of climbing through storms and heat, battling boredom, exhaustion, relying on the kindness of strangers, the gods and Saints that look out for wayfarers, the blessing of the American people. I've lived, as Beryl Markham put it in *West with the Night*, a life of "discomfort in such lavish proportions." I've wallowed in road grime, gallons of sweat, my pounding heart and heaving lungs, an aerobic drama that was sometimes easy and sweet, a two-wheeled dance into the heart of everything that matters. I pushed on and dreamed and worked towards a horizon that seemed forever out of reach.

Until now.

I keep these pedals turning. My legs burn with the effort, but it is the sweet sensation of life, the spice of my desire to live fully. How strange in this modern, fully industrialized world of ease and comfort that I find myself yearning for difficulty, striving for the obscure pleasures that only a familiarity with discomfort can bring.

Cottonwoods flare in gold down in the canyon bottoms. Scruffy chaparral covers the slopes hard on the road as I crawl by, hardly breaking four miles per hour. I'm overwhelmed by my need to finish, to gaze at last on the Pacific, to hold my wife, Jodi, in my arms again. But I'm held back, too, disbelieving that the journey is almost over. For so long I've faced another state, another town, another time zone. How could it end? Is it possible? My sweaty hands grip the bars, hold the line. I briefly close my eyes and slip into the trance of give and take, gravity and muscle. The light bleeds through my lids, the bike weaves, I open my eyes again and correct my course. Spin and spinning, my legs, now efficient pistons, respond to my demands, my incessant demands. The ocean is over there, somewhere. I just have to keep moving.

Prologue: Making Life Difficult

"All you need is ignorance and confidence, then success is sure."

Mark Twain

"Beginnings are always messy."

John Galsworthy

Points of No Return

I stared into the glowering eye. The computer mouse lay under my right hand, my right index finger hovering over the left button. On the screen, the arrow sat firmly on the "Buy" for a one-way plane ticket to Bar Harbor, Maine, USA. No refunds allowed. The cheapest ticket I could find. An eight hour layover in Boston, midnight to eight am. One change of plane in Texas, another in Boston. The idea was to maroon myself on the far side of the continent, a stranger in a strange land, and fight my way home. I would do battle with all manner of weird, savage people, navigate alien cultures, sail the American states in a ragged lightning bolt from the Northeast to the Southwest. I'd ridden Mojo over 1,500 miles in the preceding months. Besides a big ride to Vegas with Jodi, I'd pedaled a good chunk of the California coast and done regular training rides, too. I was physically ready, and I had the time off from my teaching post at the college. Although she was dreading the impending separation, Jodi was prepared to see me off on this quixotic mid-life madness. We both understood that this was *something I had to do.* Ever since my mid-teens, I've had a sense that life is short, that I need to pack it with vital, challenging experiences. From that early age I've had a surging urgency within that tells us we've got no time to waste. Still, I hesitated over my purchase. My finger twitched, refused to move down onto the mouse. My heart was pounding. I felt lightheaded, swooning, giddy, lost. *Press the button, for Christ's sake!*

Getting to this point had not been easy. Ever since we "decided" that I would do the ride solo, we had a strained undercurrent between us. Jodi knew I had to go, understood my motivation, was happy with all the activities in her life, but there was this beast between us, the unborn child of the tour that occupied my energies, my thoughts, my dreams. I wasn't really home. I was long gone. Who was this tall fellow stalking the rooms of our house? I inhabited a strange limbo, a place walled in by the past and the future, the force of years of planning and the keen edge of anticipation. I went about my daily activities, moving, for the most part, as if nothing were different, nothing had changed. And nothing *had* changed. The dishes still needed to be cleaned and put away, the animals fed, the floor swept. I did these things as I had always done them. Take out the kibbles, pour them noisily into the stainless steel bowl while Django sits nearby with sharp-eyed intensity. He knows in every cell of his body what this ritual is about.

But with each action, each moment that slipped into the past, I was one moment closer to departure. Briefly, just briefly, I would forget what was hanging over me, the long flight and unthinkable return. I knew that I had to do this AA style, one day at a time, but still the enormity of it all squatted in my consciousness like a grinning water buffalo, 2,000 pounds of dark muscle that would not be denied, the glinting black eyes and sweep of horn. I knew a little about the men who hunted this most dangerous kind of animal, the Cape buffalo in Africa, usually found in deep thickets where it could charge without notice. The hunter, when faced with the on-rushing animal, had no time for fear—if he wanted to live. He simply had to *get busy*.

So the antidote to anxiety is action. True enough. I found, at this stage, however, that most of my business in preparing for the tour was over. My bags were packed, the bike soon to be shipped. I had too much time on my hands. *Let's get this damn freak show on the road, shall we?* But the plane would leave when it would, and I could not hurry it. I hung in the margins between sunrise and sunset, between home and away. Jodi said that I had been "gone for months."

Maybe. This condition sat in my gut like a poorly digested piece of potato. *Please, dear ghost, show me the shadow of bicycle tours yet to come.* I didn't know, didn't want to know. The point is in the discovery, the slow unveiling of the mystery, the epiphanies and revelations. Everett Ruess, an adventurous young man who vanished in the Four Corners region early in the last century, said, "I am always being overwhelmed. I require it to sustain life." That young man knew his religion. You can't be overwhelmed if you know exactly what's coming. The unknown is the voltage of life. Sometimes we must be strapped to that table and lifted up into the storm and lightning above. What species of monster was this? I was the monster, the gargoyle squatting on the castle wall, waiting, waiting...waiting. Neither in nor out, I hung on the edge.

I took a deep breath and let my finger fall onto the cool, yielding plastic--"Thank you for your purchase!" I wiped the sweat from my hand and looked away from the screen.

*   *   *

The evolution of this trip had been a long affair, hatched first in the primordial slop of our touring-addled brains years ago. From the beginning, this was to be a tandem sojourn, Jodi and I and the faithful hound, Django, riding across the country, having a great big old adventure. But the direction of evolution cannot be predicted, and so it was with my trans-continental dreams.

Unlike many long distance cyclists, I am married, with a home, a job, settled in some very conventional ways. Not a student between colleges or fresh off the stage with a newly minted degree, not hanging in the abyss between jobs or careers, what the hell was I doing taking off for three to four months—by myself? How does such a thing happen? Had I been served with divorce papers, or was that my desire upon my return? Fortunately, none of these applied, but the path was not without its obstacles, pot holes, flat tires and headwinds.

Jodi's career as a holistic nutritional consultant had been growing like a summer squash on steroids. Besides advancing her education beyond a basic master's, she was doing a lot of writing for Bauman College and working closely with its founder and her mentor, Dr. Ed Bauman. Dr. Bauman offered to pay for her advancing education and asked that she help in writing a book and articles for the college. Like a mafia don, he'd made an offer she couldn't refuse. And she loved it. She's good at what she does and wanted to develop her knowledge and connections. She simply did not want to leave while everything was developing so wonderfully. Who could blame her? But what about the tour, our journey? She said that I should go alone. Hmmm.... Well, okay, I could do that, I guess.

But simple sounding resolutions are rarely so. When I began obsessing about the trip, planning, posting questions online, I could feel Jodi getting upset as the reality of our separation began to set in. Her natural resentment at my departure, envy at my impending adventure, home duties she would have to face mostly on her own while I was out having "fun"—all these came boiling to the surface on more than one occasion. She would be in tears, I, in mute anxiety, wondering, in my typical, klutzy male fashion, how to deal with this overflow of emotions.

At one point, I decided that I would not do the long ride. I'd do something shorter, plan a couple of trips, one solo, one with Jodi. That would be great, of course. I could live with that. Compromise, right? A good thing. But a splinter was lodged in my brain, festering. I'd dumped a dream. Something in me, deep inside, needed to try this, no matter the risk of failure. I walked with Django on the steep mountainside above our home and stared out over the valley. *Can I let this go? Will my life be complete? Can Jodi and I work through this?* After all the planning, time invested so I could take a leave of absence from work, I just couldn't let go.

Ever since becoming a mountaineer and rock climber in my mid-teens, I've been drawn to big dreams and plans, adventures that pushed me in deep, meaningful ways.

El Capitan, Half Dome, peaks in the USA and Canada, I found the best moments of my life, times of such burning intensity and joy that I cannot imagine a life without them. And many of these times were with Jodi. But I never did take that really big expedition to the Himalayas or the Andes. I never felt what it was like to push over 20,000 ft. In a way, that particular kind of dream had morphed into this continental crossing, a ride of ridiculous length and scope. As Werner Herzog, author of *Annapurna*, said, "There are other Annapurnas in the lives of men." I will never climb an 8,000 meter peak, but this ride could be *my* Annapurana. I could only hope that I had the good luck, physical attributes and determination to see it through, although I wanted to keep my fingers and toes, appendages lost to Herzog after he achieved the summit of his desires.

So I went back to Jodi and said, "I don't think I can give this up. I need to ride across the country." She understood, but that understanding came with pain, the knowledge of a separation longer than we had ever known, and this pain and worry were mine, too. I didn't shrug off her concerns easily and delight in my own "escape." Besides some physical breakdown that would nullify my dream, my greatest worry was leaving her, the woman of my life. I imagined moments, stopped in the middle of an Iowa cornfield, really needing her by my side, wanting her input, intelligence and good sense of humor. I suspected that such times would provide genuine challenges, maybe the toughest. I tried to rationalize my feelings and wondered if such contortions worked for Jodi: *It's ONLY a few months-- not the rest of our lives. We can both work through this...blah, blah, blah.*

But still the emotions sat there, staring back at us, creatures often deaf to the ranting of our rational selves. As Jodi has taught me, however, we have to let the feelings run their course. We would be okay. We just had to let our emotional side get used to the idea.

July 2006

I pedaled intently through the backstreets of Van Nuys, California, wasteland of the San Fernando Valley, porn capital of the world. The usual beige dome of heat cursed us all as I worked through the gears, concentrating on how the bike handled. I strained my imagination. A year hence, a thousand miles into the journey, would this be the best machine? Pressure points? Balance? Feel? Soul? The wondrous Teutonic two-wheeler carried me smoothly: the HP Velotechnik Street Machine Gte. Full suspension, disc brakes, the BMW touring sedan of bicycles. Yeah, a nice ride all right. I hoped this test would help me decide. Down the road, airplanes roared and grumbled along acres of tarmac. Nondescript businesses, stucco and dark glass, lined my route, but my concentration was inward. *Was this the one?*

I quickly caught up to a young man working the same street on a BMX bicycle, the typically tiny frame, seat too low, knees churning up high nearly cuffing his chin, baggy denim shorts, loose shirt and jaunty black cap tilted up high on his forehead. "Hey, man," he called out, "that's a coool bike!" I liked his smile, and we rode along together as I told him my plans.

"I think this is the bike I'm going to ride across the country."

"Really?"

"Yes."

"By yourself?"

"Yeah."

"Wow, man. That's *crazy*! What if something

happens?"

His question stayed with me a long time: What if something happened? Indeed, what if? He voiced a typical concern for my safety, perhaps my sanity, but he said more than he knew or intended. What if something happened? That was precisely the point. I wanted, needed, craved the happening of things. I wanted to taste and feel and smell, to throw myself across the miles and into the life and land and people of my country—although that possessive pronoun is a strange one in this context. *My* country? Mine? I own it? Or does it own me? Most of it was a blank to me beyond scrambled images gleaned from books and movies. I had no comfortable sense of ownership as I might have with my shoes or an old knife my father had given me. No, I needed to invest myself in the landscape of America to be part of it, to belong to it more fully. Questions, risks, dangers lurked across this dark continent. Me? Alone? On a weird bicycle? What if something happened? Something sure as hell better happen or I'm asking for my money back.

This is a strange longing. Modern day penitents we are, chained to our bicycles to expatiate sins of lethargy and sloth, of ignorance. What other than a religious fervor drives us? When you see us on the road, burdened by bags heavy with gear, nothing to justify our struggles but vague romantic dreams, what do you think? Do you curse the fact that we occupy the road? Do you, somehow, wish you could join us? You could do worse than be a "swinger of birches," as Frost put it. What else is the long-distance cyclist but a child swinging from branches—on a continental scale? Swing on, brothers and sisters! Yelp your yawps to the heavens and scream in crazy joy down the mountain passes. In four billion years the sun will expand to toast this spinning rock, and then what will anything matter? No time for vast, slow empires, no time. You need no charger for this chariot. A sack of food and foot to the pedals will take you where you need to go. Snag a dream with taut sinews and heave that unwilling carcass into the journey.

On my return to the bike shop, I knew that this rare recumbent bicycle would be my chosen steed, this odd amalgam of wires and tubes, chain and rubber. Now all that remained was the long wait until I left on the flight bound for Bar Harbor, Maine—that...and riding thousands of miles by myself. Someone had to do it. I churned through the hot, sticky afternoon and felt a slight tightening in my stomach. This was a big step, a serious monetary commitment on the path to my dream. I would later christen the bike, "Mojo" to signify the energy and spirit needed for the ride. His name is an acronym, too, for "more jo', more java, more *coffee*"—a good thing. Mojo and I together would face down the miles. In my dreams we would perch on one side of the country and then on the other and drink deeply the experience in between. I made the final arrangements for how I would appoint the bike.

Then I waited for something to happen.

The Love of Maps

The road-smitten, the hikers and cyclists, the world wanderers and compulsive wayfarers know the condition, this addiction to maps, the unquenchable thirst for topographical knowledge. We spread out these magical sheets of paper and gaze into their meandering lines, the town sites and rail lines, rivers, canyons, that steep ridge clearly indicated by closely packed contour lines. At points familiar we can rest our fingers and say, "Ah, yes, I know that turn!" Perhaps it was a corner in Winslow, Arizona, where a fine young thing in a flat bed gave us a good once over—don't leave!—as we stood with a dusty pack and three weeks of beard hanging in the breeze.

In grade school a teacher whose name I cannot recall but whose lesson rings on showed me how to read maps, especially the topographical variety. These were special, the Holy Grails of the cartographer's craft. With the right imagination you could *see* where the land went up or down and get a sense for its steepness. With a compass and a little trigonometry you could find your location—all without a satellite or battery powered gizmo. Traveling often in the mountains of western North America, I have rarely needed a compass—maps, yes—but not often a compass. By simply identifying the significant landmarks, usually an easy task with land forms like major peaks and rivers, I could always orient myself. Once, however, I would have been truly lost without that little magnetic device.

Jodi and I arrived at road's end somewhere in the vicinity of Mt. Adams in Washington State, a heavily glaciated peak and third highest in the Cascades at over 12,000 ft., but there, standing in the thick fog, we could have been anywhere. Dark, dank conifers vanished in silence into the snow and mist. Visibility was less than fifty yards. Where was the north face of this grand peak we hoped to scale? *The map says it's there, right over...there?* Out with the compass, set the map in the proper direction, set a heading from the map to the base of the Adams Glacier, start hiking. We took turns leading up through the snow and fog, always focused on the needle, instrument flying on faith and physics. We broke from the trees, and suddenly we could see even less-- whiteout, a pale, fuzzy realm without corners, horizons or depth. Shortly after entering this world, we set up camp in a light drizzle and hoped for the best. The next morning, the clouds lifted just enough for us to see the icy toe of the glacier, right where it was supposed to be. A day later we would stand on the summit, alone on an ice cap above the clouds, first climbers up that season. The day after getting down, the clouds locked in again and it rained for over a week.

As a cyclist, I am no less fascinated by what maps can tell me, the dreams they inspire. This is a very old impulse shared by the great names of history. What must it have been like to have those old maps, the ones marked "Terra Incognita"? In one sense, thankfully, until we ourselves have been there, each map represents a sense of the unknown because the maps cannot tell us everything. Korzybski said that the "map is not the territory," and he was right. As a thoroughly modern person with some knowledge of the sciences, history, geography, I *know* that there be not dragons yonder, not real dragons, anyway. Now, dragons as metaphor, that's another story altogether.

This suggested, implied world of the maps is what keeps us coming back. They can imply, tease, lift a veil to reveal a hint of another world. *What is that really like? Is she all insinuation or the fulfillment of my desires?* The maps lead us to places both outward and inward. When we seek to cross continents, then this map business takes on ever deeper shades of meaning. Once, while walking down a hallway on my campus, I came across a rather large map of the United States, perhaps five or six feet across. This shape, with its odd bulges, dangling appendages, and disembodied lumps, has been so thoroughly burned into my brain that I practically cease to notice it while, paradoxically, it has taken on a sort of concrete life of its own. *My country, my people.* What? How could this be? What are these strange lines? How does California become Nevada? Iowa become Missouri? We come to see the cartographer's product in a strange light once it has been hammered over by the forces of politics, wars, disease and migrations. Occasionally, in human time, geology plays a noticeable role, obliterating an island or blocking a river. So I stared in wonder and disbelief at this construct of consciousness, generations of brooding and striving, taking and building that carried it at last to this sprawling map and my befuddled eyes tracing a line I hoped to cycle, mile upon mile--Maine, New Hampshire, Vermont, New York, Pennsylvania, Ohio, Indiana, Illinois, Iowa, Missouri, Kansas, Colorado, New Mexico, Arizona, and home, my Ithaca, Tehachapi, California.

To make this journey possible, I needed maps, lots of maps. The most important of these have been produced by Adventure Cycling Association, an organization out of Missoula, Montana, dedicated to promoting bicycle travel. I hoped to follow a goodly slice of its "Northern Tier" route as far as Muscatine, Iowa. Then I would take the "Great Rivers Route" until I could connect with the famed "Katy Trail" of Missouri, over two hundred miles of car-free bliss cutting across the center of the state. From the end of the Katy Trail, I patched my own route to get to Manhattan, Kansas, to visit my nephew who was attending vet school there. Then I would connect with the "TransAmerica" route, which I would follow using AAA road maps as the route is a simple, straight shot into Colorado. Then my own route finding would lead me through New Mexico and Arizona. At the Arizona border, Adventure Cycling's "Southern Tier" route would carry me to the Pacific at San Diego. The last leg, if I had the legs for it, would take me north up the "Pacific Coast Route" to Ventura and east over the mountains and back to home.

Every day I pulled out one of my maps and studied, tried to imagine what I would find, the people I would meet. Would the natives be friendly? Would I be able to handle their strange customs? What would happen if one of them insisted I marry his daughter or face a slow death? Would he understand that I was already married and could only handle one wife at a time? Would I have to eat the raw organs of some unknown beast? Would the chief take MasterCard? I stared at the maps and wondered.

A Training Day

Sometimes the stars align, the winds shift, and the patron saint of cyclists smiles down upon us. This ride was one such occasion. I had a free day to myself before I wanted to be at my mother's place in Carson City, Nevada, to visit and help her pack for the big move. She was leaving her home of the last ten years, the place where my father had died. On the forested Sierra crest visible from her front door, we had scattered his ashes. She liked to look up and see that place and think of him, although she was no longer physically capable of walking to the crag where we had set free the dust of his body on the clear mountain breezes.

So this trip had some meaning beyond the usual good times I found in the peaks and valleys of the East Side. This was one of my last trips up to Carson City to visit her there and stay in the house where I last knew my father.

Although I had strained mightily on a three day tour into the mountains with Jodi, I was keen to get in one more classic ride on the way north, so I left Jodi at Pearsonville and drove up through the hot desert afternoon--strangely hot for April 2nd, the low 90's down in Creosote Country. The warm weather and good forecast held promise for excellent conditions up high where I wanted to ride, the Jeffrey pine and sagebrush volcanic lands north-east of Mammoth. The cycling gods blessed my bittersweet journey, and I was given a day to cherish.

The night before was frosty cold at 7,000 ft. I huddled in my bag as long as I could, but the growing day would not be put off. I turned on the heater in the van and got dressed, brewed coffee. Clad in a down jacket and thick polar fleece pants, I went for a walk in the bright April dawn. The Sierras were transcendent in their winter white, gullies, ridges, gleaming craggy crests of snow and rock. From a high knoll, I could see the White Mountains, too. A typically dry range, this time it held a snowy mantle and lived up to its name. The sun climbed and warmed me. Finally, it was time to pack and drive to the start of the ride. In short order, I pulled into the June Lake turn-off and parked at a deserted visitor center.

I extricated the HP Velo Street Machine from the van and busied myself with dressing, collecting gear, applying sunscreen--the habitual stations of the cross for all my rides. To the west, a snow-plastered Ritter Range pierced the blue sky. In the parking lot, I stood in fantastic warmth. The heat of the sun cut through the high, cool air.

My route was simple: From the first (southern) June Lake turn-off, head north on Hwy 395 (huge shoulder/light traffic) to Hwy 120 and take that east to Sagehen Summit, over 8,000 ft. high. From the summit, drop back to 395, jog north to the other end of the June Lake Loop Rd, and follow that back to my vehicle--the one that burns petroleum.

What transpired was a strenuous joy of effort and solitude, cycling nirvana. The smooth shoulder of 395 carried me quickly down the few miles to 120. Once I left the main north-south route, I left virtually everyone behind. Thirty five, forty minutes at a stretch with not another soul on the road. I paused frequently for pictures and wide-eyed gaping. I stood in the middle of the road and didn't give a damn. Mono Lake mirrored the sky. Distant ranges, rank upon rank, faded into silences unexplored. The bike clicked and whirred and carried me upward through a landscape painted by Salvador Dali: stout Jeffrey pines jutted from a light gray sea of pumice spread beneath soaring cinder cones ringed by broken teeth of harder rock. I was grateful for this smoothly paved trail through an otherwise impossible country. A cyclist hitting the shoulder here would go down in an instant. Although there might be some wisdom to the adage that leaving the path is the way to find one's path, it's bad advice for pedal-powered pilgrims in this neck of the woods.

Too quickly I reached the summit and drank in once again the panorama of my favorite place in the world, my one true home. *Okay, mate, down it is.* The descent was hampered by cross and headwinds, but even so, I arrived at the base in minutes, concluding a pitch that had taken me over an hour to climb. I was struck yet again by the strange bi-polar disorder of bi-cycle travel, how one aspect can require so much effort, so much muscle-burning, soul-searching struggle, while the other is simple as sin. Here's the rub: Do we need the pain in order to enjoy the pleasure of surrender to gravity's insistent desire? If the path to enlightenment is as difficult to walk as a razor's edge, can it be accomplished with spoked wheels and a chain? The philosophy of kinetics does not yield easy answers, especially when the philosopher is clipped to an HP Velotechnik Street Machine Gte and hurtling downward through Dante's Vulcan playground. *No time for deep thoughts, Captain. Hold your line, dodge the dragons, and flee these infernal regions! Down, down, down...*

Jog right on 395, left on the Loop, into the snowy peaks and granite gaps. Switzerland? Norway? This Range of Light folded me into it arms and held tight, a gentle climb and cruise lakeside, a safe passage through avalanche-prone narrows, precipitous alps draped in snow looming impossibly high. Warm sun and cool winds swirled across faceted lakes and flashing cascades...and I was virtually alone. Everything was shut down--too little snow for skiing, too early for the swarms of summer campers that infest this area from June through August. Chalets and motels stood empty. Vacancy signs hung everywhere. A lone dog wandered down the road.

I, however, was slapped with the steepest climbing of the day, hard, ornery rollers that tested what was left of my reserves. I took the signed bike route, which avoids the main hamlet of June Lake but, of course, offers more climbing. Still, the views were grand, the road empty. Then the hills gave up, checked out--TKO, recumbent cyclist. I zipped down the last hill and so back to where I began.

I camped out in the sage and enjoyed a fine German lager while clouds danced on the highest summits. It's not just me, I don't think, but hasn't the St. Pauli Girl gotten hotter over the years, retooled with a bit of the *Cosmo* aesthetic? Not that I mind, certainly not. Still, some deep thoughts are worth considering after the riding is done.

Life without Motors

For those of the right frame of mind, the human-powered touring life has immense appeal. It is, at last, a deeply meaningful mode of travel because one earns the experience in a very personal, physical way. A kind of *Protestant work ethic* for the tourist, relying on human power pays dividends unavailable, perhaps even unimaginable to those dependent on motors and combustion to see the world. Morally superior? Not in my view, especially since we are all dependent on petroleum and its discontents to one degree or another. So is the use of petroleum a kind of moral failing, one to which we are all party? Extreme? Perhaps—but not too far a stretch when we consider all the ills the use of petroleum brings us. We love the toys and power that oil makes possible, but our affair with the slimy ooze comes at a price. Environmental concerns aside, my point here is how that reliance affects the traveler.

I am no saint. I, too, wear the dripping oily "P" on my shoulder. But in my explorations, I've found that to leave the car, bus, train, plane, moped, rocket ship behind is to get more from my traveling experience. I feel the land, smell, taste the air, encounter the people in a way that is not possible when sealed up in a car. I can't speed through, ignorant of the topography, the heat, the cold and wind. Besides the factual knowledge of the places we explore, the main purpose is the emotional landscape created by the new places and people. Emotions are called "feelings" because they are physical responses. The more physical our relation to experiences, the deeper, more lasting the emotions, the more valuable, on a personal level, our attainments. On May 14th, 2005, Didier Desalle, flying a French Eurocopter AS350 B3, landed on the summit of Mt. Everest. While this was no doubt a thrill for Desalle and a meaningful aeronautical achievement, how can attaining the summit in this fashion compare to the experience of fighting up from the base, relying on one's nerve and muscle?

Contrast the Eurocopter adventure with that of Goran Kropp, a Swedish mountaineer. The helicopter flight required a few minutes noisy climbing from the base, about four minutes on top, then—zoom—back to base. Been there, done that. Kropp, however, had a different vision for his ascent of Mt. Everest. His book, *My Everest Odyssey*, tells the epic tale of a journey that sets the adventure bar to a new standard, one yet to be repeated or equaled. Riding a stout mountain bike with a customized trailer packed with all his mountaineering gear and, he hoped, food enough for the hike and climb, Kropp set off from his home in Stockholm, Sweden, pedaled across Europe and Asia to Nepal. Once he had ridden as far as possible, Kropp loaded his food and gear onto his back (a burden well in excess of one hundred pounds), marched into Everest and proceeded to climb it without oxygen--*solo*. He did accept some food from another expedition at one point after his first summit attempt failed, but after his subsequent success, he hiked back out, loaded up the bike, and pedaled home to Sweden. The helicopter flight set a new record, the ultimate record, for a high altitude landing, but the achievement was more about the flying, the equipment and engineering than the mountain or the land or the people of the region. No doubt, the flight had intense meaning for the pilot, and he has made some high altitude rescues of climbers, so the technology has a genuine human value, but if your goal is a lasting travel experience, an opportunity to learn about yourself, different cultures and places, which ascent of Everest provides the best means? "There is more to life than increasing its speed," said Ghandi.

Inspiration

I ponder often on what keeps me motivated, what inspires all of us to get out there and live life intensely. I was blessed by a father who took me into the woods when I was young, hunting and hiking. While most of the other hunters who used the ranch where we hunted would storm off in their 4X4's, Dad and I would rise at 4am, quietly pack our light day packs—he used to love those chewy, layered raisin cookies—shoulder our rifles, and slip off into the fog shrouded forest. The early, groggy feelings, the growing sense of excitement at the possibility of finding a deer or wild boar, the long, quiet walks through the oaks and tall grasses all filled me with a sense of wonder and connection with the outdoors that has never left me. We almost never got anything, though there were some exceptions, of course. The greater point was in the ritual, in spending time together, in blending into those grand and rugged hills.

Like an addict, I kept upping the dosage of my outdoor activities, and by the age of fifteen, I was hooked on rock climbing and mountaineering, but before that I had sampled some cycling in my local area. Once, at about the age of twelve or thirteen, a handful of us strapped sleeping bags to our bikes and pedaled many miles away, spent the night camped in the dunes by the Pacific, and pedaled home. That freedom and sense of power were important lessons for me. Before we could drive, we could ride, and *look how far we could go*. Now, I'd rather pedal than drive if I can help it. I've entered my second childhood, it seems, and none too soon. H. G. Wells said, "Every time I see an adult on a bicycle, I no longer despair for the future of the human race." Damn straight, old man. When gas is $40 a gallon, many more of us will rediscover the joys of the bicycle.

I did a few other overnight bicycle tours in my twenties, and once rode part of the Oregon and California coast but failed at my tour due to knee problems. I liked the idea of human power. I hiked and climbed all over the western US and Canada, and on one long drive up Hwy 395 just north of Susanville and headed for Canada, we passed a lone cyclist. There in the vast basin of sage and juniper was a single, solitary young man, a lean figure of muscle and sinew, baggy shirt and shorts flapping in the wind, his bike fully loaded with panniers front and rear. I found something so pure and fantastic about this unknown cyclist. He was up out of the saddle and pulling for glory, no motor, no sag wagon, just the dry wind and scent of sage to fuel his dream.

That image never left me, and I have since had the joys and pains of riding that same country and other wild, remote parts of the western states. The promise of his example has held true for me time and again. I am so grateful to have a spirit and body that allows me the privilege of such travel. To the sedentary public, our struggles often seem foolish, crazy. Why bother? *Because it is a totally, thoroughly, brilliantly transcendent experience.* The Mahayana of the bicycle takes the spirit where it would not otherwise go, from painful depths of exhaustion to sublime peaks, often, of course, at the same moment. That's it, that moment when effort and awareness and the flow of life combine in a timeless, electric current. This is not mediated, modulated, pixelated, *virtual* experience. This is life, straight up in a dirty glass, three fingers deep and burning down your throat.

Recently, while strapped into one of my smog-belching boxes, I caught a glimpse of another touring cyclist, in my own town of all places. Again, a solitary male, bike fully loaded, cut a sharp turn and cranked for the big valley to the west. A lucky bloke, that one. We were in an unusually cool spell for June. I knew what he was going through, the great expectation of the big descent, the satisfaction at having broken another pass. Ride well, brother.

I wondered who else on the road that day really *got*

what he was doing. Not many. Perhaps that is part of the appeal. Cycle tourists travel on the fringes, the edges of a thoroughly motorized society. Still, many, many people are interested and inspired, even if they themselves will never attempt a long, human powered journey. And this is good. It gives me hope.

Taming of the Screw

     I had too much time to imagine how things would go on the TransAm. It was months away, with lots of living to do between now and then, but I kept jumping ahead to the day when I would board the plane. I thought about a joke made at The Bard's expense--about "sticking your courage to the screwing place." The actual line, from Macbeth, reads: "Screw your courage to the sticking place." The good lady was inspiring her husband to get busy and kill all the nobles and guards in the castle so that he might take the throne. The inversion of the expression, however, has some interesting implications, ones that climbers, military personnel, and various others can appreciate, even adolescent cyclists.

     We can, if we dream ourselves into the right frame of mind, attempt some very impressive deeds. But if our luck is bad or our preparation inadequate, this mustering of courage can put us into desperate circumstances, screwing places, i.e., places where we get screwed, whacked, hammered, shown who the REAL daddy is. Arctic explorers (wasn't one of them named Scott?), Everest climbers, skate boarders jamming rad flips down concrete steps—all of us can find ourselves in "Oh, shit" moments when our reaches have exceeded our grasps, when nerve alone was not enough or too much. This, of course, was Macbeth's problem, too. Once the spot is in, there's no getting it out.

     Any seasoned adventurer can provide a litany of such experiences, and these tales form the spice of life, the narratives for late nights around the campfire. Since I am here to write these words, I have always been able to escape the ultimate price. I have a number of nerve-shredding tales from my years climbing and some from cycling, too: I was twelve, and I left my friend Danny's house high on a hill above my home. The rain was pouring down, the streets slick, treacherous, but home was close, just a wee bit down this steep hill—*I'll be home in no time. No worries*. I jumped onto my trusty three speed—a cool lime green number my father had cobbled together with a Sturmy-Archer hub, drop bars, hand brakes, and nice, shiny, smooth, plated rims. I loved that bike. So with the cavalier courage of youth, I pushed off. Faster, faster, and faster still into the stinging rain I plunged, a fine rooster tail of water flinging off my rear tire, splashing my back. *It's time to slow down now. Let's put on these brakes.* Nothing. A truly sickening nothing. Where there should have been a satisfying resistance, a rubbing or squeaking sound, there was just the increasing rush of the air across my unhelmeted head and the more painful sting of the rain. The grade only got steeper.

My mind, a rat on crack and cornered by a cobra, scrambled about for solutions. There was the turn. *Okay, okay, you can stop this thing, right? Drag a foot? Run it out to the bottom? Crap, not that, too much cross traffic. Those bushes? Just ram this rig into a hedge? Drag my foot? Too fast, too fast. I'll just try to make my turn. When the road levels out, I'll drag a foot.*

My eyes flooded, my heart pounding, slippery fingers still bearing down on the levers, I leaned into the corner—smack into a station wagon that had just pulled up to the intersection. Thump! Crunch of steel, snapping spokes, a scream—I was airborne, free from earthly restraint and somersaulting over the wagon. Then, in an unplanned move that would have done Buster Keaton or Jackie Chan proud, I landed on my feet on the opposite side of the car. A 10! Too shaken to truly stick the landing, I sagged to my knees, a quaking, terrified kid too lucky for words.

The driver, an equally terrified woman, burst from the car to see how I was doing. "Oh, my God! Oh, my God! Are you all right?" I stood up on uncertain legs and surveyed my frame. I was fine. Everything bent in the proper direction. No colorful fluids issued from fresh openings. I walked gingerly around the front of the wagon to survey the damage. I had come in at a sharp angle and hit the side just ahead of the front door. There was a dent in the door, and a strip of plated window trim was bent back. The front wheel of my bike was "potato-chipped," one of the pedals was bent terribly--but I wasn't. The woman followed me home the couple of hundred yards to my door as I dragged my broken bike through the rain.

I never made that mistake again.

So we experiment, take risks, fail, and get back on to try again. When I got off that plane in Bar Harbor, would I be pushing off a hill, only limp brakes and polished rims to stop my fall? Over thirty years of experience between then and now told me no, but there was always that thread of doubt. Sometimes I tug at this thread, worry the suture of uncertainty. Pull too hard, and the wounds can open up, the garment unravel. Sometimes it's best to ignore it. Or take a razor and cut it free.

Launch or Hurl?

My last day before lift-off was spent cleaning house, keeping busy. The humming birds swarmed around the property, the day perfectly sweet, a nice cool spell after weeks of heat. Being August, of course, it wouldn't last, but I'd take this parting gift from the weather gods, a foretaste of autumn. Already I was beginning to sense a change in the quality of light, even if it was more feeling than fact. When I returned, we would be fully into another season, closing in on winter. The other morning I stepped out before the sun had risen—an alarm clock gift in the form of two pounds of psychotic kitty—only to see Orion for the first time dominating the eastern horizon. Normally I would be gearing up for classes, reviewing rosters, class notes, plotting tactics and strategies for the coming semester. But little was normal this time.

I was reminded of my internal state when I faced the vertical face of El Capitan in Yosemite. I was just eighteen, hardly needing to shave, and I camped with new friends in The Valley's infamous Camp 4. El Cap, as we called it, loomed in ways that are hard for the non-climber to imagine. The casual tourist looks up and thinks: Wow, that's big. The climber poised for an ascent staggers about with a gut full of acid roiling and boiling within. He's calm and cool to his mates, but inside he's raging, plotting, striving to anticipate what he'll need to do, how to handle the challenges and fear, doing everything he can to keep the uncertainty under control. *You've just got to step up and do it*. How did Goethe put it? "Boldness has genius in it"? Good words to remember when we challenge ourselves. Plot, plan, train, anticipate, then take the leap. Although there can be risk in the leap, the risk of the leap not taken is the greater.

Preparing, devising, executing an expedition like this is a convoluted undertaking. Somewhere, somehow, the seed germinates in your head, and you decide that, yeah, *I've simply GOT to do that.* But between thinking and doing there often exists a fearsome chasm. It's one thing to think about having sex with a squadron of super models. It's something else to git 'er done. A full life means seeing these things through.

But now, at long last, the game was afoot. Tomorrow I would stand on the eastern edge of the frontier. What strange creatures and customs would I find? The natives friendly or hostile? The adventure would tell.

Part I: The Northeast

"New England has a harsh climate, a barren soil, a rough and stormy coast, and yet we love it...."

Henry Cabot Lodge

"I [pedaled a *really cool* recumbent bicycle] to the woods because I wished to live deliberately, to front only the essential facts of life, and see if I could not learn what it had to teach, and not, when I came to die, discover that I had not lived."

Henry David Thoreau

"[C]ontinuous cycling is productive of a superfluity of exhilaration."

Thomas Stevens (1887)
The first man to pedal across the
USA and around the world

Departure

A powerful undertow of anxiety, sadness and fear pulled against our spirits during these last hours together. The unspoken possibility was that something terrible would happen, that these hours would be our last—not just for a few months—but forever. What the hell was I doing? Simultaneously I was excited, edgy, ready to jump into that plane and get started. I was a tangle of barely corked emotions, and I knew Jodi felt the same. I held her tight and memorized the feel of her body against mine. We would talk, but her touch would be only a memory for thousands of miles.

Bound in knots of anticipation, I paced the house in the hours before Jodi drove me to the airport. I'd flown only two or three times in the last twenty years, so this first phase of the trek felt like a big undertaking. And I had never seen the Atlantic or touched our eastern shore, that other side of this continental country. My panniers were packed, wedged into a massive duffle that I'd check and schlep from terminal to terminal. I had a carry-on consisting of my seat bag with a shoulder strap and sleeping pad for that eight hour layover in Boston. I had some food, a water bottle, my camera and mp3 player, a journal, a book, a sweater and the clothes on my body. All the other gear was crammed artfully into the duffle. Mojo was already in Bar Harbor, packed in a box, waiting for our reunion. I kept looking at my watch.

The three of us—Django clipped into the back seat— slipped out of the Tehachapi Mountains and into the vast Mojave desert, thousands of square miles of creosote bushes, sand, dust, rocks, trailers rotting in the sun. Here and there a twisted Joshua Tree broke the botanical monotony. The shimmering highway between Mojave and Lancaster shot like an inflamed nerve towards L.A. as we turned on the radio, checking for traffic problems. We didn't have much to say at this point. Jodi drove while I watched the parched land roll by. For weeks I'd been thinking I didn't want a cell phone, tired as I was of spending money. Besides, what did people do twenty years ago? But as we entered Lancaster, I started to have second thoughts. The words in an email from my friend Carol echoed in my head: "TAKE THE PHONE!" I imagined myself, leg broken, lying in a ditch forty miles from nowhere, cursing myself for not having this most common of modern devices. We stopped in Lancaster at a Verizon outlet to get a phone.

At last we climbed and descended into the Los Angeles basin, smoggy angels lost in the wilds of pavement and concrete, strip malls and super highways in some places *twelve lanes wide*, and still these could seize up, regular infarctions of traffic, millions of motors idling in quiet desperation, heat and frustration rising in waves into a tarnished sky. We entered the labyrinth early enough to avoid the beast of gridlock and soon, too soon, finally—*is-this-really-happening?*—Jodi stopped in front of my terminal, the end, as always a beginning, too. "So, this is it," I said, master of the obvious.

"Yeah," Jodi said, her voice constrained, a rim of tears in her eyes. *Get this over with, do it, now*. I kissed her and looked into those eyes that so often mirrored my own.

"I love you. I'll call you when I get to Bar Harbor." I leaned back between the seats and gave Django a kiss on his furry forehead, grabbed my bags, and stepped out into the blinding Burbank, California, sun. In our purple Subaru, Jodi and Django eased into the traffic and vanished, back into the maze. Suppressing a tight feeling in my throat—*get a grip, Scotty*—I hoisted my bulging duffle and staggered into the building. In the back of my mind was the knowledge that I was going to be pedaling this load—and more—across the country. My stomach tightened at the thought.

Hundreds of people milled about, bags over shoulders, bags hanging heavily in tired hands, bags on wheels rumbling like tiny wagons behind their owners. I did a sort of Quasimodo duffle-shuffle to the check-in counter and abandoned my bags to the airline gods. Whether or not they would arrive in Bar Harbor was an open question. Had we sacrificed the appropriate animals, recited the checked-luggage incantations? My Last Supper had been a fine barbequed steak, so a proxy sacrifice had taken place. I insured the bag for bundles of money and hoped for the best. Then I stood in line for security check, passed my explosive Teva sandals through the scanner, and found an empty seat among the other passengers. I supposed like the rest I wore a non-descript expression. Most looked tired, bored. Inwardly, I, for one, was on fire. *Shit, man, this is it! You're getting on a plane for the goddamned east coast!* I played it cool, ate some left over Last Supper, and scribbled in my journal, a fat spiral-bound notebook that was to be my closest companion for the next three months.

These are fine moments when we stand on the edge and look out into the darkness, anticipating, dreaming, yearning. Not often enough do we feel this alive. To challenge, risk, reach for a vision is the essence of life and why we need to find ourselves time and again in these situations. Sedentary complacency is death. Move it, man. Get yourself out there. Don't wait for tomorrow, some day, when you retire. Now is the only moment you'll ever have. The pen in your hand, the glass separating you from the tarmac and the slowly approaching jetliner—this is it, crossing the threshold, the edge of an unknown world. Suck it up. Follow that rabbit and roll through the portal to see what's on the other side.

The engines moan and roar, tires grumble, the fuselage shimmies as my stomach settles back into my abdomen— and *no one* screams out in wonder and fear. We are all tilted back into our seats as the horizon takes on a freaky angle. My heart pounds in my chest. What an experience, yet so many seem not to care. In minutes, we are beyond the reach of Everest. Hardly two feet away, the smooth housing of the starboard engine guzzles the thin, icy atmosphere that races by just inches from my elbow. With a heave and mighty grunt this amalgam of distilled bauxite and petroleum burns across the continent, accomplishing in hours what will take me months to reverse. What a distortion our technology creates in our relationship to the land. When I speed down the road in a car, an hour behind the wheel means a day on the bike. At almost six hundred miles per hour, an hour in this plane covers more than ten times the number of days I would need to pedal. As the jet flies, however, is not how the cyclist pedals.

I stare out the window with hungry eyes and follow familiar lines—Old Route 66, the Amboy Crater, bleached, sun-blasted. In minutes, I'm looking down at Prescott, Arizona, a town I'll not see again for almost three months. Flagstaff, Sedona, Oak Creek Canyon, one after the other gives up its topographical secrets. Monsoonal clouds build into ethereal mountains to the east, a mutable landscape of the soul. This awesome speed and altitude leaves me nearly shaking with wonder. My shipmates doze, read papers, scrutinize computer screens, all seemingly detached from this fantasy made real. *Wake up! Look, everyone! Mountains! Deserts, for crying out loud!* I keep my wonder to myself and watch the planet reel away beneath our wings. Can I possibly ride back all this way, just Mojo and me? Do my legs have the power, my own beating heart and lungs the endurance? I crawl into this uncertainty and try to face it down with philosophy, bravado, and denial, the essential cocktail of all adventurers.

Clouds and shadows, shifting lakes of darkness roll and spread across a land of canyons and arid watercourses, the grid-work of roads, emerald patchwork of irrigated fields, the green-eyed geometry of crop circles. We work and strain and bend the land to our will. I gape and stare at the strangeness of it all, grateful to be here to see it.

Dallas International Airport was a blur of movement as I walked off the plane and carefully navigated my way to the next terminal for my connecting flight to Boston. On the final approach to Dallas, I saw a surprising amount of greenery, lush lawns, strips and stands of forests. This was a much wetter place than I'd imagined. Some sections of my connectors from terminal to terminal were not perfectly sealed off from the outside atmosphere, and I could feel the heat and moisture of an August afternoon in Texas. The light cut obliquely through the glass as I stood in a gently rocking rail car that traversed the massive airport. Soon I would be flying into the night, rushing to meet the dark side of the earth. Would my bag make the transition, too?

I took my seat near the noisy rear of the plane. A couple of seats over was a fit young man, slim, bearded. We were the only passengers in our row. I struck up a conversation. The cycling gods had provided me with a guide to the other side, my own velo-Virgil. Phil, a music student working on his master's at Tuft's University, had just completed his own trans-continental bike ride and was on his way home. What are the odds? We both grinned and shook our heads. Although I'm not superstitious, this was a very good omen for the start of my tour. Instant brothers, we talked for a long while about cycling, music, how best to pull meaning from our lives. All the while, the darkened cylinder roared and swayed and seared across the night sky at 31,000 ft. to drop us—if all went well—in Boston by midnight. Cinderella's carriage courtesy of American Airlines. Clouds and the inky void meant no views as we neared the east coast, but towns and roads glowed through the fog like new born stars in a distant nebula.

With a rattling thump and squeal of super-accelerated rubber, the Boeing airliner flopped onto the runway in Boston. I'd made it, this far at least. I wished Phil all the best and made my weary way to the baggage claim. This was going to be a long night. Like the other walking dead pulling graveyard in the bowels of the terminal, I stared trance-like at the slowly rotating conveyor belt until—grand, glorious miracle—my plump black duffle bulged through the split fabric opening in the wall and moved up to my place along the line. I heaved it clear and fought my way back up the stairs, through a parking garage—darkness, strange moisture in the air, cabs, vans, more zombies—to another terminal where I would die a slow death for several years until dawn and my last flight to Bar Harbor. Damn, at least I had my panniers. Somehow, I was going to be reunited with Mojo and start this damn tour, damn it.

Insipid lite rock music droned through the mostly deserted halls. The luckiest of the undead had claimed a few cots left out for people like me, the lost souls caught in the purgatory of a layover between midnight and morning. I found a spot out of the main hallway and behind a stainless steel cart of vague purpose and lay out my sleeping pad. With a bit of shade from the glaring lights and silicone earplugs jammed deep, perhaps I would get some rest. The cart on one side, tall windows overlooking a vast parking garage on the other, I tried to get comfortable—and didn't get even five minutes of sleep. Periodically, in a faintly English accent, an official message boomed over the loud speakers: "Please, do not accept packages from strangers." Yeah, especially if they are heavily bearded and dressed in long flowing white robes and mumbling in an Arabic accent about infidels and Allah. *Okay, yeah, I get it. Now just let me sleep!* Minute after minute, hour after hour, I struggled for sleep, rest, some release from this torment.

Like a wino rising unsteadily from a park bench, hours later I crawled out from the dubious protection of the cart and into the nauseating glare of fluorescent lights and the never ending pop drivel. The hero, in order to be fully prepared for his quest, must be nearly destroyed at the threshold, the no man's land between worlds. Cast into the belly of the beast, he appears to have died. Any connection with the old self is shattered, and he must claw his way out or be carried to the other side, the realm of the adventure, the new environment of challenges, intrigue and danger...

Bleary-eyed, rumpled, foggy-brained, I pulled myself weakly to my feet, and there, mere yards away, beckoned my salvation, a faint promise of life: Starbucks. I staggered over on wobbly legs. There, a goddess-barista said in a sweet New Yorker's brogue, "Can I help ya?" Yes, yes, *yes*. The hot cup at last in my hands, I sat and slurped the elixir of caffeine

44

and chocolate and watched the other addicts drift in to receive the black sacrament. Teenagers in baggy shorts, pot-bellied businessmen, crones and codgers dragged their caskets to and fro. I was envious of their wheeled cases. My lumpy black beast sat like a dead rhinoceros at my feet. No mechanical advantage here, no sir. This inert mass had to be kicked, dragged, hoisted like a penance for sins long forgotten. The punishment is always more diabolical when you can't remember the crime. Kafka, the bastard, knew all about this. He also said all novels should leave you contemplating suicide. *Screw him. I've got coffee, see? I'm on a mission. I've got places to go, miles to ride. Kafka needed a good bicycle, that's what. Clear his morbid head a little. Christ, I feel like a poisoned cockroach.*

Eight AM and I stared out at rain and deep gray skies hanging over the tarmac. This was real weather. I hadn't seen rain in weeks. How would it be in Maine? Probably worse. The crew of the nineteen passenger, twin engine Beechcraft (with *propellers*) lowered the stairs, and we jogged out through the rain to board for the short jump to Bar Harbor, Maine, end of the line, the start of my long ride across America.

The stairs leading up into the plane didn't feel sturdy enough, but after just a few steps, I slipped through the small portal and into the plane, tight, narrow, dark. At six feet four inches, I barely fit. A pinched aisle led for a few yards between two rows of tiny seats, the sides of the fuselage curving in sharply. This wasn't a plane. It was a bloody beer can with wings. I was looking for my seat number when a slim, bespectacled gentleman in a suit said in an Australian accent, "Oh, take whatever seat you want. Nobody cares on these flights." Holding my meager carry-on luggage, I sat down across from him, the ceiling almost touching my head so that I felt like I had to lean into the aisle. Outside, the rain spattered across the wings and vast puddles on the tarmac. I couldn't remember the last time I'd seen such heavy rain. The engines rumbled through the seats, and down the aisle the pilots chatted over the controls in the cockpit. No security door here.

Soon we taxied into position, the pilot pushed forward on the throttle, the egg beaters jumped into a raging blur, and we raced onward and upward, seat-of-the-pants barnstorming, by God. The clouds took our noisy penetration with damp indifference as heavy moisture smeared onto the windshield to be squeegeed off by our high speed. The engines roared and pounded the interior of the cabin with a droning throb. Half yelling over the engines, I struck up a conversation with the man in the suit. He worked in a research laboratory on the island but was originally from Australia. Although he had been born and raised in Australia, he loved Bar Harbor and even liked the winters, which he said weren't too bad. It was very quiet then, after the tourists had gone. The beautiful Maine coast and Acadia National Park were big draws. Another man seated ahead of us said, "We might not be able to land in Bar Harbor at all because of fog." It had happened before. Great. Just what I needed.

We climbed higher. The plane bobbed and shook, bounced, dipped, climbed again. Heavy clouds gave way to pockets of sun until we slammed into another cloud. Shake, sway, drop, climb, drop...in moments I began to feel sick— really sick. *Hold on, man. Get a grip. You are NOT going to toss your Starbucks here. You...are...not. Keep it together.* I breathed deeply. I studied the distant cloud tops—when I could see them. I thought about solid earth and things that did not move. A green, gooey, noxious creature was growing in my belly and clawing its way up my throat. *Jesus, Scotty, you can't puke. Don't even think about it.* With every brief moment of calm, I struggled to center myself. There! The ground. Trees. A road. We had lost some altitude. I was gastrointestinally grateful for the brevity of the flight. And we would land in Bar Harbor after all—well, at least just outside it where the airfield was located. Starbucks bucking but still in place, I woozied my way off the plane and into the small terminal where I drank some water and waited for the nausea to pass. Shortly the bags were unloaded, and I waited for mine to appear in the staging area. And I waited. And waited. *Uh, excuse me, but where the hell is my duffle?* "I'm sorry," said the placid woman behind the counter, "but it couldn't fit in the baggage compartment, so it will be coming on the next flight"—hours later.

First impressions of Maine? Not good. No panniers meant no rain gear. The world outside the terminal was gray-green and damp, the clouds low, dark, pregnant with still more precipitation. I could see a lot of trees across the road and on the other side of the runway. My stomach was still in a battle with the surging air currents aloft. It was only mid-morning, and I was not keen on waiting around in a boring terminal for my bags to arrive. I talked to the placid one: "You'll send them along to the hostel? Great. I'll be waiting." I caught the next shuttle bus out to the island. I was recovering from the motion sickness, but I felt isolated, alone, a castaway by my own design and not too happy about it. I was tired down to my bones.

The free shuttle service was efficient, and after a short ride through rain showers and corridors of thick trees, we pulled into a small town, quaint shops across a small central park, Bar Harbor, Maine, at last. The would-be cyclo-tourist hero stumbled off the bus and headed for the main street across the park. Instinctively I headed for a gazebo where I could see some young cyclists had gathered to wait out the rain. I walked with some speed as my polar fleece sweater was already getting wet. My first day on the east coast and I didn't have rain gear. Classic. The riders told me where to go, and I headed out. I was thrilled to see the heavy woodwork and shingles of the local architecture, but my mood was twisted by a creeping exhaustion. Since it was still early, I was determined to get my bike assembled then get to the hostel and get some sleep. A solid half mile of walking brought me to the bike shop. With some relief, I stepped in out of the rain, my hair and cap ever more plastered to my head, and into the familiar world of pedal-powered hardware, a couple of shop hands in aprons back in the work area. I talked to one of the young men behind the counter. "Hi," I said. "I'm from California, Scott Wayland, and I had my bike shipped out here about a week ago?"

"Sure. It should be in back. I'll go check." A few moments later, he emerged from a dark doorway with my big bike box in his hands—good old Mojo. The shop hand laid the box on the wood flooring. I quickly surveyed the packaging: one small hole in the box, a few dents and scrapes, but it looked okay. I started opening the box. "Uh, I'm sorry," said the wrench in the apron, "but you can't do that here."

"What? I can't assemble my bike here? It's raining outside."

"Sorry, can't do it."

Huh? What the hell? I might frighten a couple of customers by assembling a bike in—holy crap!—a bike shoppe? *Well, quaint fucking Bar Harbor Bike Shop, thank you very much.* "Could I at least borrow a wrench set and a screw driver? My bags are still on their way from the airport. Thanks." I dragged the box behind the building to an area suggested by the shop flunky but couldn't find any real shelter. I finally set up under a tree branch against a fence and began pulling the carefully packed and padded components from the huge box. Time and again, sheets of rain raced across the town, shaking the trees and pouring through the leaves and branches overhead. Fumbling with wet parts, wet tools, a soggy brain and short fuse, I somehow put Humpty Mojo back together again. I couldn't attach the chain as that was with my bags, but at last I rolled him back to the shop and left him there until the next day when I could finish my work and take him away for good.

Then I had to walk about a mile through the pouring rain.

A couple of hundred yards down from the bike shop, I stepped into a café and natural foods store to get something to eat. I sat on a stool at a very narrow counter that looked out on the street. People were still out, at least in my feeble state they looked like people, most of them, I noted with envy, in rain gear and toting umbrellas. The turkey sandwich had almost no taste---not because it actually had no taste but because I was about to collapse. I couldn't remember the last time I had been so tired. With robotic movements, I crammed the food into my mouth, chewed it out of a sense of duty and knowledge that I needed the calories, and forced myself back out into one of the worst storms of the summer on the eastern seaboard.   From Boston to Bar Harbor, power lines were knocked down, trees mangled.   I trudged along through my final baptism, the crushing of the spirit to impress upon my dim consciousness that everything was different now. The old life was over.

The squelchy trans-continental dreamer arrived at last at the hostel, shelter from the storm—but only in his dreams. Lock out. *Oh, sweet Jeeeezzzus, I need sleep, I need to get dry*. I looked around in desperation. There wasn't even a covered porch or anywhere I might stand, so I went hunting. Maybe in the back? Not much there, but what's this? There, on the side of the two story building was a strange kind of recess or alcove about four feet deep and reaching to the roof. The outside was constructed of an irregular wood grid with some of the openings covered in plastic, some open. Down at lawn level, a couple of spaces were open to the street, and I could see a somewhat dry strip of dirty concrete, a couple of paint buckets, some random sheets of plywood. *Any port in a storm, eh, Scotty?* Once more playing the role of the random rummy, I stepped through the grid, arranged some of the plywood to block the rain and wind as best I could, and set up my pad on the narrow strip of concrete. Not perfectly dry but good enough. There was even an electrical outlet, so I plugged in my new phone to get it fully charged after calling the airport to alert the delivery person about my location. I covered my eyes with an extra shirt and promptly fell asleep to the sounds of driving rain and wind-lashed trees.

My coma was briefly interrupted by the arrival of the cab with my duffle. I moved the plywood door to my hovel, crawled out to retrieve the bag and then retreated back into my coma. I don't think I would hold up well to torture. Deprive me of sleep long enough and I will do anything. A couple of hours later, the storm in retreat, I was admitted into the hostel, a shower, a new lease on life. A low budget ruled my adventure, so I set up my tent on one of several tent platforms in the back, only ten bucks a night. Because I estimated about one hundred days for the tour, I had to economize where I could. There were two other bikes and tents already pitched, and later I would briefly meet Chris, a hardcore Dutch cyclist who was near the end of a year-long circumnavigation of the lower forty eight states—fantastic. I wasn't the only crazed pedal pusher around here. Chris, slim, blond, smiled in the dark as we talked briefly about our plans. We were at opposite sides of the adventure curve: He was 95% finished and would ride to New York over the next couple of weeks and then fly home to Holland; I was edgy, pumped, about to blast off. Here at the edge of the country we each inhabited our own edges, the marginal zones of life and transformation.

That night I called Jodi and we talked. I sat in a strange hallway in a strange town and felt her familiar voice flow into me from thousands of miles away. Hearing her was comforting but so unnerving because I knew how long it would be until we could speak face to face. Later, as I was going through my bags, I came upon a card that she had slipped in under the radar. On the cover, a snow-plastered, icy road vanished into a frosty white forest. On the bottom it read: "Every step of the journey is the journey," a Zen saying. Inside the card, she'd left these words:

> To my sweet, transcontinental, no trans-fat husband,
> I wanted to send you off with a little surprise note,
>> which I hope you find before you're too far along on your journey.
>>> Truly this has ended up being a journey for us both, from which we've already grown tremendously. No matter how I react emotionally from time to time, that's almost always old business that I thank you for nudging to the surface to be dealt with. Sort of like skimming the scum off the pond.
>>> What I most want you to know is that I love you dearly and support all your efforts (so far, anyway) to express your SELF to the fullest.
>>> You are in my heart, and in my thoughts,

every hour of each day.

As you test your mettle on the pedal, I wish you so much more than luck; I wish for you the fullness of experience, the learning, the transformation, and all the rest you so desire. (It's so much easier to write all this than to speak it.)

Tailwinds, my love— Jodi

I felt a stabbing pain in my chest and carefully put away the card, wondering what I'd done to deserve her.

The next morning, I emerged into a day as fine and bright and promising as the day before had been heavy and oppressive. This was it. I'd finally crossed to the other side and the journey could begin. My mood and excitement carried me in light steps through the cool morning. To the south, a tree-studded granite shoulder bunched up against the horizon. I walked north past shops, restaurants and galleries, the colonial seaside architecture that was so different from the bland stucco and tile of my home, the generic development of a western land seemingly without a history. The vast majority of the structures built in my home region date from after the 1950's, a good many of them from the last few years. But here? New England? Restless Europeans had been pacing these shores for more than three centuries. My earliest ancestor came over on the Mayflower and landed not far to the south. This is where the American experiment began.

I liberated Mojo and performed final adjustments, put on the chain, got him ready to ride—all under a brilliant Bar Harbor sun, tourists walking by, people in shorts and sunglasses, folks renting bikes for the day. I, too, set out for a ride, a shake-down cruise to see the island and make sure Mojo was in working condition. Mt. Desert Island, home to Bar Harbor and Acadia National Park, is a split granite lump just off the coast. In the late 19th century it was a getaway spot for the wealthiest of American families—Vanderbuilts, Astors, Rockefellers. Ultimately, it was designated a national park, the first east of the Mississippi, and John D. Rockefeller, Jr. financed and guided the construction of a fifty mile set of carriage roads to help visitors explore the island. This involved granite bridges, entrance gates, retaining walls. These smooth and scenic roads now provide access for bicyclists and pedestrians to all corners of the island—but all motorized traffic is forbidden, a rule to warm the hearts of cyclists everywhere in this car-crazy culture.

I started out on the paved loop road and stopped for lunch on a granite shelf overlooking the Atlantic, leaving behind the heavy weekend traffic to lose myself in the deep blue ocean and crisp breeze. Hardly a cloud marked the sky. The coarse orange stone felt good and solid under my feet. To the south, rock climbers played on a sharp little escarpment while boats cruised the gentle chop. I strained myself for a view of Europe, somewhere over the horizon. Why couldn't I stay here forever? Become a Mainer? If only the whole tour could be like this, cool, brilliant. I planted these sensations firmly into my tour data bank for later examination. There would be hard days ahead, and these memories would help keep me moving. After a dozen miles of pavement and traffic, I bailed onto the packed dirt carriage roads and rolled happily on the smoothest dirt I'd ever seen. I zipped through trees, smiled into sunlight filtered through pines, maples, a host of hardwoods I couldn't identify, and for the first time I became aware of a spice in the air, a smell unique to my experience and unlike anything I'd smelled in Western forests. For a few minutes, I stopped to watch otters play in a pond in this enchanted garden.

After my carriage road exploration, I dropped back into town, hit the library to update my blog, check email, and later found my way to the water's edge. I needed to perform the ceremonial dipping of the wheels. The bike had to touch both oceans, a baptism for the bike, a symbol of initiation and completion. Would I make it to the Pacific, over four thousand miles away? I could hardly bear to think about it.

That night in the hostel I organized gear, making sure everything was in its place, wondering how these two bags, pretty small, all things considered, would carry all my possessions for the trip. Now they were stuffed with food for the first leg of the journey, a rambling route south along the coast. These simple acts of packing, placing, zipping, checking seemed freighted with importance. I wasn't headed off to a trackless wilderness, but somehow it felt that way. The real wilderness I was facing, of course, was within, the dark corners of a funky monkey mind that would chatter and ramble, joke, complain and cajole me this way and that for months of solitary pedaling. Could I even stand that much time by myself? Was I good enough company? My longest solo effort had been about two weeks long through some pretty barren desert country, and I'd finished with reasonable sanity. Perhaps this trans-continental foolishness was evidence to the contrary? Or was it the conclusion of a logical line of development? Logic? Who the hell was I kidding? There's nothing logical about pedaling an eighty pound two-wheeled Lazy-Boy across a continent. No, that's lunacy, romance, dream and delusion. I slipped my bags under a bench seat in the hallway and stepped out into the night. Tomorrow was the big day.

Lying down but wound up, I worked on relaxing my thoughts, breathing slowly, fighting the noisy jerk working the late shift at the filling station next door. Friends rolled in at 2:00, 3:00AM? and they talked in loud, obnoxious voices about who-the-hell-knows-what. I rammed the earplugs deeper and deeper and somehow picked up a few hours of sleep in fitful spasms. Not a good night. By 5:00AM, a dim light bleeding across the sky, I was up, rolling my pad, stuffing the bag. For practice I did this inside the tiny one-man tent. No doubt I'd have to face these chores during some rainstorm, so a dry run seemed like due diligence.

I wolfed down last night's left-over pasta and finished packing. At this hour, the hostel was quiet, but the concierge did come down with some laundry while I finished breakfast. She wished me well, and I stepped out into the early dawn. The bags cinched tight, pad and tent in place, every-single-last-freaking-thing accounted for, I pushed the portly Mojo through the rear gate and out to the street, the cleats and hard soles of my cycling shoes crunching against the gravel, clacking on the blacktop. Disbelief, fear, burning excitement pounded through my veins. After years of planning, scheming, day-dreaming, countless hours of staring at maps, trolling bike touring chat rooms, the moment was finally here.

First Things First
Aug. 10th: 60 miles

August 10th, 2007, 6:45AM, I settled into Mojo's thick padded seat and leaned back. I stared at the pedals, gripped the bars, felt the heavy, swaying tail end that I'd have to get used to, breathed in and out deeply, in and out. *Okay, then. First pedal stroke, bloke. Clip in and make this tour happen. The journey of four and a half thousand miles begins with a single turn of the pedals.* I pushed my right shoe in and up— "CLICK!"—looked over at the hostel, gave a solid push, lifted up—"CLICK!" the left shoe, and rolled away, turned left past the hostel and up the street into the chill morning air. Balance and roll, the sweet slide of delight, Mojo and I began our long conversation, the quiet tires on the pavement, the positive click of the shift, the gentle whir of the long chain that bound me to my travels, that transferred my muscles, my will and resolve into forward motion and another coast, another beach a continent away.

So began this solitary journey into the heart of America. No marching bands, no reporters, just a lone cyclist on a deserted street. He checked his mirrors, turned left again for the short climb past the town park and out beyond the village. He shifted down and felt the first serious pull of the loaded bike resisting his intentions. Desire and concern, longing for experience and knowledge, a deep yearning led him into the morning light and these United States.

Climb, descend, turn—Bar Harbor was gone. I wondered if I would ever return, but action and anticipation were stronger impulses than thinking about where I'd just been. For many weeks to come my energies would be—

needed to be—forward leaning. This was all about the next turn, that far bank of a river, a town on a map that would become a place in my life once I'd been there, making the world real through direct experience. It was time to *live* the land.

Coastal Maine is convoluted and corrugated, cut by rivers and plowed by glaciers, no road straight or flat. It's all about turning and climbing, something new around every corner. For me, a neophyte to the Northeast, it was a fantastic land of old, weathered barns, the reach of dawn across the Atlantic where it butted up against walls of dark evergreen growing right up to the shore and everywhere the air redolent of a mysterious spice. A strange dampness hung in the air—humidity?—a strangely thick atmosphere alien to this boy of the West where fresh bread turns to toast in minutes out of the bag. I pushed on through and let it wrap around me like a blanket, a weird slipperiness.

I made the mistake of taking Dutchman Chris' recommendation of Route 3 off the island. Some tight traffic, places with poor shoulder. He must have a higher tolerance for such conditions. Once off the island, I left this line and vanished into the back country, the quiet rural lanes that I craved. Immediately the trees closed in, and I stared with wonder at the dense growth—tree upon tree upon tree so closely packed that no light seemed to enter. Since I hoped to find wild camping most of the time, the packed forest came as a shock. There was no way I could push Mojo into these trees, nowhere to pitch a tent. Everything was so much more spaced out in the west. I was getting an education fast.

Tight purse strings and desire for adventure meant that most nights I would seek out free camping. Jodi and I called it "stealth" camping, "commando" camping, or, my favorite, "guerrilla" camping. I knew that in some places I would camp in town parks, the occasional campground, but we always prefer the special hidden place away from prying eyes, noisome cars and lights. But here, in these woods? I shook my head and kept on pedaling. I wasn't going to camp for hours, but I felt some gnawing doubt creeping in. Each day begins with a set of vital questions that must be answered: What route will I take? Where will I find supplies? Where will I spend the night? If I'm abducted by space aliens, will they confiscate my bicycle? Finding the answers can fuel some anxious moments, but they also provide much of the charm of cycle touring. This is life distilled, a course of action whittled down to the bare minimum, a haiku for the traveler: ride, eat, sleep, ride, lather, rinse, repeat. Do this often enough and the pedal pusher can circle the globe. Like the Japanese poem or a Shakespearean sonnet, the limitations force creativity and insights in ways often hard to imagine. Some play well, others flop. The variety and contrast form the beating heart of the journey.

Along Western Bay and up the reach of Union River Bay to Ellsworth put me into the groove. The tour was on. As I approached the town, I was attracted by the stately brick and stone buildings flanking a tight intersection where my route cut left. I needed some alcohol for my stove and so searched out a hardware store. I finally procured the flammable stuff and added even more weight to the bike, a quart through which I would slowly burn and so lighten the load one meal at a time. I had to be careful getting off and on Mojo. He was feeling a bit tippy, ungainly, a handful too spirited across the beam. But it was only the first day. What could I expect?

Surry, East Orland, Orland, Bucksport, the poetry of places urged me on. I arrived in Bucksport by lunchtime and ate beside the Penobscot River across from Fort Knox, less famous than its Kentucky relative but still a fine fortress built in the mid-1840's to guard the river. A high grey ceiling of clouds had moved in to block the sun as I set up my victuals on a park bench overlooking the water. It was still early in the day, but I'd covered almost sixty miles, a good start, so after lunch, I asked a couple of teenagers walking by if they knew of any place I might camp, maybe down by the water? "Sure, there's a beach a few miles beyond the bridge. Look for a road that drops down to your left right before the railroad tracks cross Route 3." And so it came to pass.

A new suspension bridge crossed the Penobscot River, sleek granite towers and radiating lines of thick white cables spanning the dark water. It was a thrilling experience to roll through such startling geometry. A couple of miles beyond, feeling the humidity, I found my road and dropped off toward the shore. The ocean was not far away so this was as much tide water as river. Long, low-slung ridges dense with trees marked the edge of the water near and far. After a couple of false starts, I found the beach access and rolled down to a parking area, which looked a bit exposed for camping, but at the far side I found the end of a nature path that didn't look to get much use. I pushed Mojo up to a bench and changed out of my cycling clothes and waited for the evening to come so that I could pitch my tent. I sweated even as I sat still and wrote in my journal.

Before long, I saw a figure coming down to the bench where I'd spread out my kit. Stewart French, heavy set, thinning blond hair, a kind, round face and powerful hands, introduced himself and asked about my journey. Here, right into my afternoon had walked the one person I most needed to meet. Stewart was eager to talk about his state and the waters below our perch. He came from a long line of Mainers, Revolutionaries, and Mayflower voyagers. "Oh," he said, "if you count second and third cousins, I've got two or three thousand relatives in the state!" His pride and sense of place were clearly central to his life. "This area, down in Camden and Belfast, was where most of the ships were built for the Revolutionary War. In fact, just a couple of bays over there to the south was quite a battle with the British. They sank a few Yankee ships. Later, during the night, some Maniacs—the word comes from the wild fighters from Maine, don't you know—rowed out there and set fire to the British ships and sank several!" He grinned at this, proud as if he'd done it himself. His mood rubbed off on me.

"Go Yankees!" I said. I showed Stewart my map and intended route and received his blessing.

"Camden is the most beautiful place in the world," he declared with total certainty. He turned a bit melancholy then, talking about his life, how he used to be a champion body builder, but now he was just "old and fat." His approaching sixtieth birthday seemed to hang over him like a dark cloud. For all that, life had been good to him, and he'd been able to retire at forty because of good real estate investments.

He talked to me about the New England character, what it meant to be a *Mainer*. The real, down-home residents were wary of outsiders, and when someone moved into the state, native residents would say, "He's from away." It was considered a great betrayal to sell land to someone "from away"—though a lot of that had been happening over the years, mostly on the coast. "Once you get inland a bit, you'll meet some *real* Mainers." I asked him about the weather here, especially the winters. "Oh, not so bad here on the coast, kind of a 'banana belt' really, but you go inland ten miles or so and it's twenty feet of snow all winter long." In this immediate area, his father had helped build the first bridge across the river as well as the now abandoned and rotting docks that reached out into the river before us— heavy-timbered stumps, weathered, split, home to gulls, cormorants, the stately osprey that patrolled the shore. Once tools of commerce, now the remnant docks served another purpose.

The afternoon was getting on, the sun low at our backs, slipping away from the ocean—a strange orientation for me. Stewart bid me safe travels and ambled down the path to vanish in the wall of foliage. I swatted a mosquito and smiled at my good fortune. Good man, Stewart French.

At Stewart's suggestion, I loaded up Mojo and muscled him down to the beach to avoid the mosquitoes. They didn't get the memo. Still, I was happy to be right next to the water and pitched my tent beside a bleached log and cooked my first meal on the road: rice, kippers, and broccoli seasoned with olive oil, garlic and Parmesan. I sparked up the alcohol stove made from salvaged Pepsi cans, watched the blue flames pouring out, and set the pot on to boil. Gulls squawked, cormorants clacked, and the sun set on this Revolutionary shore.

"The Most Beautiful Place in the World"
Aug. 11th: 117 miles

I awoke to the cries of sea birds and a dim glow behind a foggy ridge of trees across the bay. The ocean had slipped back to somewhere else, so my beach was bigger than the night before. Although the sky was clear, the inside of my tent was soaked, really dripping wet. What the hell? I slipped gingerly from the tent and surveyed the general moisture. The only time I'd experienced this kind of condensation was on very foggy days on the Pacific coast, conditions where you could directly see the stuff swirling through the atmosphere. But this was a magician's trick, great puddles of water conjured from thick air.

I stood still for a moment looking out over the mirror-smooth water and honored this experience, the only Atlantic sunrise I would witness in its entirety. I heated water for coffee and began the customary packing ritual, a process that would become rote science before long: dinner and sleeping gear on the left (nighttime stuff), lunch, breakfast and cooking gear on the right (daytime stuff). As I puttered about my chores, I soon realized my tent and sleeping bag were not going to dry, not in time for a decent start on the road. I had a country to cross, for goodness sake. *Laundromat later, me boy*. I packed the gear damp and muscled Mojo up through the weedy slopes and out to the smooth morning road. Time to get after it. Today I would leave the Atlantic behind. I had no idea if I would ever return.

A windbreaker to take the edge off, I dug into the cool morning shadows, clicked through the gears, and rolled through Stockton Springs and the harbor where the Yanks had fought back so effectively over two centuries before. Searsport fell quickly with hardly a whimper, and by 8:30AM Mojo and I pulled into Belfast. On that morning, I could not have imagined a more perfect town. Founded in the 18th century, it rises above Belfast Bay like a dream, a collection of boats in the harbor and handsome Victorian structures defining the old town, a requisite blinding white church steeple piercing the clear August sky.

I'd made contact with a fellow through the Internet before leaving California and decided to make good on my threat to look up Alex once I landed in town. I got him on the phone and before too long I was cranking up a frighteningly steep hill to his house. I'd read that the East would provide the hardest riding, and I was beginning to see why. *Low gears, Scotty. No heroics.*

Bearded, bespectacled with intelligent, bright eyes, Alex made me feel right at home and quickly opened the garage so I could park my bike. He introduced me to his friendly wife, Diane, who had the good sense to leave a couple of bike nuts alone while they prattled on obsessively about gear and the cycling life. But as I was unloading, transferring my wet gear to his dryer, Alex gave me the CliffsNotes edition of his life: At ten years old, he escaped with his family from the former Yugoslavia. He struggled with the new language at first and took every speech class he could find to perfect his English. He was an *American* and wanted to sound like one. I detected no accent, so his efforts had paid off. In college he majored in literature and had the incredible good fortune to hear Jack Kerouac read and then shared some drinks with the famed Beat master. I, too, was *On the Road* and intrigued at these minor degrees of separation between myself and the famous writer. Of the generation before mine, Alex encountered Vietnam in a way I never could. Patriotic, motivated, he joined the Army Rangers and served two tours as a medic, drowning in the worst that conflict had to offer. One hip was blown to fragments, so it was now plastic. Agent Orange left its mark, one he battles with still. The nightmares retreat with medication. I sat in awe of his experience and what he had endured for our country.

But Alex's problems would not hold him back. Until recently, he and Diane lived for fourteen years on a boat, sailing up and down the Eastern Seaboard. Health concerns for himself and in-laws put an end to the seafaring life, but his time on the waves had introduced him to Belfast, so here he and Diane made their home. He took up cycling with the fervor of the newly converted and rides year-round, the Maine winters be damned—Alex, a Ranger still.

I left Alex and Diane's under a hot, late-morning sun and pushed for Camden, where I planned to have lunch. There I found docks thick with schooners, a green leading down to the bay, and a waterfall pouring down granite slabs under a restaurant, the patrons seated on the deck above. Cormorants and gulls perched on the slick rocks and floated on the gently moving ocean below. Most beautiful place in the world? Like flavors of ice cream, that's a hard one to argue, but it was the most beautiful place in my world on that afternoon, so I found a spot of shade on the grass and enjoyed lunch. Shortly out of Camden, I'd leave the Atlantic for good. Better soak this in nice and deep. Many people stopped to ask me about my trip, even offering help, a place to stay. The drivers, too, seemed relaxed, very considerate, giving me lots of room on the road.

Later I cruised shaded lanes below outrageous domiciles of the fantastically rich, colonial homes with impeccable landscaping, scarcely a leaf out of place. It was a glimpse into a world I could hardly imagine. I made my mortgage, got the car payment covered. My life was not a hard one. But this? Back in Bakersfield, anything called "estate" usually meant a trailer park, meth addicts, wife beaters, desperate cases. While there may be meth addicts and wife beaters here, you couldn't tell it by these genuine *estates*. Folks here knew how to dress up their vices.

I picked up Route 90, and the coast was toast. So was I, soggy toast under a damp burning sun. On to West Rockport, Warren and Waldoboro. Studying the map, I was impressed by the number of towns. In the desert Southwest of my home, burgs can be fifty miles apart, sometimes farther. One stretch of road north of Baker—home to the world's tallest thermometer and a Bun Boy! restaurant—presents the cyclist with a grim warning: "Next Services 72 Miles." Here? One couldn't throw a rock without hitting some little village or other.

Tired and sweaty, I stopped in Waldoborro to ask a fellow trimming trees if there were someplace I might camp nearby. He lowered his clippers and smiled, kind of shaking his head: "You could camp over there." He gestured to a stand of trees where we could see a tent.

"Oh, another cyclist?"

"No," he said, "I think that's guy's more interested in Milwaukee's Finest."

I laughed and said, "Well, have you got any ideas where I might set up for the night?" He recommended a spot near a parking area not too far away.

"But it's up a big hill," he warned.

"Oh, man, that's all I need!" I cried. He laughed. I looked him in the eye: "Hey, are you laughing at me?"

"Just a little schadenfreude." He grinned and looked at his feet.

I couldn't recall *anyone* ever using that term in conversation—go Mainers. I took the man's advice, picked up water and a beer on the way out, and started up the hill, which looked bad from below, but the angle wasn't severe, and I powered up with confidence. At the parking area on top I balked. A total wall of trees, the identical situation as I'd found leaving Bar Harbor. *Nope, not throwin' down here.* The evening was coming on, the sun down below the ridges, and I needed a camp—now. I pushed on, anxious, water bag sloshing, and checked out a lawn behind a mortuary—too exposed. *Okay, this is getting desperate. Where the hell am I going to camp?* Then I espied a double track dirt road leading towards a cell tower in the trees. I cut off the pavement and into the forest. There at the base of the tower was an open area not visible from the road. A chain link fence topped with barbed wire circled a concrete building. Above loomed the cell tower, icon for this era of mobile communications. I stopped, looked around, felt the sweat trickle down my back. Home sweet home.

My circumstances seemed marginal at best, so why was I happy? I camped not one hundred yards from a busy road. A cell tower brooded overhead as I lay sweating in a nylon cocoon. Periodically an air conditioner groaned to life, cooling the inflamed bowels of the cellular technology housed in the pebble-studded bunkers behind the wire. My body was momentarily fooled by the sound, so familiar from hot spells at home. With each jump and rush of the machine, my nervous system expected the cooling relief. But that gift was not for me. Hidden, soulless circuitry received that periodic blessing. Like a sinner trapped in Dante's *Inferno*, I suffered the miseries of the damned, the exquisite agonies of the Contrapasso wherein each sinner is tortured by that which he pursued. Like an alcoholic surrounded by kegs he can't quite reach, I was reminded of the promise of cooling air but denied it every time.

Even so beleaguered, I was happy. How could this be? Because discomfort is not reason enough for unhappiness. The heat would ease, the night cool. Earlier I cranked Creedence Clearwater Revival on the mp3 player, opened a cold beer—at least I had one—and cooked my dinner. I washed with cool water and bandana. For now, this was an abundance: Adventure, challenges heaped high on my cycling platter, fine encounters with the land and its denizens in the great state of Maine, the simple pleasures expanded to their proper magnitude. *I'm on my way and I'm going to ride Mojo across this country.*

Sweat and Storm
Aug. 12th : 176 miles

I stepped in my own crap this morning.

Oh, the joy of the woodsman's craft poorly executed. *Reminder to self: Don't stagger backwards after doing your business, 'kay?* I buried the waste and spent too much time cleaning my sandals. Maybe I wasn't so happy at this chore, but finally, my gear cleaned and loaded, I headed out into the quickly warming day, 7AM and already in the low 70's. I braced for a challenging ride.

Climb and descend, climb and descend, Maine set the rhythm and I followed as best I could, dropping into my lowest gears time and again, riding in my "granny" as we call it, playing hot, sweaty games with that small, toothy gal. At the top of each grade, I'd catch a breeze and cool off on the roaring descent that followed. The rewards were undeniable as I devoured the landscape and the towns of perfect beauty—New Castle, Damariscotta Mills and others, New England clapboard colonials and brick commercial districts, lakes, ponds, rivers, a wealth of water everywhere.

Outside of Litchfield Corner, the heat was getting to me. Time for a break. I turned off in search of a store indicated on the map but found instead a roadside farm stand and stopped to get vegetables for dinner and borrow a patch of shade. Clint and Rebecca Heenie of This and That Farm welcomed me into their small place and gave me chair to sit in near the pungent garlic shed, its rafters draped with the fabulous vampire repellant. These were real Mainers, the first I'd met with the distinctive New England accent that everyone out West joked about. Whenever I told people I was starting in Bar Harbor, they said, "Ah, Bah Hah-bah!" and laughed as if no one had ever made such a joke. Up until Litchfield Corner, I'd met no one with this accent, but when I asked for Swiss chard for my evening meal, Clint called out to Rebecca, "Hey, this man wants some chaahd!" Apparently, not many people went for the greens. For a couple of dollars, I had a bag full of organic produce. I ate lunch and enjoyed the shade while Clint and Rebecca told me about life in Maine.

Clint said that Maine is one of the poorest states with the highest tax rates. Most people are forced to commute long distances because all the towns I was enjoying no longer provide good jobs. They both raved about the education system: "Oh, we've gaht great schools," he said, "but ah number one export is educated young people!" Clint lamented the economy, and Rebecca explained that the "fahm" was a small side business. They both had jobs elsewhere. I learned that the shoe industry had once been central to the Maine economy, and Clint told the story of his brother who spent his days hand stitching shoe leather with a double-handed technique: push in hard with needles and stout thread in each hand; pull out and away with both hands to cinch the stitch—again and again, thousands of times a day, year after year until one final stitch collapsed his lung and he fell to the workroom floor, dying. Only the good luck of a nearby medic saved his life when the crafty and determined aide rammed a tube straight into the gasping brother's lung to re-inflate it like a misbehaving air mattress. The medic pushed the vent through skin and muscle between ribs, *right into the lung*—no anesthesia. For a few moments, Clint said, his brother preferred to die. "Mainers," he added, "are known for working very hahd at menial tasks."

While we talked, ornery geese led a pitched battle, a muscular black cat lay languorously upon a narrow bench, hollyhocks and sunflowers glowed in the high noon heat. How this place could be buried in snow was beyond me. The previous winter in minus 45 deg. F weather, Rebecca and a friend were in the hot tub outside, Rebecca's hair frozen solid. Clint was stepping through the back door to join them in the blizzard when the cat, an abandoned stray, came bolting in out of the cold and made himself at home. Now he earned his keep as an excellent rat catcher.

After lunch, I went back to work on the steeply rolling terrain, topographical waves in a storm crashing into Mojo and me. Head down, bow into the swells, I strained into the sweltering afternoon, wondering what people thought about me as they drove by in their air conditioned splendor. Did they have any sense for my struggle, or was I merely a curiosity, a random oddball quickly forgotten?

Late in the day, climbing above the Androscoggin River, I was on the hunt for a bivouac spot and found my chance—maybe. A low, rotting shed was being overcome by trees, consumed by what had produced it like bodies reclaiming lost bones. I explored beyond the shed and discovered a flat spot of grassy land, an abandoned concrete stock tank, a crumbling foundation. Camp it would be. Out over the shallow river valley and vast expanses of dense woodlands, thunderstorms expanded to fill the sky to the west and north. Immense dark wings of brooding clouds reached out from a glowering center to embrace the horizon as heavy sheets of rain blended into the distant trees.

The forests and grasses, the flowers and mosses, the insane riot of life was intimidating to this boy of the arid West. It seemed the people here were barely holding their own against the encroaching trees, that if they ran out of gas or some malevolent force broke all their mowers and chainsaws, every person and town would be engulfed in days, lost to an all-consuming greenery. The storm grumbled while I pitched my tent in the long swaying leaves of grass, sun and shadow racing over the land. *Remember this, Scotty. You'll never be here again.*

The Hero Falters
Aug. 13th: 228 miles

Idiot! Stupid! MORON! How could you be such a jackass? Have you ruined this tour? Do you want it to be over—right now? You can murder your dreams acting like that...

I left my wild camp by 6:30AM, damp, grey skies pushing down. The riding was fun, easy, dark woods lovely and deep. Pushing through the rural beauty of the Waterford townships, I felt like I had landed in heaven as I cruised along lakes and fields, remote lanes bordered by stone fences and overhung by trees. Beyond Sweden, however, I crossed a line and became my own worst enemy.

They were only a couple of bumps on the map profile, a little steep looking, sure, but even moderate grades could be distorted on these maps. I rolled past a broad grassy field decorated with a house-sized granite boulder, turned a corner and looked straight up a wall, a backwoods blacktop Mt. Everest that begged for nylon ropes and pitons, Sherpas, oxygen tanks and several well-stocked camps on the way to the summit. Something clicked in my brain, a primal challenge like a crazed bull goaded into the narrow streets of Pamplona. *This bitch is going down.* I dropped into my lowest gear and attacked, a recumbent Pentani, Lance with a load on his ass, a raging supine lunatic with a single-minded agenda: ride this precipice like a man. Pull, push, groan, beg to the gods, yell out in agony...for all the drama I was moving less than three miles per hour and struggling to stay afloat. *Mayday, mayday....* But I hung on, rode the tsunami and tagged the summit. I stopped on the crest, gasping like an asthmatic strapped to a hookah. But I'd done it! But what had I done? I felt a serious point of tenderness behind my right knee, caused, no doubt, by the insane pulling on the pedals. *Oh man, Scott, what have you done?* A solid tendon pull could end the tour. I'd battled with ligament and tendon injuries before, spent months, years limited in one way or another. Hard rock climbing had permanently compromised my fingers. *Dammit, fool, why didn't you just walk that hill? What did you have to prove? Is this how the tour ends, not with a bang but a whimper? Oh, shit....*

I tried to stuff my fears of doom and pushed off to the west, down the sharp slope of this double-humped Sweden Rd., a punishing dromedary of cycling pain. Isn't Sweden a flat country? As a blast of rain swept down over the hills, I scrambled for rain gear, pedaled—oh-so-gingerly—only a short distance up the next incline, nausea-inducing steep, and walked sensibly to the summit. I could stretch to touch my toes, but any extra movement sent pain shooting up my hamstring. *Okay, okay, don't stretch like that! Leave it alone. Pedal smart. Back off. Walk.*

When I dropped into Lovell (pop. 974), still mid-afternoon, I resolved to camp. According to the map, this place had all I needed—food and a library. I did a quick update of my blog, picked up supplies, and searched the area for a possible camp. Right in town, on the far side of the park, which had running water and a blue booth for basic needs, I found a backboard for playing handball. Behind lay an undeveloped forested area that was uncharacteristically open, nice spacing between the trees and a fine carpet of pine needles underfoot. Behind the backboard was ideal— out of sight, shade from the afternoon sun, over a hundred yards from the road, places to set my beer and hang my gear. I staked a claim.

As happy as I was to find such a camp, my mood was tainted by the knowledge of the injury. How bad was it? I could walk around, pedal easily and feel no symptoms. But good grief, I still had all of New Hampshire and Vermont to cross, not to mention New York, the White Mountains, the

Green Mountains, the Adirondacks—unknown mountains for many days. I couldn't walk them all, could I? I decided to be optimistic, to wait and see. I'd take a short day tomorrow and then a rest day. I'd focus on my pedaling technique and avoid *any* pulling. Take it slow, rest, stretch very carefully. I had to continue. This was my one shot at this, at least for a number of years. This was going to work out. It had to.

Action is the antidote. Put on some music. Slice and dice that garlic and onion. Sauté in olive oil. Crack that beer. Music, my good man, music! This camp was all I could ask for. And the ride was going to continue. It had to, didn't it?

My Own Private Walden
Aug. 14th: 266 miles

Cool, drier air greeted my last furtive miles in Maine, although afternoon storms were already brewing in the morning, gorgeous white clouds that slowly congealed into forms more threatening. I set out gingerly, soaking in the morning. Say your prayers, make offerings to the gods, keep your insurance paid up and set sail for ports unknown. The confusing net of roads led me astray near the New Hampshire border, and for some time I wondered where the hell the state line was hiding. I finally realized my error and so enjoyed an extra eight miles I hadn't planned on. I repeated a mantra: *Check the map at all the intersections. Check the map at all the intersections. Gotta take it easy today, old man. Rest day tomorrow. Get yer ass to New Hampshire.*

The first state is always a big milestone, a definitive statement that you're going places, not just on a ride but an epic journey. My knee complained only vaguely and seemed to respond to my careful tactics. Lakeside homes, cottages in the trees, dark green pines against blue and white skies played across the big screen all morning. Then I saw it: "Welcome to New Hampshire." Oh, the fine reward of progress for this pilgrim, for all of us on our journeys. Here was a sign! Unambiguous, bona fide, fantastic. I'd pedaled across Maine. One state down, fourteen to go.

Cute, clean, set in a bowl of high mountains, the resort town of Conway was next on the menu. I stopped at a coin-op laundry and assessed the situation while my clothes were purged of a special scent developed over the first week of

71

riding. But I needed to get clean, too. The laundry had a large, lockable bathroom with a deep sink. Bird bath time. Pack towel, soap, bandana, razor, I had all I needed. Like Superman changing in a phone booth, I entered the restroom a grungy cyclist and emerged a much cleaner scoundrel. There was no disguising the type, however. The cyclist has that faraway look in his eyes, fingers twitching for the next gear shift, leaning into corners even as he walks. He studies road surfaces compulsively, assessing risks, ride quality—smooth? Rough? Broken? Sandy? What's the traffic? These thoughts and the shock of wonder play across his features and might be construed for mental illness.

A garish neon beanpole in rubber pants, I collected my clothes, strapped a still-damp pair of socks to the outside of a pannier, and rode down the street to an information center. Campgrounds: $24. Hostel (Hell): $21.50—too expensive for this penny-pinching pedaler. It was too early in the tour to be forking out good cash for a place to flop, so I found information on the surrounding National Forest and soon located a lake not far out of town. Maybe there?

First I had to ride several miles more out of my way to get to a grocery store for good grub and plenty of it. I wasn't going to move for at least twenty four hours, so I was forced to pedal up and down hills, loaded with food and water, my knee taking the abuse, somehow. I pedaled, too, across my first covered bridge, icon of New England. This was not a thrilling experience. What's the big deal about a bridge with a roof on it? They're just sheds with big doors on two sides. The art-deco masterpiece of the Penobscot River, now there's a bridge for you. Or the Golden Gate? Aye, that's a bridge. A few boards thrown together over a creek? Please. Okay, nice, quaint, but—yawn. More exciting were the dreaded steel grated bridge surfaces I'd confronted on a few occasions across Maine. These open welded grids of polished edges were meant to shed snow and ice. They also shed unwary cyclists, and I nearly went down when I first came onto such a span after a gentle turn. I was fanatically careful after that.

In long evening shadows, a lingering glow on the White Mountains thousands of feet above, I left Conway in search of National Forest land, a free-for-all stealth scenario. Good news: the road was blocked but only for through traffic, not for bicycles. I heaved Mojo—truly bulging now—over a ragged patch of rail work and stopped for a few minutes on the other side to call Jodi. The cell phone was becoming a vital piece of kit. How could I have ever done this without one? Being alone most of the time, I cherished this one (usually) reliable link to home, something I needed. Jodi's voice jumped from the dense lump of plastic and I smiled. So good to hear her voice. I jabbered excitedly about my injury, the beauty of New England. I was worried how she was doing, but she seemed okay, upbeat. For a few minutes in the press of evening I was home, too. But then I had to go. I signed off, closed the phone and was once more alone and nowhere yet to spend the night. This was a strange, unsettling feeling.

A gentle climb led up into the trees, a home here and there in open patches hacked from the forest. Red Eagle Pond was my destination. Ponds, such the eastern term. The only ponds we have out west are faux installations in landscaping. We've got *lakes*, by God, and up high, *tarns*. Though some of these eastern "ponds" were a good deal larger than many lakes I'd encountered. Still, when you're heading for a pond, you're in the East, cowboy.

Soon I entered the National Forest and encountered more of that green density I'd come to expect. It was getting good and dark. I passed one possible access through which I could see a sliver of water, but I held out for something optimal. Rest days must be optimal. I took a dirt road past the lake—still nothing. I turned again, the night bearing down seriously now, my stomach a knot of uncertainly. *I will not camp in some ditch*. I pushed hard, scanning feverishly for a spot. Once darkness took over, I'd be screwed. No finding a great spot then. The slopes on both sides of the road were loose, uneven or too heavily treed. Mojo's rear end was heavy with fresh food and a celebratory malt beverage of not insignificant volume, and I worked hard to control him on the shifting surface. He rode like a skittish colt. *Calm down, boy. We'll get there.*

But where? I slipped and slid, corrected and pushed hard into the on-rushing night. Then the dirt ended and I was back on the pavement, coming full circle. *Keep at it.* I came around to the first rejected access point and slipped into the trees. This would have to suffice. Ah, fantastic. Flat, easy, plenty of room for Mojo and the tent and far enough from the road. Tent pitched, I made a brief reconnaissance down to the water, not expecting much. When I stepped out of the trees, I was stunned. There, rising above the mirror of the pond and a dark line of trees, stood the green pyramid of South Moat Mountain over 2,000 feet above. My own private viewing platform of the White Mountains, a name that probably made more sense at a different time of year. I took a deep breath, grinned into the mountain night, and hiked back up the slope to cook dinner.

Life the next day in Camp Thoreau began, of course, with a steaming cup of French roast in hand (fair trade, organic, of course). I grabbed my pad and sauntered down to the water's edge in the heavy gray before dawn. I would sit by the pond, write in my journal, and watch the sunrise over the White Mountains. My knee felt good as I settled into the serious business of doing nothing, everything, all that mattered then: to sit and be still, to watch mist drift lazily over the calm water, to listen to the haunting echo of a loon's cry, to contemplate the dark band of clouds moving in.

The light grew by steady degrees until the sun's first rays tipped the highest trees and, behind me, a band of bright gold illuminated the forest floor.

Tomorrow: Kancamagus Pass and the deep mountains of New Hampshire.

White Agony
Aug. 16: 356 miles

The strange dissonance of "Kancamagus" rattled pleasantly in my brain as I began the long climb to the highest pass on this eastern leg of the tour. A few stacked bicycles shy of three thousand feet, by Western standards it didn't amount to much. But the East has a flavor all its own, a hidden punch, brass knuckles in the velvet glove. Kancamagus pass is gentle, seductive at first: a fun frolic along the Swift River, water rushing through polished boulders, views up to green ridges. But the riding was too easy. Where's the business on this mountain? A few miles short of the top, the grade kicked in and provided some solid journeyman cycle touring. Other cyclists appeared, all on light road bikes out for the day, all passing me with frequency. One wheelman's comment: "You're brave!" Huh? *Yeah, that's right. I'm stormin' a machinegun nest on Omaha Beach. I'm swimmin' with blood-thirsty great whites. I'm Indiana-freakin'-Jones on a queer bike.*

After a blazing toboggan run down the west slope, I stopped in Lincoln to replace my slowly delaminating cycling shoes. A small gap had appeared around one toe, and I couldn't afford a blowout in a remote location. At the bicycle shop in town I talked to another cyclist who was on a fund-raiser, which explained the frequent pedal traffic I was seeing. I asked him about the next climb. "Oh," he said, "it's not as bad as the last one."

Cyclists are usually the only reliable source of information regarding road conditions, the nature of the topography, distances. The motorized public simply has NO idea what it's like to pedal over land they may drive every day, which, of course, is another reason to ride a bike. But this bloke could not have been more wrong if he'd plotted with twisted malice to break me in body and spirit.

Internet café and coffee in North Woodstock then up the next easier climb. *I'll be in Haverhill by mid-afternoon.* The long 7—8% grade of the first pass had been a challenge but nothing serious. Anything easier would be no problem. Innocent at first, like a young woman in a breezy summer dress, hair flowing lightly, a sweet come-hither look in her eyes, the pass quickly showed her true colors: a leather-studded, whip lashing sadistic dominatrix. *What the hell is this?* I was punching it out for a pitiful three miles per hour. *Easier? Screw you!* This was the hill I'd come to die on, two solid miles at an unbelievable 12%. I was getting spanked—*hard.* With one long break at an expensive geological tourist attraction, which I skipped, I somehow battled my way to the summit without exploding my knees—or my entire cardiovascular system. Humbled, contrite, granting the eastern mountains their due, I gasped on the summit in the chilly late afternoon breeze, Mt. Moosilauke brooding greenly above.

Like a long, tedious courtship followed by sex, which *never* lasts long enough, miles of descent flew by in minutes, a fleeting ecstatic contrast to the grinding effort of ascent. Did I respect myself for this relationship? I couldn't think clearly enough to know. Another short hill left me pushing for a few yards, my fragile pride now lost in a fog of lactic acid and aching knees. These eastern mountains would either kill me or turn me into cycling steel. At this point I couldn't tell which way it would go.

In North Haverhill (Have-a-heart-attack-after-that-hill), I cast about for sleeping options. The gray skies had returned, damp, dark, and descending. One nice local with a friendly dog offered accommodations right away, but his place was miles back up the road. More serious riding was out of the question. Another local suggested a bicycle shop where I could find information, perhaps a place to stay.

And so it came to pass.

Tom and Noreen of High Intensity Bicycles offered me refuge—and none too soon. The rain was coming, and shortly I was rolling Mojo onto the sales floor of the shop, which was about to close when I first arrived. Initially conceived as a B & B, bikes and beds, the bike business had quickly grown too large, and they had to scrap the bed part. Their home and business were housed in a barn and old farm house. Since the shop was directly adjacent to the home, the couple had a tough time keeping out after-hours customers. "If you're home, you must be open, right?" said Tom. He then stepped out and rolled a huge dumpster sporting a giant "CLOSED" sign out the driveway to block would-be intruders. "It's the only way to keep people out."

Noreen was a bit frantic with in-coming stock and getting ready for the annual Mt. Washington hill climb, which Tom and his sister were going to ride on a tandem. I quickly learned that this is considered the toughest mountain climb in all of cycling, almost eight miles with an *average* 12% grade, long sections of 18%, and final headwall of 22%. The road is so extreme that race officials won't allow riders to descend. They must have pre-arranged and qualified support to drive them off the mountain, a place known for some of the worst weather in the world, home to the highest wind speeds ever recorded: 236 mph. Support vehicles must have acceptable width and braking characteristics. Hummers, for example, aren't allowed. Tackling this climb on a tandem was outrageous as two-seaters climb much more slowly than singles. I would never try it on my recumbent. To attempt it on a fully loaded Mojo is the stuff of late night beer-goggle thinking. No, I was content to let the pros take on that particular challenge. Tom had the resume: Over thirty years of riding experience including time as a professional top-ranked downhill mountain biker. He looked fit and relaxed in the face of his impending suffering. He said that he'd been diagnosed with a heart disorder when he was young, and the doctors recommended he stay away from strenuous exercise. I wondered if the physicians knew how he turned out and that tomorrow, Tom, now in his early forties, would be riding the toughest climb in the world. Don't let the bastards keep you down.

A young adolescent, Keegan, was helping Tom store bikes in the upper level of the barn from the outside, the boy lifting the bikes up high for Tom to grab and hoist into the loft. Keegan was a bright, happy kid in love with bikes, a "shop rat," as Tom put it. The boy had no father in his life, and the combination of bikes and a friendly older male figure were irresistible. Their banter and upbeat relationship were a pleasure to observe. The boy had landed in the right place. Tom's warm, easy presence made everyone comfortable, and I slipped into the scene as if I'd always been there. Keegan called home after a ride with the boss and another employee and ended up staying for dinner, the night, and breakfast the next day. He was surgically attached to the shop and spent more time here than at home.

For some reason, my cooking of broccoli at dinner was a major disturbance. Everyone hated the smell, yelling: "Oh, that stinks!" "What are you cooking?" "God, I HATE the smell of broccoli!" The good-natured ribbing was relentless, but there was little doubt my cruciferous vegetable was no favorite in the house. I had the veggie, rice and salmon. Everyone else had pancakes and sausage. I went to sleep that night to the sound of steady rain pouring down on this quiet New England valley.

In the morning, a boney Keegan shuffled around dressed only in a pair of baggy cycling shorts and made a comment about eggs for breakfast, but it was clear he had no idea how to cook them. With a grin, Tom looked him in the eye: "You can't make 'em, but you've got no trouble eating them!" Then Tom started pulling out peanut butter and tossed him a loaf of bread: "Can you make that?" Tossed him a package of instant cocoa: "How about this?" We were all laughing at this point. Keegan grinned sheepishly, so Tom and I provided sage advice about taking a home economics class at school. "You know," Tom added, "you're gonna get kicked out of the house in about three years. You've got some things to learn." Keegan started spreading peanut butter and heating water. Outside, a gray morning became somewhat less gray.

I was excited to be going but reluctant to move on. Good people and places do that to travelers. Still, the road was calling, waiting, pulling me onward. I said my farewells and pushed off into the residue of last night's storm.

A Green Mountain Boy
Aug. 17 + 18: 458 miles

Moses may have parted the Red Sea, but Mojo and I parted the storm clouds of New Hampshire. We pushed out of the murky funk and into a day of radiant beauty, clouds and blue sky, everywhere the deep green of meadows and forests, a flood of pulsing chlorophyll as we cruised above the Connecticut River Valley. I grinned myself stupid and took it all in, the absolute best of what I'd hoped to find. When I crossed the river, I entered Vermont, my third state and thought then I would be reincarnated as a Vermonter. Or maybe I'd spread myself across the whole of New England. Ethan Allen on a strange German recumbent, I charged the Green Mountains. A flurry of Thetfords crowded the map: North, East, Thetford Center, Thetford Hill. I climbed away from the river and into the heart of Windsor and Orange counties. Much of this country felt close-in, cut off. I was used to the twenty, thirty, sixty mile vistas of the high desert. This was a more intimate landscape asking the traveler to look closely.

Outside Sharon, I stopped at a roadside organic farm stand to get green matter for my evening meal. I was determined to eat well and fuel this body. I crunched down the gravel and stopped beside a long, low building. Through an open door, I could see produce spread out on shelves, in bins. A self-service pay box was placed against the far wall, and a refrigerator held the more delicate lettuces and tomatoes. No one was around. The honor system. I selected some green beans, a potato, a couple of carrots and slipped a few bills into the metal box. As I stepped back into the sun, I met the principal farmer: a huge smile, easy laugh, a man enjoying his life. Lean, a scruffy beard, ragged jeans and blue t-shirt, all capped by wide straw hat, he introduced himself as "Geo."

"Like geo-positioning system?" I quipped.

"Well, it's a long story," he grinned, taking my bad joke in stride. I liked him immediately. Vermont was feeling like a place where I belonged. Maybe my next life.

We talked about the local environment, and I commented on the incredible vegetation. Geo was quick to point out that they were having a drought. What?! "Oh, yeah," he said. "Look at that"—pointing to a handful of dry grass at our feet—"that's a drought here. This place should have a lot more grass right now."

I was headed west and asked if he knew where I might stay in Bethel just up the road. Geo was about to call a friend when he turned and said, "You could stay at our camping spot down by the river—unless you need to make some more miles." The road will provide.

"Yes, thank you!" I filled up with water and prepared to head down the dirt road. Geo was off to cut some hay. "Watch," he said, "it'll rain and get the hay all wet before I can get it bailed." He walked down the hill to start his tractor.

I rode and pushed Mojo down to my camp beneath the spreading trees. That night, the storm moved in, and the rain fell gently on my tent in the Green Mountains.

A sodden morning seeped through the heavy dripping foliage. Nothing to do but deal. I rolled, packed and stuffed all I could while inside the tiny shelter and crawled out into a light rain to finish the morning rituals. Except for a quick scramble to pitch the fly when the rain started, I'd passed a good night. Time to confront the last of mountainous Vermont. On today's menu: Middlebury Gap. I pushed Mojo up through the high wet grass and out to the road. Tricked out in full rain gear, I settled in for a day of soggy cycling. I was awarded a day of clouds, rain, bright sun cutting through the storm here and there, a day of high beauty and drama.

The library in Bethel provided shelter for an hour, but I couldn't stay too long. I had miles to go before I slept.

Cool, chilly headwinds kept me busy, and at Hancock I started the big grind up "Bread Loaf" hill, a 1,000 ft. climb with—*a curse on the seven mad gods who rule the mountains*—a two mile stretch labeled 12%. A couple of hundred yards shy of the summit, I was good to my promise and got off to push. I found the act strangely liberating. Park the ego, use the gray matter, stretch the legs. I paused briefly on the summit, a special place for me. This was the last of the worst, at least until I reached the western mountains. I was on the cusp of New England. More was still to come, but I'd crossed a threshold. New York was a certainty tomorrow. A few more days of riding would put me in the flatlands beyond the Adirondacks. Climbs aplenty would hurt me in those mountains, but the absolutely punishing pitches of the East were over. And I was still standing, still sitting, still pedaling. The tour would continue.

I zipped up my wind shell, pushed on gloves, and plunged down the west slope towards Middlebury, Robert Frost country, a waking fantasy of twisting turns into dense forests. At the Bread Loaf Campus of Middlebury College where Frost gave writing seminars, I paused and gazed with deep academic envy and wistful wonder at the perfect verdant lawns, the chairs scattered about under the spreading trees. This was the polar opposite of the scruffy dry campus of my home, a place where "Panorama Drive" looks out onto blistered oil fields of dead grass tangled with pipes, pumps, and wires sagging in the scorching heat. I looked out to the Green Mountains and understood in my bones why Frost had become a Vermonter. He wrote in his poem "Away" words to fit my journey:

> Forget the myth
> There is no one I
> Am put out with
> Or put out by.

Unless I am wrong
I but obey
The urge of a song:
I'm-bound-away.

A Yankee Meets New York
Aug. 19th: 506 miles

On a dark May morning, hours before dawn, a few dozen men and two leaders moved up and down the river until they could secure a boat hardly big enough to move them to the opposite shore, but it would have to. Hearts pounding, sweating in the spring chill, they rowed across the inky waters. They had a dangerous task to perform, and all of them knew they might not live to see the day end. It was 1775, and Ethan Allen and Benedict Arnold had rallied the Green Mountain Boys to attack Fort Ticonderoga in what would later be called New York, although at the time boundaries and jurisdictions were in dispute. What was not in dispute until then was the garrison of British soldiers holding the fort. The small group of patriots was determined to change that. The story goes that the lookouts and other British troops up at that hour were easily subdued, and Allen went directly to the commander's quarters and confronted Deleplace, who appeared in a nightshirt. Allen secured his victory without a single death. If only the other battles would go so smoothly.

On the high ground overlooking Lake Champlain and, on the other side, New York, the Adirondacks, I surveyed my last piece of New England. Down there, in those trees, on that water, the modern history of my country was written. I tried for a moment to put myself in that group of men, flint locks and powder horns, worried about keeping my ammunition dry, fearful of the reception awaiting us at the fort. Then I looked down at Mojo and felt the centuries slip away. I rolled down into the humid green hills and tried to imagine what it was like to be a revolutionary, but the feeling wouldn't come. I was a product of a different age, and that couldn't be changed.

I caught the ferry across the lake and climbed into the mountains of upstate New York, an expanse of 3,000,000 acres protected by the state. I cycled through green corridors punctuated by clear lakes reflecting a bright August sky. There was still some wilderness up here, deep forests haunted by bears and mountain lions. There were cabins along some of the shores, the docks covered like garages overhanging the water. Here and there blocks of mossy granite bulged out of the trees. "I am hopelessly and forever a mountaineer," said John Muir. Even in these relatively mild eastern ranges, I felt the pull of the high country, the thrill of peaks and ridges, mountain streams. Muir was speaking for me, too. I tried to pack these feelings deeply into my heart, the tug and push of the topography. I was going to need this energy in the cornfields of Ohio towards which I struggled so steadily.

The Intruder
Aug. 22nd : 627 miles

The Adirondacks slipped into history and the whirling wake of my tires. Steady stepped descents led me out of the mountains, the last I would see until Colorado, too far away to contemplate. My finest encounter was with a gray-haired cyclist nearing the end of her cross country ride with a large, guided group from the Adventure Cycling Association. She had pedaled about 1,500 miles to join the group for the official start in Washington. Now she was in the last couple of weeks of her tour. Somewhere in the middle of the country, she turned seventy. When so many of her generation already had one foot in the nursing home, she was over 5,000 miles into a continental ride. You go girl. I could only pray for such power and resolve in my later years.

In this convoluted corner of New York I felt too far from home, isolated, facing something that was too much. I'd made good progress, but New York was still *the East*. That's the wrong side of the country. What was I doing here, all by myself, nothing but my legs and a whacky bike to carry me home? To make the crossing possible, I had to see it in manageable stages. Or better, as an evolving process, a challenge for each day, a blending of planning and improvisation. The general direction of the narrative was clear enough: Head west not-so-young man, head west. But the individual scenes, the character development and conflict were to be written as each day evolved. One moment I was searching for a camp that felt too far away. Instinct and emotion told me to drop that course, and in a few moments I was surrounded by members of my own tribe, cyclists on a quest. I was taken in by smiles and boisterous shouts, an international gathering of kindred souls. How does this happen? Mere chance? Or was my decision to search for a different camp driven by something else, an alternate sense that I needed to be with these people? A message sent on the mountain air? I couldn't say, but the road seems to look out for travelers like me. We need a careful mix of resolve, determination and flexibility, an eye for opportunity.

After the group left camp, the septuagenarian riding away at a steady pace, I thought about the value of riding with a big group, the ready company and support, but the variety of my experience was more valuable to me at this point. Would I camp alone under the stars? Or would I stretch out on the floor in the living room of a young engineer just making her way in the world, as I had done in Middlebury? No sure calculations, no absolute predictions, just the unfolding mystery, the dance of the journey revealed.

The mountains of New York fell into darkness behind me, and, as always, I searched for camp. The park in Booneville was non-transient friendly, so I pushed on, searching, hoping, anxious. Huge big-top tents in blue, white and red bands appeared to my right. Fair grounds. Fair game. The tents and concession stands were empty, not a shred of cotton candy anywhere. This could work. The place was dead and felt odd, my presence faintly illegal. *Stuff that uncertainty, Scotty, and find a camp.* I rolled all over the compound to find someone to ask about camping. Nothing stirred but the dust raised by my tires and the faint flapping of the empty tents in the breeze. It felt post-nuke creepy. Flesh-eating zombies or no, I decided to stay put and pitched my tent in an obscure corner behind a monster hanger signed for livestock, a faint odor of which hung in the evening air. A small creek gurgled nearby—perfect for cooking water. I had all I needed. I rejoiced in the mildly illicit act of sleeping in unconventional places, an adolescent's dream of escape and adventure, making do on the road, Huck Finn with wheels and a chain. All I lacked was the corn-cob pipe. I popped open my evening beverage and set about cooking dinner.

Then, late in the night, came the intruder...

Rustle, shake, clink! rustle. *Huh? Damn, something's in my trash bag. Stupid 'coon.* To save my trash further molestation and general spreading about, I unzipped the tent and stuck out my head—Whoa! Death on a stinky stick—skunk, polecat, *Mephitis mephitis*, the dumpy form and bold black and white striping clear enough under the security lights. What to do? What to do? I couldn't just lie there, letting it strew my garbage willy-nilly, could I? I squirted some water in its direction to no effect. Then I thought better of my actions and made a tactical retreat. Though my own odor at that point was formidable, I knew that prudence was the better part of valor. But then the toxic beast came gunning for me, sniffing and snuffling, waddling its skunky waddle towards my tent, towards me. Sniff, snuff, waddle, sniff—right up to the mesh door, my own quivering form just inches away, holding my breath, bug-eyed with fear. *Oh shit! I've got chocolate in here. The little fucker's got a lock on my candy bar. Please, please, please go away!*

I tried flashing my headlamp. Nothing.

Now, I'm not without my own manly intensity or ability to face down danger and conflict when I must. I'm as tough as the next tough in a pinch. I might do battle with all manner of creatures to defend my honor or my garbage. Squirrels, rabbits, raccoons, small bears, Godzilla—bring them on, I say. I've been known to grapple mano-a-mano with that masked bandit the raccoon on occasion, stepping up for some close-in work. I once smacked one between the eyes with a heavy metal spoon, clonked him four square, I did. That was one sorry 'coon, I tell you. But this? This furry, four-legged bundle of biological mass destruction? The first rule of combat: Know thy enemy. In this case, I had sufficient knowledge to concede the field of engagement with few regrets. As deeply attached as I was to that plastic bag and its contents of wrappers, scraps, and empty can of salmon, I had to accept the loss, take the casualty like a man, and live to tell the tale. Retreat with honor.

Finally, I let out a silent prayer to the patron saint of bicycle tourists, St. Shimano, and Skunky retreated back to the creek, its arsenal locked, loaded, and un-deployed.

Misery Mine
Aug. 23rd—25th: 780 miles

A grey, congealed slab of meat hung over the world, a fetid sky like an enormous beef steak gone bad, dampening enthusiasm, tempering groggy optimism. Still, no rain yet and cool enough to start, so put spurs to Mojo and set out to chase the sun. Rolling farm country, green, forested corridors, the promise of my first ever Great Lake led me onward. Bass fishing seemed to be king here as I surmised from the number of big-mouth style mail boxes.

Nearing Lake Ontario, I paused on the edge of a massive, amorphous dark presence. The sun had pushed at last through the decaying flesh of the morning, but now I faced an ill-tempered wall of grumbling attitude. Thunder growled in evil tones that quickly sapped my desire for more miles. Reluctantly I resolved to take the closest camping option down near the lake and set up before I had to take a beating on the open road. I rolled into Selkirk Shore State Park, paid my $15 (the leeches! the stinking leeches!), and pedaled quickly to find my site as the first rain started to fall. Camp loop after loop led me at last to the lake shore where I found my site next to a busy group of adults and children. I smiled and waved, leaned Mojo up against a tree and stood for a moment to catch my breath and take in the scene.

Immediately, Mike and Dave came over to say hello and get a good look at my rig. Mojo was proving a great way to meet people, but just as we got into preliminary introductions, the grey beast overhead made good on his threat and poured rain upon us all. I scrambled to get Mojo under the awning my new neighbors had set up. Safe under the tarp, we watched in astonishment as the flood came down, a Biblical hosing like I hadn't seen since New Hampshire. The two families took me in, and we laughed and cheered as one of their daughters, a blond girl about seven years old, pedaled a small pink bike in furious circles around the paved loop, plowing through the biggest puddles and begging for more, a huge muddy stripe up her back from the spray off the rear tire. In a soaked t-shirt and shorts, her arms akimbo, she bent her head down and cranked with all her might round and round. I recognized once again that we are all born with this enthusiasm for physical adventure, for wild nature. How do we ever grow to lose it? I took a sip from my beer and smiled as the girl took another lap.

Mike and Dave were old friends, and every year they came with their families to the lake to fish for fresh water salmon. Dave told me that the water had once been very polluted but that an accidentally introduced mussel (a filter-feeder) had reproduced like crazy and saved the lake. As the stormed eased, I left my new friends and walked down to the shore to get a close view of this amazing body of water. I pushed through the dense trees and down to a strand of pebbles pounded smooth by countless waves. Beyond the rounded stones stretched the ocean. A lake? No, too vast for that. No other shore across the way limited my view. Nothing but a watery horizon and the slowly breaking thunderheads. It was humbling. I squatted by the small waves and felt the polished rocks, selecting, at last, one to bring home for Jodi. I gazed out over the calm, blank water, felt the damp air on my skin, in my lungs, and climbed the steep embankment back to camp.

Mike and Dave came over as I set up my tent and prepared to cook. They were fascinated by my journey, and Mike especially couldn't hear enough about it. I showed them my maps and the little alcohol stove. Dave had read about this design on the Internet and was keen to see it in action. Mike asked: "So do you camp out every night?"

"Usually," I said. "I don't often stay in campgrounds. Most of the time I pull off somewhere, or I meet people who give me a place to stay." I sparked the fuel, and we all watched as the flamed burned first yellow then a hot, clear blue.

"Look at this!" exclaimed Mike. "The guy's got everything he needs. He loads up his bike and just heads out. Damn, that's great." There was a wistful tone in his voice, a longing that I understood too well. I was fortunate to be able to feed my wanderlust, my adventure addiction. Mike talked with some regret about his business, the constant press of obligation, responsibility. I thought of his beautiful children and the good relationship he seemed to have. His life had compensations, but there was no denying our shared desire to get out. We didn't necessarily want to run away from our problems. We just wanted to run. In the end we all make choices, grab life where we can. If when God closes one door, he opens another, the opposite must also be true: When he opens one door, he *closes* another. The art of life is in making peace with the worlds given to us through the doors we choose—even if we don't have a choice.

The next morning I stepped into an atmosphere of phantom piranhas, invisible flesh-eating devils that hovered above the damp forest floor. Clad in bike shorts and a light top, I danced a River Dance jig, gulped coffee between hops and got the hell out of there. What *were* those things? I never saw them, but for the rest of the day—and into the next and the next—I raked my nails across ravaged calves when the itching overcame me. No one ever said the road to enlightenment was easy. This day would prove the truth of that axiom.

The landscape was pleasant enough, barns and fields, dark stands of trees, ivy climbing up the old buildings. But as the day blossomed into all its fiendish intensity, I ceased to fully appreciate the bucolic countryside. The heat and humidity joined in a deadly embrace, became a burning, choking sack of misery that closed around me. I couldn't breathe. Shade hardly took the edge off. My strength oozed from flooded pores and fell to the scorching pavement. A test of will, character, resolve, call it what you will, but every physical adventure has these moments, the times when elements and terrain conspire to ruin your soul, defeat you, leave you whimpering for relief, escape.

But there was no escape, only endurance. I drank water continuously and pushed on. A handy mausoleum came into view at the edge of a large rural cemetery. Feeling a bit too close to my compatriots behind the heavy stone walls, I slumped into the little patch of shade thrown by the small boarding house for the dead. This day could end any time. I'd had some grand ideas about mileage, but the weather gods had other plans. What's the old proverb? If you want to hear God laugh, tell him your plans? The good news, the important point I had to keep in mind was that I was under no orders to make the miles I'd first considered. The Nazi's weren't running me down. No cyborg from the future was intent on snuffing out my sweaty little existence. I could slow down! I could stop! Sodus Point a few miles down the road would be it for the day.

As I closed in again on the lake shore, the temperatures eased a bit, and I pedaled around the small town. Sunday, no library, no air conditioned refuge. *Go ahead, kick a man while he's down. Go ahead. Do it and laugh.* I landed at a park right at the end of the point where the main feature was a well-preserved 19th century lighthouse. The park, contrary to what a local said, was not conducive to my style of camping. A beautifully preserved sailing canoe parked near the lighthouse slowed me down for a while with its dark wood and sleek, lacquered lines. Inside the lighthouse, I found a pair of middle-aged women, docents, who were more than kind and determined to find me a cheap place to camp. I pitched them with my now-standard line: "I'm a teacher riding across the country, and I can't afford to pay for every night's camp. Is there some place around here I can throw down my tent for the night?" All the while I exuded boy scout good cheer, earnestness, anti-psycho energy. *I'm a good guy, really. I only need a wee patch of grass for the night then I'm gone like the wind.*

I must have struck the right chord because after calling around a little, one of the women, Edi, said that I could camp in her back yard—score. After a cold shower down by the lake at a public beach, I pedaled back across town and up the hill to Edi and Bruce's home. I introduced myself and they showed me around to the back yard, a broad expanse of lawn walled in by tall, densely planted cypress. Quiet, private, ideal—at least so I thought. Edi was friendly but seemed a bit wary of this tall stranger she'd invited to her home though later she and her husband introduced me to their son and his girlfriend before the whole family went out for the evening. A few mosquitoes and the threat of a big impending storm meant I had to pitch the tent. After dinner, I crawled in and began one of the worst nights of my life.

No air moved through the yard, the heat terribly slow to dissipate. I stretched out, gasping in the stifling confines of my nylon sarcophagus, sweat pouring off every inch of skin.

And then the itching ...

Burning, raging, mind-bending itching radiated across my calves and shins. I played head games, went totally Zen, checked out Lamaze breathing, prayed for a sudden psychic split so some other personality might fight the maddening sensation in my legs. Nothing worked. *I will not scratch. I will not scratch.* Over and over I repeated the mantra until I snapped and lunged for my legs and clawed for relief—which didn't come. I sweated, I itched, I scratched, I bled, the four horsemen of my personal dermatological apocalypse. No escape, only endurance.

Clouds built and grumbled, but I was denied the cooling of even a thunderstorm, although I heard later that some parts of the state experienced severe flooding. I was merely taunted. Lightning flashed across distant clouds, a counterpoint to a neighbor's barking dog getting paid by the bark. Sometime in the early morning hours I passed out due to sheer exhaustion.

By six am I was up and packing, determined to get moving. Gouging fingernails across my shins, I lay into the pedals and left the still quiet home behind. I worked hard to escape the bad dream. Movement seemed to help. I never wanted to stop the tour, but I sure did want this itching to stop. As an adolescent I'd once severely sun burnt the backs of my legs, the painful red fruit of hours floating on an air mattress down a river. Then and now, I told myself that the pain would pass, the experience recede into history, a memory unable to resurrect the actual physical discomfort. Cooler morning air helped. *Take the miles, push, ride, forget.*

Clinton's Folly
Aug. 21st—22nd : 877 miles

I've got a mule, her name is Sal,
15 miles on the Erie Canal
She's a good old worker and a good old pal,
15 miles on the Erie Canal

We've hauled some barges in our day
filled with lumber, coal and hay
And we know every inch of the way from
Albany to Buffalo.

"Erie Canal"

Ten, fifteen, eighteen miles per hour, a light grey contrail of dust drifting out behind me, I pedaled the crushed limestone towpath along the Erie Canal, a steady rolling crunch under Mojo's tires. Reclined on a bike that probably tipped the scales on the wrong side of eighty pounds, I flew along with an ease and speed that my ancestors could have scarcely imagined. For me, fifteen miles was an easy hour's work. At the dawn of the 19th century, this freedom of movement was unthinkable. DeWitt Clinton, governor of New York from 1817 to 1823, was the central figure in making the canal a reality. Stretching over 360 miles from the Hudson River to Buffalo, the Erie was the longest such waterway in the world. So expensive was the project—$7,000,000 at the time—people called it "Clinton's Folly" or "Clinton's Ditch." Version 1.0 was only four feet deep, but even then it reduced transportation costs by over 90% and led to an explosion of commerce, opened westward settlement, and turned New York City and Buffalo into the economic powerhouses of the day. Clinton's folly, indeed.

Early travel on the canal, however, was not via high-tech German couch bike. Mules like good old Sal towed barges mile upon plodding mile up and down stream. Today, the mules are gone and so are the barges as the advent of the railroad made the canal obsolete. Now only recreational traffic takes this historical route. The astounding locks and motorized bridges of the improved canal remain, rising and lowering to accommodate boats during the warm weather. Winter shuts down the whole enterprise. Since the Great Lakes can themselves freeze over, ice in the canal would be impenetrable.

I dreamt of ice as I sweated under the damp August sun, but the sky was a perfect blue scattered with harmless downy clouds. Car-free miles led into the land of religion where the devout take their faith seriously. Churches, cathedrals, temples, towers and stained glass dominated seemingly every corner and tree-lined avenue. In Palmyra, a single intersection sported a different church on each corner, a different denomination battling for the lost souls of New York. In the birth place of Mormonism, however, not a single temple to the Latter Day Saints was to be found. Joseph Smith had been run out of town, and I imagined him sprinting for his life, pursued by a mass of pitchfork-wielding villagers, a scene out of *Frankenstein*. To the townspeople, Smith's doctrine was the monster and he its embodiment. The irony of religious persecution in the land of the free was no doubt lost on the angry mob. I thought of my own Mormon relatives, and the connection to this place seemed strange, improbable, but it all started here. Like Smith, I headed west.

In Albion, I rolled beneath needles of ornate stone, antennae of the faithful to transmit their prayers, God's old time wireless network. One church sign proclaimed that its spire was the tallest in town, almost two hundred feet of holy rollin' steeple. No dropped calls here. No admonitions against pride either, the divine conflict between theory and practice. Pulling a lazy u-turn through a confluence of churches, I gazed up at a fine stone edifice of Catholic glory as a man in t-shirt, jeans and heavy tool belt yelled out: "Hey, look at that!" Brian Brewski hailed from beneath a broad-leafed tree. I gave him the basic outline of my journey, and he gave me the good-natured joke about his name: "Yeah, all my friends say, 'Let's go have a brewski, Brewski!'" Brian was an arborist and worked on trees up and down the canal, mostly for various churches. I remarked on the handsome Catholic structure. "Oh, you should see inside," he said.

"Can we?"

"Let's see."

Soon we were walking between the pews in cool shadows, the stained glass windows of the saints glowing in the afternoon light. Brian went on at length about his life in this cathedral where he had been baptized, where he had been married, where he had mourned with his community the loss of his father and young niece, gone recently before her nineteenth birthday. From the joyous to the grievous, the stone, glass, and care-worn benches had provided a grounding point for his entire life. I found myself envying this friendly woodcutter as we gazed at the ornate columns, the huge organ with a bristling forest of gleaming pipes. We lingered for a moment in the quiet space and stepped back into the blinding light of day.

"That's quite a trip you're taking," he said.

"Yeah, a once-in-a-lifetime adventure."

"You'll meet some good people and some assholes, too."

"Well, I've only met good people so far."

"Trust me, there are gonna be *some* assholes between here and California!" he laughed. With a big smile and slap on the back, Dan Brewski sent me on my way.

Easy miles along the canal walled in by overhanging trees took me down the line. Squat canal boats with names like "Hemlock" puttered leisurely towards Lockport, Buffalo, and the open water of another Great Lake. I quickly outpaced the boats and found myself in Lockport. Free camping by the canal left me plenty of time to run errands in town, and by the post office an enthusiastic woman named Lil helped me find the library and followed along to make sure I found the place. She was thrilled about my adventure and leaned out of her window to make sure she had the correct address for my blog.

"I've lived out of my truck before," she said, "and it's wonderful, to have that freedom to deal with people—or not—if that's what you want. I'm seventy-five, you know, and I'm just getting started. Life is just too short!"

"You're right," I said and leaned in towards her like a conspirator. "Go kick some ass."

She laughed and said, "I'll pray for your safety. I'll have the whole church pray."

"Prayers gratefully accepted," I said, and she drove off.

I felt buoyed up, cared for in ways hard to explain. Whatever the challenge, whatever the risk of this journey, more and more I felt like the whole country was looking out for me, women like Lil with a laugh and a prayer to see me off, role models of how my future might be. This ride was about a lot more than simply riding the bike.

Buffalo Shuffle, Oh?
Aug. 28th: 931 miles

Woods to hoods and Canadian Mounties defined my ride to the shores of Lake Erie. By mid-morning I was pushing over the bridge from one country to the next. I would be in the land of hockey and maple syrup for only a few hours as I rolled along the Niagara River past the great falls and into the USA at Buffalo. Like a full-fledged automobile, I took the center of a lane and pulled to a stop across from a mustachioed Canadian official glaring down at my heavily loaded recumbent form. I had no passport for two reasons: One, I hadn't even considered the need, and two, a tourist back on the canal had said that I could get into the country without one. Besides, what bomb-toting terrorist comes in on a touring bike? I looked up sweetly, said, "Hello!" and hoped for the best.

"Passports are required for entry into Canada," he said sternly. "We are a multi-cultural society and as such we have to treat everyone equally." This wasn't good. I'd worked out an alternate route that avoided this foreign land, but the Canadian side of the falls was supposed to have the best views—and a long bike path. I was getting in, I had to. The world champion recumbent cyclo-tourist would not be denied. I pleaded my case, flexed my bulging quadriceps, the Guns of Navarrone. Surely, he must submit.

Mounty the border agent worked his moustache and fell into his rote speech—again: "This is a multi-cultural society and as such we have to treat everyone equally." A robot? How many times did he have to recite this line in a given day? Was he tested by a middle-manager, forced to stand in front of the class and recite? There had to be some way around this situation. The other lines of cars moved smoothly across the border while I jockeyed for position. This guy was human. He could see I was no threat. *C'mon, man, do the right thing*. Then, suddenly, my opening. "I do a lot of riding myself," he said, his tone easing by a very small but noticeable degree.

"Yeah, it's the best way to see the country!" I added enthusiastically.

"My friends and I go out for two-hundred kilometer rides all the time."

So he was a tough guy. Time to work that angle. "Wow, that's some serious distance. I'm not usually up for that kind of effort." Play it smart, acknowledge his superior power. He's the man.

"Okay," he said (Yes! Yes!), "I'm going to let you in. But next time, remember the passport. Welcome to Canada."

I fired up the big guns and began the international portion of my journey.

Signs in French, kilometers slipping out all over the place, "eh?'s" and "aboots" on the breeze, it was good to be back in Gretzky-land. I had all the food I needed and wouldn't have to change any money, my only duties to take in the famous falls and make it to Buffalo. As I approached the falls, a rift in the earth's crust where one oceanic lake drains into another, I was slapped with a fearsome yin and yang of the modern world, the wild, the untamed hard up against the worst kind of commercial development.

My senses hungrily sought out the rumbling blue wall to the east, but I couldn't get past the abomination of Las Vegas on the Niagara. *What the hell?* Space needle, amusement rides, animal displays, the worst of kitschy krap kreeping relentlessly along the shore. I paused to photograph a barrel that some mental patient had ridden over the falls, an attraction I expected. On the New York side, a long observation deck hung precariously out over the water. A tethered observation balloon floated even higher, the whole scene like something out of the Pan-American

Exposition held in Buffalo back in 1901. For all the visual noise and confusion, the falls were still there, still dumping millions of gallons of water into a churning caldron, moving, pumping seething as they had for thousands and thousands of years. I walked right up to the edge of the drop and stood transfixed by the rolling lip of muscular liquid pulling my spirit over the edge. My heart pounding, I imagined the flow and slide into free fall. Almost two hundred feet below, a boat loaded with tourists flowed into the vast clouds of mist roiling in the watery amphitheater hammered by four million cubic feet of water every minute.

Who would volunteer for a ride over the lip? That someone sat down and actually thought the plunge was a good idea left me breathless, the death wish, the giving into that hidden wire from the beyond that tugs at us all. I shuddered and stepped back. *Who were these people?*

The falls roared that day, one hundred and seventy eight years before, as they had for millennia, the throbbing, mesmerizing primordial power. Goat Island, a wedge of rock splitting the river, sported a new fixture, a ladder suspended 125 feet out over the water. Sam Patch, the New Jersey Jumper, eyed the rickety scaffold, the cold blue water. At twenty-two, he'd built a certain fame and reputation for daring leaps—over falls, from tall masts, buildings, whatever he could find. That autumn day, he looked down and thought of the first one to attempt a jump such as this. He had died. Would Patch's jump end the same way? Not as dangerous or as high as going straight over the falls, his leap was still pushing the edge beyond what he'd tried before. Death lurked in those waters.

Suddenly, one of the heavy cables supporting the cantilevered ladder snapped under the strain, and the last fifteen feet of the scaffold plunged into the river below, giving the small crowd a taste of what was to come. Not to be put off, Sam crawled out on the swaying steel, stood on the end over the water, and jumped. The sickening pull of gravity sucked him down, the air rushed over his ears, his eyes wide, focused on the landing, arms out guiding is fall. Time stretched but space did not. In an instant he slammed into the water feet first and vanished beneath the surface, lost under the churning waves. Moments later, he clawed back to the top and up onto the shore, the first man to survive a leap near the falls. The gathering of spectators was too small for his taste, so he successfully repeated the stunt later to a crowd of 10,000, who cheered when he finally pulled himself out of the river.

Like all men addicted to the edge, he kept jumping, but not for long. A month later, in November of 1829, he stood atop the 99 foot falls of the Genesee River, a cuddly bear cub in his arms. He felt its warm fur in his hands, looked down at the churning river below, at the small crowd, and hurled the little bear into the void. The terrified, squirming brown form splashed into the roiling water, a tiny disturbance so far below. Miraculously, it swam to the surface and made it to shore. Sam followed, also successfully. But the crowd was small, the income disappointing. The only thing to do was to spice the punch.

A week later, on Friday the 13th, he built a tower to increase the height to 125 feet. This time, before a crowd of 8,000, he climbed, spotted his landing--the crowd shouting "Jump! Jump!"--and leapt. He fought for control, the fractions of a second spinning wildly, his arms pinioned, but he tilted, came off vertical and slammed into the water on his side, a huge splash marking his impact. For long moments the crowd held its breath, looking, gaping. No Sam. What trick was this? Had he slipped away? Hidden somewhere out of sight after swimming underwater? They waited and waited and finally wandered off, feeling somehow cheated, confused, worried. Where could he be? Months later, his frozen body was discovered downstream near Rochester. The Jersey Jumper was through.

The first person to go directly over the falls was a sexagenarian teacher by the name of Annie Edison Taylor. Desperate to set aside some money for her later years, she struck upon the scheme of riding over the falls in a barrel. Constructed of oak and iron, it resembled a stretched wine cask. In October of 1901, she followed Sam Patch's example and first sent a cat named Lagara over the falls. One can only imagine what that was like for the kitty. Lagara survived, and so, on October 24th, Annie wedged herself into the mattress-padded barrel, and her assistants screwed the lid tight. It must have felt something like a coffin, totally dark, a second womb. The helpers then pressurized the barrel with bicycle pump and slammed a cork into the filling hole. In a stunt more typical of testosterone poisoned young males, this rather dour-faced Victorian woman in her sixties set out on the ride of her life. We can imagine that in those moments before the fall, the water rushing, the cask bouncing, the complete, utter blackness, Annie Edison Taylor likely regretted her decision. But she had made her choice. There was nothing to do but pray and wait for the fearsome acceleration over the lip and the 178 foot plummet.

About thirty minutes after setting out, bruised, bleeding, but alive, Annie emerged from the barrel. Hungry for every detail of the harrowing plunge, the press crowded around. "If it was with my dying breath," she proclaimed, "I would caution anyone against attempting the feat... I would sooner walk up to the mouth of a cannon, knowing it was going to blow me to pieces than make another trip over the Fall."

She never did make her fortune. After a few speaking engagements, her promoter vanished with the barrel, and Annie went broke paying for private investigators to locate the icon so necessary for speaking engagements. Contrary to her earlier pronouncement, she contemplated another barrel trip but never followed through. She lived another twenty years and died in a nursing home in Lockport not far away from the falls.

Others ignored Annie's advice and took the big ride, some died, most did not. Perhaps the most incredible journey over the falls was by Roger Woodward. He did not plan his ride, did not scheme to make a fortune in speaking fees. He was seven years old, and he fell into the water by accident while on a boating trip. In July of 1960, he and his teenage sister, Deanne, were out on the river with a New Yorker at the helm when the outboard motor of the small aluminum boat could not fight the current. The boat drifted, caught on a rough shoal and capsized, throwing all of them into the turbulent rapids. Gut-wrenching panic shocked their floundering bodies, the falls not far away. Roger wore a life vest and bobbed and bounced along, getting bruised and beaten by the rocky bottom. Deanne swam for her life, unable to help her brother or the man who had taken them out. Accelerating toward the edge, she came into view of tourists at the railing on the edge of Horseshoe Falls on the Canadian side. They began to yell at her to swim harder. People were running up and down the shore in futile panic, watching the boy head for the falls, praying the girl to swim to safety. Deanne pulled with everything she had. John Hayes, a New Jersey truck driver, jumped over the railing and yelled out to Deanne. Flailing, gasping, she started to close the distance, the crowd looking on in stunned horror. Twenty feet from the rolling cusp of oblivion, Deanne grabbed the Jersey truck driver's thumb and started to pull. The mist and rocket roar of the falls filled the air. Straining, about to lose his grip, Hayes cried for help. John Quattrochi, another man from Jersey, jumped forward, and together the two men pulled the young woman to safety. She called out for her brother. Quattorchi whispered: "Pray for him."

Down below, incredulous, horrified, the riders and captain of Lady of the Mist spotted a small body in a life vest bobbing in the water beyond the falls. They fished Roger from the water and found him alive, battered, but alive. His story became an international sensation. The pilot of the small boat was killed and forgotten.

I stood near where the Jersey truck driver had leaned out over the rushing river. No drama unfolded for me, only the usual bland tourists taking photographs, looking as I did at the impressive moving wall. No signs of the life and death struggle. Only whispers in fragile old papers stored in libraries, a few pixels on the web remained. Further down the road, a concrete piece of evidence of another near disaster stood a couple of hundred yards off shore. A barge, the "Niagara Scow," gave testimony to another frightening event eighty nine years before. A tug boat, the Hassayampa, had lost power when the current shifted the barge that carried newly dredged sediment. The stout line connecting tug to barge stretched, strained and finally snapped under the constant pressure. Slowly the barge began to move down stream with only one destination: the falls. The two workers aboard the scow scrambled to arrest their progress, at first throwing out an anchor that merely bounced and dragged along the bottom without catching. We can only imagine their nauseating fear at watching the line feed out, no final setting of the anchor, the falls drawing closer. They opened the hatches on the bottom of the scow, hoping that the doors would catch on the rocky bottom—no use. Swimming was not an option— too far from the shore. It was a slow motion death sentence with far too much time to contemplate the end.

A mere six-hundred yards from the falls, the anchor caught, the line went tight, and the scow swung to and came to a stop. The two men aboard had to pray the anchor would hold. What ensued was a twenty-four hour rescue effort. At first a fire department came from up river and tried to shoot a line out to the scow, but it fell far short. Finally, another crew arrived with a bigger line gun and succeeded in firing a thin rope out to the scow. This cord was not heavy enough to provide a safe rescue line, so one of the men, a more experienced seaman, fashioned a winch from equipment on the scow, and the pair began the unbelievably laborious process of hauling over a heavy line, a few inches for each revolution of the crank. Through the long, dark, desperate hours, willing the anchor to hold, the men took turns at the winch. Finally, the rescue line secured, the men were hauled to safety. One never went back on the water; the other made a living for a while on the lecture circuit, another survivor of the falls seeking fortune from his experience. Today, filled with sediment, planted like a slowly rusting island, the Niagara Scow told the story of a desperate rescue almost one hundred years before my passing.

I was glad for the lack of drama in my life in comparison and set out with Mojo for the Peace Bridge back to the States. Canada and I would have only a one afternoon stand this time. After lunch, I called Jodi from a park and for the first, last, and only time I was able to say this and mean it: "I've got to shuffle off to Buffalo." On the way I had a funny encounter. Needing to use a restroom, I pulled into a construction site to use a blue outhouse. A hardhat-wearing foreman emerged from a nearby building.

"I just need to use the outhouse," I said.

"Sorry," he replied, "but you don't have proper protective equipment." I laughed and pointed to the helmet on my head, surely sufficient for the radical dangers of a wee tinkle in a booth of blue plastic, but he would have none of it and sent me packing. Canadians are tough.

On the bridge between countries, I stopped and looked out over the impressive panorama: Buffalo, New York, the wide Niagara River below fed by Lake Erie to the west, a thin, diffused moisture suspended in the air, an overflowing, floating abundance of water everywhere, an alien atmosphere. The dampness on my skin told me I was far from home. I pushed over the crest and rolled into the United States to do battle with border agents.

A world class Ninja recumbent cyclo-tourist will not be denied. While others languished in stultifying boredom and mute anxiety, I was quickly cleared to enter even though one bloke had warned me that getting back into the US could be worse than getting into Canada without a passport. In five minutes, I was cutting a big corkscrew on a ramp leading down to street level...and the 'hood. Low-riders, rough sidewalks, trash-strewn gutters, graffiti, decaying brick buildings, iron bars on windows. What strange place was this? Risk sensors on high and hyper-alert navigating traffic, I received only friendly waves, yells of encouragement, a happy toot of a horn and smiles. I could live with this 'hood for a while.

I frequently stopped to check the map and navigate my way to Justin's place, a host to pedal-powered wayfarers like myself, a fellow devotee to the chain and the spoke. In an earlier call, I'd confirmed our meeting, although I was a bit early. I rode slowly and let the scene sink in, the broken glass, drunken patrons staggering from darkened saloons at mid-day, weed-choked lots. The wooded bliss of the

Adirondacks seemed another life, but this ride was about everything, not only the comfort of wild places. I needed everything, wanted it all. For now, Buffalo was where I needed to be.

A hundred years before, at the opening of the Twentieth Century, Buffalo was a very different place. Home to the great Pan American Exposition, the town was the first electrified city in the country with Tesla's impressive dynamos providing the power. The first modern "high rise" structure was built here. This was the golden age for the city that boomed once the Erie Canal was finished. In 1901, it was one of the largest cities in the country, and with the twin enchantments of the hydropower and the great falls, Buffalo was a natural choice for the Exposition. Some of the wealthiest families in the country had homes here— Stanford, Rockefeller. President McKinley, however, would find Buffalo less welcoming.

At the dawn of the Twentieth Century, when everything seemed possible in this showplace of the future, a crowd gathered around to greet the President, who went down the line, shaking hands. He reached out to one fellow, Leon Czolgosz, who answered the gesture with two pistol shots, one glancing off a rib, the other driving deep into McKinley's abdomen. Czolgosz was punched to the ground by an unemployed waiter. McKinley, who did not fall, was immediately led away. Although the city was electrified, no lights were available inside the buildings, so mirrors were employed to bring light to the operating room. The doctors could not find the bullet, which had become lodged somewhere in the president's back. Strangely, although Edison's x-ray machine had been invented, and one was on display at the Exposition, it was not used. Perhaps they feared what the strange new machine might do to the president. Whatever the case, he was stitched up and taken to a nearby home to recover. In fact, McKinley did remarkably well for days, gaining strength and staying lucid. Optimistic press reports were sent out. But the wound had become infected, and after days of building hope, the president died. In modern times, he would have survived.

For all the advances on display in Buffalo that September in 1901, one that had yet to appear was antibiotics, so we lost another American president.

President Bush was hale, hearty and bullet free as I cruised the edgy streets in 2007. Whatever wonders and shine the place had at the turn of the Twentieth Century were gone now, at least in this quarter. Buffalo was changed, a faded prom queen gone to seed. I stopped a couple of times to get my bearings and finally located the correct street. In moments, I rolled to a stop in front of Justin's house, a two-story clapboard structure with a narrow, overgrown porch, chipped paint, a weedy patch of grass, a brick drive shot through with grass on the side leading back to a garage with rooms above. No one seemed to be about. I stood for a moment, feeling the hot, sticky August sun beat down. With time to kill, I crossed to the other side of the street and parked Mojo under a tree. A lively group was gathered on the steps and lawn of the house nearby. Small children ran about yelling, the young mother in short-shorts and tank top yelling: "Shut the hell up!" Several young, working-age males lounged on the steps and smiled and waved as I greeted them. A bulky older woman set about laying out a water slide for the children who quickly started taking running leaps onto the water-slick surface. I wondered about the men, all healthy, sitting around in the middle of a work day, but the implications were clear enough. One fellow with huge Dior sunglasses with jeweled ear pieces asked about my bike, and I gave the short version of what I was doing. Then he said, "Hey, I got a nice video recorder. It just needs a cable. You wanna buy it?"

"Oh, thanks," I replied, with an easy refusal, "but on a bike I've got to keep the weight down. No place to carry it, anyway."

"Hey, that's cool," he said.

I then asked if I could take their picture in order to document my journey. "Oh, hey, ha, ha, nooooo, I don't think that's a good idea. Take a picture of the kids!" Grandma, a Rosanne Barr type, stood with the achingly cute children. I wondered how their futures would play out in such a family. *Shut the hell up.*

Soon, a lean young man on a bike stopped across the street and whipped off his helmet to reveal a head of shaggy blond hair. He leaned the bike against the fence and crossed the street when he saw me with Mojo. "My place is over here," he said, giving the motley crew on the steps a hard glancing look.

"We're just hangin' out," said Dior Sunglasses, sounding a bit defensive. I could only guess at the subtext whirling about. I bid the Stoop Meisters good day and rolled over into Justin's world.

In his twenties, a recent college graduate, Justin and I had much in common even though we were born a generation apart. He worked a landscaping job to earn money and stayed rent free in the loft above the garage—no insulation, no running water. An acolyte of adventure, he worked to save money, his dreams set on New Zealand for the coming winter, a summer escape in the southern hemisphere away from Buffalo's notoriously hard winters, most notorious in recent times being the big blizzard of '77 when winds up to seventy miles per hour and many feet of drifting snow buried houses up to their eaves. In many cases, only snow mobiles, snow shoes and skis would do for travel. In an average year the town receives ninety inches of snow.

Now we both stood sweating as he let me into the narrow, dark garage. Suddenly out bounded a huge brown, goofy hound--Dutch. Right away I had another friend in Buffalo. In the back of the crowded, narrow room, Justin led up the stairs, almost ladder-steep, to the loft: a big couch for me, an entertainment center backed by a hanging sheet to separate the "living room" from the bedroom, a single table with a laptop. A large window was blocked by a massive fan, the only cooling for this apartment of bare framing backed by bits of drywall and thin boards. The air was hot and still. For a bachelor interested in zero rent, it would do for the summer. Sub-zero winters would make the lodging an extreme survival sport, however. As I stood in the hot, damp, close air, summers didn't appear to be a pleasant affair either.

That night, after visiting with his parents (his father, Jan, a recumbent rider and bike nut, too), Justin took me down to the Elmwood district, where the locals go to eat, socialize, soften brain cells at a number of watering holes and restaurants. These few blocks were bouncing with activity. With the college semester due to start in a couple of days, a young, hormone-twisted multitude was out enjoying the cool of the evening and the last moments of freedom. Some would find more value in the bars than the lecture halls, but the energy of the busy street was infectious, and it was good to have a young, savvy local as my guide to the nightlife of Buffalo. Lines poured in and out of bars. Two story rooming houses overflowed with boisterous youth, chairs scattered across balconies and lawns. Errant bicyclists jousted with slow-moving pedestrians while streams of fully loaded cars rolled slowly up and down the avenue, a scene out of *American Graffiti*. Justin and I ducked into a dark, loud pub to sample suds on tap. We ordered up a couple of light-toned ales and got down to the business at hand: *Who the hell are we and why are we here?*

As I had done with other people I'd met on the road, I quizzed him about life in Buffalo, what he liked, what he didn't. Justin had been through a lot for a man barely halfway through his twenties. The party life he'd been through in college had sucked him in, and he found himself in a time-wasting limbo. He saw friends in a similar, unproductive spiral and began to doubt what he was doing. Then a close cousin died, then a beloved grandmother. Two other events proved pivotal.

One night, in a neighborhood perhaps best not frequented after dark, he and a friend, Shawn, went to sell some electronics. Instead of reaching for money to complete the sale, the buyer pulled a pistol and shot Shawn in the chest. In a blind panic, Justin grabbed a knife he happened to have in his pocket and began stabbing the gunman. Screaming, thrashing, blood, noise, a river of hot adrenaline flooded the car. The knife no doubt saved Justin's life. Wounded, the shooter scrambled from the car and fled into the night. Unlike the late president, Justin's friend recovered, but in Justin the sound of that gunshot echoes still, a wake-up call to choose what he really wanted in life, to find meaning.

To clear his head, Justin took his bike to the West and sweated and strained his way through the glories of the Arizona desert. In the movement and effort, he found the peace and direction he needed. For now, he wanted to ride, explore, seek adventure and himself in places where he had never been. As one married for a season to the road, I understood him too well. We all come to the path in different ways, but the fundamental impulse is the same. Justin was a kindred soul.

The next day I wandered the city with Paul, a gift from the road gods for my day in The City of Light. I met him through the *Couchsurfing.com* website. I had considered staying with Paul for a night when I wasn't sure about Justin's situation, but I preferred not to move all my gear. Like Virgil to my Dante, Paul offered to guide me through the town. Paul, a therapist and psychology instructor at the local community college, was the ideal host. He had a huge knowledge and enthusiasm for his home and took me to all the fine old buildings and classic Buffalo locations. We ended up walking too many miles for a true rest day, but I doubted I would return to the shores of Lake Erie, so I didn't mind. Besides the incredible examples of art deco architecture, I was struck by the seeming emptiness of the city. Paul explained that the main downtown area was operating with about one half of the people it could accommodate, almost 300,000 souls down from the high point in 1950. Development further and further from the center, a loss of capital, movement of jobs overseas, all of these and more were draining the once vital center. Classic buildings that in San Francisco would be packed with businesses and expensive apartments stood empty—empty! A sad, anemic pall hung over the ornate brick archways and domes glinting in the afternoon sun. I was reminded of a jilted bride from Dickens.

For lunch we went out to The Hatch where I inhaled a Polish sausage and fries, the official food of many in the town, home to the world's third largest Polish population. Paul and I walked out along the wave break. In winter, he liked to put on heavy clothes and come out to watch huge plates of ice buildup like an arctic sea. I could not imagine the temperatures that would make that possible, standing as I was in shorts and a t-shirt.

That night, Justin away late at a concert, I feasted on a local delicacy: *steak on whack*, the Buffalo version of a Philly cheese steak sandwich. For some inexplicable reason, the bread was called "whack." Virgin to this particular gustatory construct, I stepped with some trepidation into The Steakout, a strange den of linoleum and vinyl, gazed up at the brightly lit menu above the counter and placed my order for what looked to be the standard version, according to Justin the classic meal in these parts—besides Polish sausage. What arrived minutes later resembled a huge gopher after a suicide bomber attack, its beige interior sprayed by center-line yellow spew—all tucked sloppily in a huge white bread roll of dubious origin. No worse than live beetles or monkey brains. I had eaten worse, sort of. It filled me up, however, and I staggered back to the loft for my last night in Buffalo, a hot, stifling affair indoors. I eventually stumbled down to the patchy lawn and passed a few hours of sleep after a round or two of Dutch slobber. Nights in the wild can be tough.

Another rancid meat morning hung low and fetid over a bleary-eyed Buffalo. Steak on whack gone greyer still, the sky closed off any options of buoyant optimism. I ate a quick breakfast of cereal and coffee and pushed off into the damp sickly limp dishrag of a 6AM dawn. The day had a distinct advantage, however: cool temperatures. After a fitful, sweaty night, I now cycled through occasional light showers. Fast, smooth, little climbing, the miles fell like housing prices after the crash. As the morning came on, I pulled away from the development, the sad run-down neighborhoods and weed-choked lots, and entered rural

America once more—vineyards, lush trees, houses and shacks tucked back from the road.

Soon I came upon a sign that said the road ahead was blocked—road construction. I had seen these before and could usually push through on a bike, but a gut feeling said I shouldn't try it this time. I didn't know how far down the road the obstruction lay, and I didn't want to be forced to backtrack. I followed the detour. The heavy green trees leaned in close over the road when I broke out and passed a small vegetable stand. I glanced, didn't stop, but again a small voice said this might be the last good access to green matter. *Better check it out.* I circled back and parked Mojo next to the stand. From behind a barn, a man in his fifties stepped out, thinning grey hair and a grey Amish-style beard with the upper lip and cheeks clean shaven giving him a distinctive look. For one dollar—he refused to take more—I had almost too much to fit in my panniers. He said he was a cyclist himself and gave me precise directions to shorten my detour and improve the ride.

I thanked him and set off, strangely shaken by this simple transaction. What was going on? A sixth sense, a hunch, an itch in my brain had said, "Stop here." Then I met exactly the person I needed to meet, maybe the only one for miles around with the information and sympathy I required. Serendipity, accident, design? *"What is going on?"* I said out loud. I couldn't know, but I felt humbled and supported and guided along by people I would almost certainly never see again. The road provides. When I regained the main route along the lake, I saw the construction area: A gargantuan trench easily ten feet deep cut straight across, absolutely impassable except with a sizeable ramp, a motorcycle at high speed, and the nerves of Evel Knievel.

An eighty mile day found me camped for my last night in New York, hardly a mile or so from the Pennsylvania border. I would rip through this sliver of the Keystone State in only a few hours, so the New England phase of my trek was over, and the enormous belly of the country, the Midwest, loomed large, flat, and long in my humid dreams.

Part II: The Midwest

"The sins of the Midwest: flatness, emptiness, a necessary acceptance of the familiar."

Stewart O'Nan

"Everything is so much quieter here than in Tokyo."

Kansas (the rock band)

"Kansas is a state of the Union, but it is also a state of mind, a neurotic condition, a psychological phase, a symptom, indeed, something undreamed of in your philosophy...."

William Allen White

The Winky-Eyed Jesus
August 31st : 1080 miles

I awoke to the undeniable reality of moisture, the wet press of oceanic lakes and soggy atmosphere. Clear save for the scattering of clouds out over Lake Erie, the night had left its impression on my tent and other belongings. As if a full night of rain had fallen, I carefully unhooked the tent fly and shook off the incredible amounts of water and realized that, unlike my native desert California, nothing was going to dry out anytime soon. I gazed out over the lake. What strange place was this? The Great Lakes contain one fifth of the world's fresh water supplies. Only the polar ice caps contain more. And the water I stood beside—whose distant shore I could not see—was one of the *smaller* lakes. Aptly named Lake Superior holds twenty-five times as much water. It beggars the imagination. Unfortunately, I knew of the serious pollution problems these lakes endured and wondered how we could harm such massive bodies. We are too many, too clever for our own good, and we've opened Pandora's box of science and technology. There's no going back. All we can do is turn this power back onto the problems we have created and hope to reclaim some of what has been lost. In the last century, Huxley, a British scientist, said that we could never exhaust the productive capacity of the cod fisheries of the north Atlantic. Today, most of the fishing grounds off New England are closed to cod fishing, the stocks nearly eliminated. We are efficient monkeys indeed and often know not what we do. Give a man a fish, and he eats for a day. Teach him how to fish and he'll deplete the whole fishing grounds faster than you can say

Ichthyosaurus. I pondered my small place beside the big water and packed for my push into Ohio.

Somewhere in the midst of my dash across Pennsylvania, I crossed a milestone: I completed my first 1,000 miles. Stopping to record the event, taking a picture of the cyclometer, I stared at the rank of zero's indicating the counter had rolled over from 999. So, there it was—or wasn't. The nothing on the tiny screen meant something, didn't it? A ghostly symbol of so much work—the mountains of New England, the insect infested shores of Lake Ontario— I'd pedaled through it all. In the absence of zeros was the presence, my presence in a strange state so far from home. *Home, Jodi*, the steep mountain country of my native California were absent and present, too. Gone, away, over 3,500 miles of strange roads and people separated us, but the gravitational pull of my history, my life and self constantly hummed, insistent, a force not to be denied. I belonged somewhere, both here and there, somehow. The road west was my North Star, a point I strove for day after day. Camped beside the Atlantic, huddled under a tree in a New Hampshire downpour, I sometimes felt alone and isolated, but the cords of home kept their steady tension.

By mid-afternoon, Pennsylvania was behind me and I slipped into Ohio. I still had over sixty miles to cover to make it to Cleveland, probably the biggest city I would encounter on my route, and I needed a place to stay. Cleveland worried me more than Ashtabula, the small town where I first landed. I rolled down a moderate hill and over a steel grated cantilevered bridge. With a house-sized block of concrete hitched to one side of an enormous lever, the bridge could be lifted and lowered to allow boating traffic into the small harbor near the town. Fishing boats sat quietly at dock, and the old part of town rose above in a cluster of vintage brick buildings. From a distance it looked quaint, like the canal towns along the Erie, but as I got closer I could see the rough edges, the poorly kept windows, chipped paint, the creep of decay moving in. Even so, it had a certain charm with the older structures and, perhaps, with some capital and motivation, it might rise again—or not.

Either way I needed a place for the night, and I needed to look up accommodations in Cleveland.

I found the library and started hitting walls. The town prohibited camping in the park, and the numbers I called for a place in Cleveland had no answer. Where the hell does a California boy with a kinky bike stay in Cleveland? I left my call-back number with the various Warmshowers hosts (a database of people willing to host long-distance cyclists) and wondered if the service would let me down this time. I wasn't even thinking that Labor Day weekend was about to start, everyone gone for the holiday.

Feeling a bit frantic, I stomped out of the library and headed for the newer section of town, determined to get more fuel for the stove and hunt up a place to throw down my bag. The acid bite of uncertainty was back. For not the first time I thought about how much easier this would all be if I broke down and got a motel. I would do it, when I had to, but I wasn't there—yet. The thrill is in the hunt. I kept reminding myself that I was on the road for over three months. I could not be flinging around cash every night for a place to sleep. Too soon the expenses would get out of hand. *Do things in order, get the job done. First, fuel for the stove.* I noticed a couple walking on the sidewalk in my direction and pulled to a stop to greet them.

They smiled hugely, revealing serious gaps in tobacco-stained teeth. He was short, under five nine, slim, in blue jeans, narrow leather belt, black t-shirt with abstract Native American symbols on the front. He used a tall walking stick that came up to his shoulders, and thick, black-framed prescription glasses hung on his nose. A short-billed white painter's cap shaded his eyes against the bright sun. She wore a lighter shade of jeans topped by a loose fitting white shirt that buttoned down the front. Her straight blond hair was tied back, streaks of grey revealing some of her years as did the missing teeth and skin with that particular quality that life-long smokers develop, the sharp, dried papery texture around the mouth. What shone through most, in both of them, was a great joy at seeing me.

I asked them about the nearest hardware store, all the while feeling the lateness of the day. They gave me directions to a store a couple of miles away. Then I asked about somewhere I might stay. "Oh," she beamed, happier than if I'd given her a $100 bill, "you can stay with us!"

"Sure, you're welcome," said her companion. He gripped and released the stick, gripped and released, tapping it on the ground.

I had to think quickly. These were not the sort of people I spent a lot of time around, but something in their happiness and their sadness appealed to me. Then I considered the prime directive of my journey—to see this country, to meet the people. I had to see this through, bear witness to this couple's life, whatever it might be. The roller coaster was headed over the top and I needed to see where it would take me. "Sure," I said. "That sounds great. You two are a couple of road angels."

"Oh, no," she said, "you're the angel! We're so happy to give you a place to stay!" They both seemed very excited to have someone to talk to. I offered to get some beer to celebrate. "Oh, sorry, we're in *The Program*. I've been sober sixteen years," she said. "Sam here for six months."

"Yes, praise God, six months." He gripped and released the stick, gripped and released, holding onto that staff like his life depended on it.

"Well," I said, "that's fine. But I'm making dinner. Where do you live?"

Sam and Alice, both in their late forties or so, had no car and walked wherever they went, covering eight to twelve miles a day. They lived back the way I had come and were headed there now, but Alice needed a Dr. Pepper. That and cigarettes seemed to get her through the day. "I used to be real overweight," said Alice, "but Sam got me walking. I don't need no cane no more like I used to." She added more details about her life. Within minutes of meeting me, she talked about a physically abusive relationship she had finally escaped.

Desperate sobriety on the hoof, they marched down the street to a convenience store while I went across to a super market to pick up a couple of steaks, some broccoli and potatoes for dinner, and, feeling strangely guilty, a beer for myself. It was the least I could do. We agreed to meet up along the way. I would speed ahead on the bike and wait for them to catch up, then roll on again. They walked slowly, hand in hand, holding onto each other and a world, for now, without drugs or alcohol.

I, on the other hand, enjoyed the beer down by the water as I waited for them to catch up. Perhaps I needn't have been so circumspect, however. After we re-crossed the river, I stopped next to a saloon. When Sam and Alice arrived, Alice said, "Hey, I'm goin' in to see if they want you to play. Ya never know." That seemed like a less than optimal place to work for a man just crawling onto the wagon, but Sam didn't seem concerned as he eased himself against a rock bordering the dirt parking area and told me about his life.

"I'm a musician, used to be real good, but when my daddy died, I got $300,000 dollars and drank it all up, one long party. Now I got nothin' to show for it, nothin'. I coulda built a studio, made some real music, but I drank it all. Got nothin' to show for it. But I found God. It's undescribable. Undescribable! My nerves, though, my nerves're shot." He looked at his hands, shaking, opened and closed them and re-clasped the stick. "Still, I got God. It's *undescribable.*"

A short distance up the next hill I pedaled past a billboard displaying the praying beatific figure of the Dali Lama, his big smile and supplicating hands. *Okay, that's it— loving kindness. Gotta tap into that, brother. You'll likely need plenty of it tonight.* I stopped in front of my hosts' apartment building and set Mojo's stand down into the gravel. Four units, two below, two above, the energy of the place spilled out into the evening.

A small boy, hardly five years old, wavered uncertainly on the steps. He looked back towards the front door and then down to the car parked in front, a rusted blue sedan with an even younger boy barely visible in the back seat. The mother, blond hair tied back, yelled in a decisive tone: "C'mon, get in! Move it!" The boy hesitated. "Git yer ass in here!"

From the bowels of this cavern of discontent staggered the father in dirty t-shirt and sagging jeans. "Where're you goin'?" he yelled, seemingly astonished that anything was wrong.

"You got a real attitude problem, and we're goin' to grandma's till you get it figured out. Now, get in here, boy!"

The child's uncertainty withered. He ran down the stairs and awkwardly, using his whole body, leaning hard, pulled open the car door and climbed in. Mom threw the battered rig into reverse, spinning gravel, and lurched into the street, bound for grandmother's house. Dad grumbled a grunt and vanished back into the night of his apartment, the screen door clattering shut.

Hoo boy. Okay. So this was it? I girded loins, battened hatches, galvanized resolve, and braced myself for impact. I only needed to spend the night, but could I make eight in such a place? I swallowed hard, unpacked the food, and waited for Sam and Alice. Dysfunction junction was home for the night. Before long, I was heading up the stairs behind my new friends.

I stepped through the screen door directly into a tiny entry area and the kitchen, a wasteland of waste—dishes and pots everywhere, on the floor, crowding the counters, packed into the sink. The acrid edge of stale cigarette smoke clung to every molecule. "I hate, hate, HATE doing dishes!" declared Alice with the conviction of a fundamentalist who lived life in accordance with her beliefs. Careful not to overturn the pots and pans on the linoleum, I moved into the living room, a much tidier space, rusty red, stained carpet. This wasn't too bad. Perhaps the worst of it was confined to the Temple of the Forgotten Dishes. Sam quickly vanished into the left of two rooms at the back of the apartment—my room for the night. Alice followed while I stood in the doorway. A virtual mountain of clothes and other items lay heaped like a moraine after a glacial retreat, a permanent geological feature, but Alice and Sam went to work, shoving, shoveling and pushing the debris to one side to clear a space on the floor. Sam grabbed a jug of blue disinfectant and sprinkled liberally over the carpeting to ward off evil spirits and errant bacteria. *Steady, Scotty Boy, steady.*

I set my gear down on the floor and joined the happy couple in the living room. They were extremely concerned that I understand where they got all their possessions. Some they found discarded; other pieces had been donated by a church. Proud of the collection, Sam patted the mustard-colored pads of the couch. "This is nice, huh? You'd pay a lot for this in the store. God brung all this into our life," he said, standing up. On a shelf behind me, under a stereo system with a complex of wires hanging like limp entrails from all sides, he picked up a small green toy, a stuffed frog the size of his hand. "Look at this!" he declared like a proud father. "God gave this to me today." He squeezed the toy, which erupted in a wheezy "ribbit, ribbit."

"Yes, look at that," I said.

Alice picked up something from the table by the window overlooking the gravel lot. She held it out carefully for me to inspect: "Look at this. God gave this to us, too." It was a small portrait of a rather Anglo-Saxon Jesus. I've always found these renditions curious since any real Jesus would have been a swarthy Semite, the kind of fellow to get hard looks from airline security or be found behind the wheel of a cab in New York City. But here was a pale Jesus. At least he wasn't blond. "Look!" she cried. "When you tilt the pitcher, the eyes open 'n' close!" Back and forth, Alice wiggled the Son of God, who winked and winked and winked, the lids dropping and drooping at different rates. Above the winky-eyed savior was taped a small four-leaf clover. "Sam and I found this clover when we was walkin'. That's good luck."

I felt like I was spinning, losing it, a lost character who'd stumbled into a David Lynch movie. I had to ride it out, stay open, let the narrative unfold. Action helps, so I went to work on dinner, cleaned some plates and a frying pan. "I hate doin' dishes," Alice repeated. "Thanks for helpin'." I was glad for something to do. Sam put some music on the stereo, Alice lit another cigarette, and shortly we sat down to a big meal of steamed potatoes with olive oil and garlic, broccoli, and fried steak—a bit tough, but filling and a big load of calories my body craved. Afterwards, Alice said, "Sam, why don't you play some music?"

He pulled a guitar case from the corner, set a clean steel-stringed instrument across his thigh, placed a pick between his fingers and began to play. A series of smooth cords at first, a country tune perhaps, a familiar swing to the rhythm. Then his fingers stumbled, he tried to sing, stumbled again, and stopped. "It's my nerves. My nerves're shot!" his voice cracking, disbelieving, wounded.

"That's okay, honey," said Alice. "That sounded real nice. You'll get it back."

Sam put away the guitar.

It was getting late for me. I had been up since well before dawn, so I thanked them both and said I'd be leaving very early to avoid the heat. I told them how much I appreciated their help—and meant it. But there was no denying my anticipation of the next morning. "Don't you leave without sayin' goodbye, y'hear?" Alice said. I promised not to and retreated to my room and the dubious refuge of thin walls and rancid carpet. I scribbled furiously in my journal and, finally too exhausted, shut off my headlamp and tried to sleep. My long journey to the dawn had just begun.

Alice and Sam talked urgently long into the night. I heard only scattered words and phrases, hints of old scars and battles undecided. Even with earplugs, too much sound pulsed through the walls. Next door, a couple lurched into full combat.

"You fucked her? You fucked her? Well, fuck you!"

"Fuck you, too, bitch!"

Back and forth, blow and counter punch, the foul invective poisoned the air and infected the walls. The deep, self-inflicted unhappiness left me counting the minutes until my departure. Later, the predictable pounding of the bed on the other side of my wall began, Sam and Alice, the other side of the equation. Then one of the F-bombing couple turned up an amplifier and assaulted the complex with seismic electric bass notes.

Hell is an apartment complex at 2 am in Ashtabula, Ohio.

After only a couple of hours of fitful sleep, I was up and packing, rolling my pad, taking careful inventory so as not to forget anything. There was *no way* I was coming back. I stepped into the living room and saw that Sam and Alice's door was partly open, a bright light coming through the gap. I gently pushed it open to see Sam face down on the bed, Alice face up by his side, the sheets pulled tight across with her arms out. A bare light bulb glared harshly from the ceiling.

"Hey, Alice," I said, "I'm takin' off. Thank you both so much."

She groggily opened her eyes, confused, then realized what was happening. "That's okay, Scott. You take care."

I eased the door shut and made my way in the dark morning down to Moji and my escape. Street lamps cast deep shadows from the balcony and trees as I carefully packed my panniers and slipped out into the quiet town. Down by the bridge, I stopped to brew coffee and watch the fishing boats motor out to the open water, the low rumble of the motors somehow reassuring. I held the warm drink in my hands and thought about the lives around me, the stories I would never know, those that now had become part of my own. We do not choose our birth. The storms of life wash over us and where do we land? I was alone in the morning night beside a great lake, only my body and a bicycle to carry me across a continent. Sam and Alice struggled against the black hole of alcohol and held to each other like ship-wrecked sailors far from shore. They knew that somewhere over the horizon people lived without the pain of addiction and constant loss. In my dark solitude I wondered if they could make the crossing.

Luck, however, was with me. Earlier I had received a message, and I now had a place to stay in Cleveland. It was time to put some miles on the road and leave this story to its own conclusion.

The Burning River and a Plesiosaur
Sept. 1st: 1151 miles

Loch Ness has its monster, a long-necked beast slipping slimily through the Scottish night, and so Lake Erie has its own prehistoric denizen, a creature strange and little known. Washed up on Cleveland's fabled shore, it remains a mystery…. In the early 1990's, Larry Petersen was walking along the lake and found a strange fish. Even as a taxidermist, he could not identify it. Birds had ravaged the carcass, but the imp and artist in the man saw something he liked, so he picked up the three foot long smelly fish and took it back to his shop where he fashioned the Monster of Lake Erie. Petersen trimmed the dorsal fin, notching it to give a more prehistoric look. He fashioned leg-like fins from flaps of skin and bent the neck to give it a Cretaceous attitude. The gag was a huge hit at the shop.

Somehow word got out, as word is wont to do, and one Dr. Carl Baugh of Texas heard about the creature and eventually traveled to Cleveland and purchased "the monster," believing all the while that he had scored the mother lode of all creationists' desires: proof that dinosaurs were not extinct, that man and these strange creatures had always lived together. Dr. Baugh's intention was to use the find in his creationist museum. He insisted various unspecified university scientists had performed CAT scans and DNA analysis—finding the creature *very interesting*. His researchers and universities apparently as dubious as his own degrees, the fish turned out to be a fresh water species known as a burbot, not common but not unknown in Lake Erie. Searches on the Internet turn up more ominous stories, tales of creatures twenty and thirty feet long with huge arms, Ichthyosaurs a-loose in the Great Lakes!

Oblivious to these threats, I rolled beside the placid waters teaming with ill-tempered, toothy serpents. I was bound for Cleveland, home to renowned sports teams, race riots and rivers that burn.

Not once or twice, not six or eight nor ten or twelve, by some accounts the Cuyahoga River has caught fire as many as thirteen times, the first conflagration occurring back in the 1880's. Choked with sludge, brackish brown, slick with oily industrial vomit, bubbling with noxious gases, the once pristine waters carried the evil fruits of the machine revolution down into Lake Erie. Flotsam and jetsam hung up on the shores and pylons. Some parts of the river were azoic, devoid of life, a stream out of Dante's Inferno when a stray spark landed in the muck and set the brew aflame. In 1952, the burning river did over one million dollars of damage. It wasn't until the 1960's and over eighty years of periodic fire on the water that Americans found the collective will to do something decisive about the pollution. The river became the poster child for the growing environmental movement and proved a vital symbol for driving through the Clean Water Act of 1972 and other key legislation, all of which has actually done some good, although I can imagine the captains of industry proclaiming the end of all that is good and holy when faced with the new regulations. Now a 33,000 acre park, the Cuyahoga Valley National Park, sits only a few miles upstream. Strangely enough, there was a monster in Lake Erie, but no prehistoric beast. A chemical stew had stalked these waters, and remnants linger still. With so much industry and development generally, I would be hesitant to join the fishermen I saw along the lake, but at least fish had come back to the river. Of course, there are other Lake Erie Monsters—a professional hockey team.

I had finally connected with Ann and her friend Mary. I had a place to flop and a guide through the city. Ann later said she detected the "desperation" in my voice when I called. She lived virtually car-free and was delighted to help a wayfaring cyclist. We met at a café, and the two of them led me on a strenuous chase into Cleveland Heights, the leafy avenues and brick homes. She and her family were having a Labor Day picnic, and my attendance was welcome and required. A loud and friendly gathering took me in like family. Mountains of food, excellent local brew and lively discussion carried me away. How could I not move to Cleveland and spend all my days with these people? "So," I asked Ann, "is Ohio considered the Midwest or just the far west of the East?"

"Oh, no," she grinned, a slim, fit woman in her early forties, "this is the Midwest, and this is Midwest hospitality." So this was it, then. The central portion of my journey had indeed begun.

Children ran around the green backyard like Sufi dancers on meth. One blond-headed boy kept racing back to the table near where I sat and grabbed cookie after cookie, pumping sugar nitrous into his tiny body, running faster and faster, chasing his siblings, rounding the chairs and tables at ever sharper angles. "Just wait," said Ann, "one of them will be screaming in about five minutes." Moments later, a piercing wail cut through the soft evening air—the evening's first casualty.

My hosts kept the hospitality coming. When I mentioned that my route would pass through Sante Fe, New Mexico, I immediately had another place to stay. Uncle Steve had retired to the Southwest, and he would love to meet me, they insisted. They made a point of mentioning he was gay. Was that all right? How could I refuse? If they'd mentioned something about beating a rap for serial murder, I might have a problem. But gay? Please. The country, the people were reaching out, offering help and support, places to land, kind words and encouragement.

The darkness settled into my tent in the still Ohio night. I was safe from the mosquitoes that had infiltrated the yard, a different world than the ornery city so nearby. The race riots of history were ghosts, a lingering stain of anger, homicide, and a different kind of burning river. Water here, too, played a role, a conflict over a glass of water that turned into a fight that left buildings in flames and bodies bleeding on the ground. Hough, Watts, Washington, D.C., Chicago, the fires of fear, anger and rebellion burned down neighborhoods across the country in the struggle for civil rights.

The spirits of discontent were sleeping when I awoke. My tent was pitched behind Joy and Phil's place, Ann's sister and brother-in-law, and Phil, tall, slim, grey-haired, was going to lead me out of the city for his Sunday ride. We had a quick breakfast in his kitchen and talked of life, cycling, our professions. He was a technical writer and had done a tour of 6,000 miles in his youth, so he knew what I was going through. The city streets were vacant as we entered our own kind of church, a two-wheeled Sermon on the Mount of Cleveland Heights that led us down to lake level. We rolled by the strangely hideous Peter B. Lewis Gehry building glinting like rumpled tinfoil in the early light and soon found ourselves spinning along the lake and up to the Rock 'n' Roll museum. We stopped to explore the wondrous ranks of other-worldly "art" guitars, sculpted instruments eight feet tall sporting alien eyeballs, urban cityscapes, weird faces, abstract shapes and bleeding rainbows of electric color that graced the plaza in front of the glass and concrete monument to American popular culture. This early on a Sunday morning, the museum was closed, but the instillation of commissioned work was worth a pause. Nearby stood the black tour bus of Johnny Cash.

A few miles beyond, we came to the end of the lakeshore bike path. Phil pulled to a stop. This was it. Time to move on. He wished me luck, pointed to the road I needed to take, and soon he was gone. I was left with that hollow aching feeling that breaking of ties requires. Although short-lived, these relationships of the road are important, and this family of Cleveland especially so. For a day, a night or two, a person, a family would take me in, lift my spirits, connect me to a place. But the journey was about the journey, the movement, the next discovery, the person down the line I had yet to meet. So the comfort of connection gave way to the uncertainty of the future, the anticipation and excitement

of the unknown.   Each tour is an unfolding ribbon of
Buddhist lessons in impermanence.

The Dead Zone
Sept. 2nd: 1219 miles

Palatial homes and estate grounds of west Cleveland by the lake faded to rural expanses and some of the flattest riding of the tour. In almost seventy miles I would gain less than six hundred feet while I encountered in a serious way the most dominant life form in this part of the country: *Zea mays*, family *Poaceae*, what most of us call corn. I'd seen patches and fields in upstate New York, but this was something different, a total domination, an obliteration of the natural landscape in favor of one crop; later, I would find soy beans almost as common. The scale of the occupation stupefies the imagination: In the year of my crossing, farmers in the United States planted 92.6 million acres of corn and 76 million acres of soybeans. This equates to 263,437 square miles—more than the total land area of Belgium, the Netherlands, France and Switzerland *combined*. Almost every ear is genetically modified—Frankencorn. Animal feed, ethanol, industrial products, chemical distillates, soy and corn infiltrate almost every aspect of modern life. Food additives, biofuels, lubricants, adhesives, inks, plastics, and on and on and on. These two plants are found in virtually all processed foods in one form or another. Used to fatten animals for slaughter, the grains sicken the beasts with an overdose of protein, so drugs are needed to keep the animals functioning until the hammer falls. And as the pigs and fowl and bovines are fattened, so too are the American people, expanding and sickening with feeding at the trough of agri-industrial food production. Today, almost three quarters of all adults twenty and older are overweight or obese. Our bodies like our country are sagging, heavy in the middle with an overdose of genetically freaked corn and soy.

The bright morning gave spurs to my pedals and miles under my wheels—East Lake, Vermillion, Huron, the towns stacked up quickly on this flat riding. I was a cycling god. Legs hardened in the eastern mountains now flew with easy joy across the horizontal farmland. I will always be drawn to the mountains, but this was a most welcome change. As the day wore on, I began thinking about camp, and I resupplied in Huron and inquired about a place to spend the night. As expected, my question was met with blank stares. People who *live* in a place rarely have a notion of how one might spend the night outdoors. I pushed on, wondering once again how this would play out.

I almost stopped at a farm house to ask if I could camp on the owners' land, but shyness overcame my good sense. I knew that others had done this, even made a habit of it, with good results. I needed to get over my reluctance. All they could do was refuse, right? I rode on and in the late afternoon landed in Avery, a more developed town with a small RV campground. Okay, this could work—but for $25? For a place to throw my tent? No way, José. I doubled back to pick up the route, made a wrong turn, and started to feel strung out, burnt out, gotta-stop-for-the-night tired. Perched on the bike, I sat there contemplating what to do and looked up to notice a strange vacancy around me. I was stopped on the edge of a huge, virtually empty parking lot attached to a huge, virtually empty and decaying mall. It had dozens of retail spaces, and all but two or three were empty. The stench of big investments gone bad oozed like a thick miasma from the weed-filled cracks in the blacktop. Millions? Easily. But where others found bankruptcy, I saw opportunity.

I pedaled slowly around the back of the building and past a tempting picnic table that was, unfortunately, still in the sun. A corner provided shelter, and I parked Mojo in a nice patch of shade. Clean pavement and a wall to lean against made a fine dining room. A few trees and endless corn surrounded the back of this dying, almost dead place, a shopping center beyond the help of life support, a Zombie Mall. The one or two remaining businesses were holding clearance sales, dead merchants selling, selling—gone. Out of morbid curiosity, I tried a back door and found it open. Like pulling back a creaking lid to a crypt, the metal door swung open to reveal piles of drywall, wire, conduit, plumbing fixtures, the dusty viscera of a commercial catastrophe entombed by financial ruin, all the wasted effort and dreams.

As I cooked and ate my simple meal, a couple of employees getting off work (for the last time?) drove by. One fellow gave me an understandably odd expression. An older woman just smiled. Maybe there would be a bit more traffic? A security guard? Drunken teenage drunks? I looked around for a safe place to pitch camp. Across the lot I saw a row of huge trash bins behind which I found a small but serviceable patch of grass hemmed in by weeds and spindly trees. It was a struggle to get Mojo wedged in behind the bins, but I was out of sight. As gnats, mosquitoes and moths swarmed, I pitched the tent and dove in, safe for the night from Zombies and errant alcoholics.

In the morning, dodging the ghosts of retail establishments long gone, I rolled over to the picnic table at 5AM and made breakfast. A simple axiom of the road: With good coffee, *anything* is possible. Out on the interstate, trucks groaned and sighed, their radiant eyes dimming in the dawn. It was time to join the pulse of the American road.

Chasing my shadow and miles beyond the horizon, I set sail due west, arrow-straight, a cool, steady cadence, Mojo and I in a silent, mile-eating mood. At the town of Clyde, I picked up the North Coast Inland Trail, a name of infinite mystery if not jest, and followed it car-free for almost nine miles to Freemont. Cyclists and joggers and rollerbladers shared the path, all plowing through occasional clouds of noxious gnats, so many at times that one jogger wore a bandana bandit style across his mouth. I passed through these patches quickly and covered my mouth and nose with one hand until I broke clear.

Trail's end, Freemont, Ohio, final location of Rutherford B. Hayes, nineteenth president of the United States. Famous for his ability to not offend anyone, he probably ruffled a few feathers when he called in the military to deal with the big railroad strike of 1877. Soldiers fired on a crowd and killed seventy workers. I suspect they and their families could find offense with the august leader. As a republican of his era, he did what he could to improve the lot of the recently freed slaves, but he probably made it worse in some ways by ending Reconstruction and leaving the South to govern itself. Hayes became well known again in my generation for being a president elected by a popular minority, taking the White House by only one very contested electoral vote. Hayes, another hanging chad of history.

To my delight, I came upon a classic American gathering: The small town Labor Day Parade. Given Hayes' attempts to break the labor movement, there was a certain irony in the event, but there was no denying the pure enjoyment of the crowds lining the street and those marching along to the cheers and music. Vintage veterans sat proudly behind the wheels of vintage WWII Jeeps, complete with .50 caliber machine guns. A line of drum majorettes in purple and white twirled batons in style, ranging from the oldest girls in front down to one tiny tot hardly five with a huge grin and saucy hips. Then staggered a collocation of zombies (refugees from the mall?), vampires, Frankenstein's monsters, mutilated corpses. Victims of a recent labor dispute? No, only exuberant youth out to promote the upcoming haunted house. Pulling up last were Freemont's finest—police and fire fighters in gleaming rigs, chrome glinting in the bright September sun.

After the last siren wailed, I saddled up and headed out of town with hours and miles still on the clock. Some distance out, I passed a strange sight. Up on a slight hill above the road, I saw a sign advertising scuba gear and lessons—in central Ohio? They must have good drugs in this part of the country. Later, I was to find that nearby was an old limestone quarry with deep, clear water popular with campers and scuba divers. The park in fact sinks new artifacts from time to time to make the diving more interesting. This seemed odd and weakly artificial, like pulling fish from a freshly stocked stream. I slipped onto narrow paved lanes between untold acres of corn, almost private bike paths, and for miles only a single slow-moving pickup passed me. I kept close tabs on the maps. One road looked just a like another, and I worked to keep the numbers straight. I was in the heart of rural America now, about as far as I could get culturally from the chaos of Los Angeles. No Mercedes or BMW's. Pickup trucks and gun racks were the norm.

Then another odd sight appeared on the road: A supremely restored ancient tractor lumbered towards me with its strange grasshopper eyes and tall knobby tires grinding along slowly, the driver smiling under a ball cap. Glowing like a red sun, it was clearly not something being used on the farm. This was a piece of lovingly restored hardware.

I turned a corner and saw a sign pointing to a S.C.R.A.P. Labor Day Weekend gathering—S.C.R.A.P. an acronym for "Sandusky Country Restorers of Antique Power." I'd stumbled across a most unusual gathering. I rolled down a dirt track between a thicket of trees and there found over 600 antique tractors and weird one-cylinder engines for running farm equipment. These motors had big heavy fly wheels and fired only at long intervals to keep the wheel turning—"chunk!" long pause "chunk!" long pause "chunk!"—the engine attached to whatever the farmer needed. In one display, a fellow was splitting shingles. The woman manning the ticket booth was enchanted by my quest and let me in free of charge. Her adolescent son was completely taken by the loaded bike and insisted on having his picture taken with me. Mom gave me a special sign: "Don't sit on this ~~tractor~~ bike!" and a commemorative plaque, which I carefully tucked away in a pannier. "The fair's almost over," she said, "but I'm sure you can camp here for the night. You don't need any hookups or anything?"

I laughed and pointed at my bike: "On this thing?"

She smiled, handed me a program and indicated a place where other campers were set up, many of them already packing to leave. "Enjoy the show."

I wandered for a long time through the rows of pampered insectile rigs, only the John Deere name familiar to me, many dating back to the 1930's. Along with this iconic brand stood McCormicks and Farmalls, Olivers, Sheppards and Allis-Chalmers, a riot of history and practical technology, tools that made this country and my life what it is. They were beautiful in their own way, a kind of "sexy-ugly" as a movie character once said to describe actors like Harvey Keitel and Humphrey Bogart. These weren't the BMW's and Porsches, the Calvin Klein super models of technology. These were the Bogies, the Edward Nortons, the Jack Klugmans of the internal combustion age—rugged, practical, efficient, beauty through practical use and accomplishment. All of these were magnificent, but some were restored to an almost supernatural degree as to give off an electric charge, the brilliant reds, emerald greens and sunflower yellows. Van Gogh understood these colors. Vincent could have painted tractors.

I encountered a group of older men taken by my transportation. One of them had founded the fair seventeen years before, starting with only seven tractors and a one day event. Now over 600 tractors came together from several different states along with thousands of people and dozens of vendors for the entire three day weekend. The standard uniform for these fellows was a plaid shirt, ball cap, and blue jeans. One looked me in the eye and said:

"Are you *protesting* something?"

"No," I replied, "I'm celebrating this wonderful country!" This made them all laugh and nod. And it was true, as true as anything I could say. This trek was a celebration of life, adventure, and the wonder of the American continent and its people. I'd read that one of the unexpected consequences of such a journey is an increased sense of patriotism. I now understood exactly what they meant. We don't need God to bless this country. She already has. I got more proof of that as evening settled in, the shadows blending into night, the last of the lumbering technology grumbling out of sight, trailers locked and loaded, kids jumping in, the start of the fall semester, homes and jobs waiting for everyone.

I set up under a covered eating area as suggested to avoid the worst of the mosquitoes, which had become fierce in this part of Ohio, a blood sucking force of nature I'd battle off and on until west Kansas. As the darkness settled in and I reclined in my tent to escape the bugs and think about my day and what was to come, I heard light running steps approach the building, hit the concrete and stop just outside my tent. A young boy's voice, the ticket woman's son, said, "Here's some water!" He set a liter bottle down by the tent.

"Thank you," I said.

Then, just before he ran off into the closing night, he said in a forceful, piping voice, "Never give up!"

And then he was gone.

I was instantly humbled and inspired and touched. Alone in my sweaty, tight little tent, besieged by insects, I was totally grateful and happy. I envied no one. However the journey would turn out, this was how it was supposed to go. The boy's words became my mantra, a voice echoing in my mind whenever I struggled. My hope for him is that he would take his own advice.

Intersecting Lives
September 4th: 1,317 miles

Before setting out on this adventure, before I had fully committed to tilting at the windmill of the continent, I'd placed my thoughts online, musing for myself and others about preparations, fears, the mix and swirl of the steps leading up to my departure. From those postings arose a minor relationship with a Marine sergeant nearing retirement, a gunnery expert, Steven Kraft. Young for "retirement"—late thirties—he'd spent the last twenty years in service to our country, many of those years at the Twentynine Palms Marine Corps base about three hours from my home. We sent messages back and forth. Steve and I shared a love of the desert, rock climbing, and cycling. He didn't know what his future would hold; he knew only that he was glad to be regaining his freedom. To celebrate, he planned to hop on his bike and pedal across the country and into his civilian future, although I am told there is no such thing as an "ex" Marine. Steve suggested that we "meet up" somewhere in the middle of the country because we would, in part, be following the same route. Of course, I would be happy to see him, but the odds seemed slim at best. Radically different start times, different routes at different times, surely we'd miss each other? I smiled at the prospect and forgot about it in the flurry of activity that consumed me.

A misty Ohio morning emerged from the darkness that marked the start of my ride. I staggered bleary-eyed from my tent at 4AM, not sleeping much in the humid confines. An hour before dawn I was on Mojo and pulling for sunrise. Distant mesas of forest rose from the corn desert floor. The light morning traffic passed safely, faceless drivers zooming in the glooming, people I would never know intent on their jobs, schools, Bowling Green University not far down the road. I motored west, content in the easy riding, my mind striving to think of nothing but movement, color, the sound of my tires purring on the smooth pavement, another day chewing at the vast corny center of these United States. Out of my pedaling induced reverie I saw a figure emerge from the low morning sun that cut through the evaporating mist. Narrow, on the margin of the road, coming from the west, I soon discerned a cyclist. We closed quickly and came to a stop opposite each other, two solitary travelers in the middle of millions of acres of corn. We looked at each other for a moment.

"Steve," I said, "is that you?" I'd never seen his picture, but somehow, I knew. He was less than six feet tall, strong, clad in bright yellow jersey and black cycling shorts.

"Scott? I thought for sure I'd missed you!" he yelled.

Elation, joy, surprise. We parked our loaded bikes and talked for a half hour in the corn, the morning heat coming on. Thankfully, the mosquitoes found other places to be while we eagerly exchanged news of the road, where we'd been. Steve had stopped for a week in Wyoming at Devil's Tower to climb with a friend. I'd missed the big storm that had flooded many parts of Ohio; Steve had huddled next to a restroom in a park while the fire hose of the gods opened up, dumping up to eleven inches in only a few hours—a fact that left me slack-jawed, knowing that my home town managed that much rain for an entire year. We talked of the war, of dreams and plans. He'd been covering hundred mile days, rising like me at 4AM to get an early start. We were both surprised how these hours came naturally to us. We wanted to talk more, share that beer we'd talked about online, but his road beckoned east and mine west. Steve was headed home for a few days, a town off the route to the south. If I had been a little slower, if he had not stopped in Wyoming, we never would have connected. But we did, and on that fine morning in Ohio, we smiled, shook hands, and set off in opposite directions. For as long as I could, I kept his image in my rearview mirror, a lean, muscular man bent over his aero bars, pushing into the rising sun.

Monroeville, Indiana
September 5th: 1,377 miles

I'd been on the bike for a couple of hours, riding steadily in my cloistered world of darkness and the tiny pool of light thrown by the bike lamp. At times I cut through narrow bands of tule fog, reminding me of winter rides at home. Pedaling in the dark is strange and pleasant, vistas blacked out, only the small light and pure sensation of riding a magic carpet. But with the full light of morning and the pressure of a big sloshing gut of coffee, I had to answer nature's insistent call. I parked Mojo on the dirt shoulder and stepped through the tall grass and into a band of trees nearby. Before I could even begin, the insects were upon me, floating blood suckers hungry for a meal. I waved and kicked, wiggled and waggled and could not even begin to relieve my demanding bladder. The bites started—one, two, three—*I give up!* Cursing every insect that ever lived, I sprinted back to Mojo, scratching already. I would hold my business until the next gas station. I couldn't reach the cool, arid West soon enough.

Late morning and Ohio was part of my history, although Indiana seemed much the same. I'd lived here once as a child but had little memory of it. My main concerns as a five-year-old were playing in the back yard and dealing with a short-lived career as a criminal, inspired as I was by a larcenous neighborhood boy to walk into open houses and pick up anything that looked interesting. Now a model citizen, if a bit odd on my couch bike, I was headed for a well-known spot on the Northern Tier—the Monroeville, Indiana, bikers-only lodging. The town was too small to support even a regular grocery store, but one man was enchanted by the regular heavily laden cyclists who came through his town.

It's hard to overstate what this backwater place means to long distance riders. They roll in from all over the country, all over the world and find refuge from the rigors of the road. Joe Clem, who recently passed on, was a founder of the cycling-only refuge. He enjoyed talking to all the different people and had a huge, giving heart. This same energy is found in the whole town, friendly people who are just happy to see you and give whatever help they can. Warren Fluttrow and Jennifer Yoquelet are two other key players in the refuge, but it's supported by the park service, too. Cyclists, free of charge, get access to air conditioning, full shower and laundry facilities, full kitchen, cots, access to the library and everything else in town within a few minutes' walk. For a couple of nights, I would get a bug-free, sweat-free sleep. I could lock my bike in the living area and walk around. Also a tradition in the center is to invite any cyclists to whatever functions might be going on in the hall adjacent to the living area. Mostly the building serves as a community center, housing weddings, family reunions and the like. We need more places like Monroeville.

After stowing my gear, I walked to the local market where I encountered a fine old gentleman, standing straight, who was hanging around the front of the store. We got talking about my travels, and it turned out I was having the honor of talking to Harold, a veteran of the Battle of the Bulge. Considering the battle was over 60 years ago, he was doing quite well. He said the army always made sure they had tobacco: "They gave us cigarettes before they gave us food!" He was a member of an armored battalion, and his tank had a tread blown off when they hit a landmine. They stuck with the tank and kept firing, providing cover for the advancing infantry. "We fired every last round of ammo!" he said. Feeling humbled by this man's service and experience, I bid him farewell and wandered off to the library. Encounters like this will not be possible in the near future.

Chris, the librarian, got me settled and shared a story with me about the building of the library, one of the biggest things to happen in this town for some time. It cost about a million dollars, the result of a state policy that sets aside money exclusively for public libraries—deep enlightenment, that. With the air of a kid with something too good to keep to himself, Chris told me about an old building that needed to be taken down next door to the soon-to-be constructed library. The town, working on some kind of draconian budget, hired *a blind demolitionist*, "Blind Bruce" they called him. He drove a bulldozer and truck--obviously not too far, but that he was allowed behind the wheel at all leaves one wondering. The entire two-story structure was taken down by hand, sledge hammers and crowbars. Pounding and yelling would issue from the site day after day. Crash! Someone yells in pain. His co-worker yells back: "Shake if off, dude, shake it off!" Finally, OSHA showed up, put hard hats on the workers and took the keys away from Blind Bruce. The building eventually came down without any serious injury to the workers.

I enjoyed Chris' company, another angel of the stacks, and whiled away the hot afternoon in the shelter of Monroeville's shiny new library. That night, I turned up the AC, lay back on the cot, and smiled into the dark room. It was going to be an effort to move on.

*   *   *

As the night once more eased into the dawn, I strained my eyes to make out the road, my headlight casting a meager beam. An imposing grey muck of a sky overhung the way ahead, and I was riding into the wind. Whatever it was, it was coming my way and didn't wait long for the introductions. A state of denial carried me through the first drops. *This will amount to nothing. Keep on moving folks. Nothing to see here.* The winds increased with the rain, and soon I was scrambling for rain gear amidst a serious downpour. Chastised, a little nervous, I pushed Mojo up against a small tree and telephone pole to get shelter. Soon the drops pierced the canopy, and I huddled against the pole, feeling a bit silly and alone. A few minutes later and I was back on the bike, determined to ride through the storm. The storm, however, had other ideas. Heavy, soaking sheets of rain dumped from the black-bottomed sky. Riding was plain foolishness. What to do? A small abandoned strip mall to my right seemed to offer shelter, a covered porch. Moving quickly, I slipped under the cable blocking the empty parking lot and wheeled Mojo and my sodden self under the overhang, dripping here and there and soaking the planks below.

I had yet to feel quite so lonely and depressed as I did crouching there as the rain blurred the sky, a chill creeping in. How I missed Jodi then. I had no idea how long this would last and tried unsuccessfully to get into the empty retail space behind me. No true escape for this lone cyclist. I could only endure, feel sorry for myself, wonder when the storm would pass.

To the southwest of where I stood, eighty two years before in March, there grew a different kind of storm. At the time, government regulations forbade the study or even the mention of the word "tornado," officials believing that funnel clouds were impossible to predict and that telling people a twister was coming would only spread unnecessary panic. Panic, however, was exactly what was called for on that March afternoon when the Hammer of God spread destruction across the land. A mile wide, and moving with an average speed of 73 miles per hour, the tornado first formed in Missouri and began its fearsome trek across three states, obliterating town after town. Almost seven hundred died with thousands injured and 15,000 homes destroyed. No other tornado in recorded history has come close to the Tri-State Tornado's magnitude and destructive power. Illinois took the brunt of the beating, with several hundred killed in Murphysboro alone. One man ran to catch a moving car when he was hit from behind by flying debris. No one records whether or not he was able to see from his eyes as they hung on optic nerves and blood vessels from empty sockets, but a savior nearby had the courage and presence of mind to pop the eyes back in and get the wounded man out of the storm. At another town, miners emerged from a shaft when the power went out only to find the town above scrubbed into oblivion, almost all of their wives and children killed. The speed, scale and totality of the destruction are hard to imagine. Houses, cows, cars, rocks, stoves, trees, people all wrenched from the ground and crushed in a cosmic blender without conscience or remorse. Almost 220 miles and three and a half hours of roaring hell on that spring day.

My worries were meager indeed. After an hour or so, the rain eased, and I slipped out onto the washed blacktop and pedaled into the clearing day. The landscape might be flat, placid, uninteresting, but the weather could provide a lethal counterpoint. Something to keep in mind as I traversed the land of corn and soy.

Cruise Missiles and Corn:
I Let Ladies Pick Me Up at Libraries
Sept. 8th: 1,530 miles

Wrong turns in the darkness of Denver, Indiana, left me frustrated, but I finally had the route and pushed on in silent effort, another day, another million acres of corn. Grey, warm, humid, the green blur of genetically modified grasses marked the morning ride. I cruised merrily through the corniferous forest, insouciantly sailed the seething soy seas only to round a corner and find three dogs startled at first by my appearance then convinced I'd make an excellent snack. Adrenal NOS blasted into my turbos and I kicked up my speed as the dogs closed in--12, 15, 18, 20 mph straight and true. In a rage I looked over at the large black one, the one still hanging with me, his snarling bark ringing in my ears. "Is that all you got!" I yelled. "Is that it? C'mon you fat-furry-four-footed-fuck, bring it! BRING IT!" I knew that I could take this snarling beast. And before long, he started to fade. I was too much work. Shortly he was just a panting black speck in my rear view mirror. I'd be the big one that got away, a story to be retold the next time devil dog and his crew gathered around the local fire hydrant. I eased back on the throttle to recover and cried out a war whoop of victory. Cerberus and his henchhounds would have to find another soul to torment.

I needed more supplies than the little towns had been providing, so I cut off the mapped route and landed in Rensselaer, home of the famed technical institute. I rolled past a deep limestone pit and into town, quickly finding a library for my customary blog update and research on the local camping possibilities. To my delight, I discovered I'd crossed into another time zone, a big marker for cross country travelers. Stepping from the refuge of air conditioning back into a sticky grey afternoon, I saw rain beginning to ooze from a dour sky. Quickly, I pulled Mojo to the protection of the covered entryway and waited for the wet to pass. Two women, one past sixty with glasses, grey hair and a kind smile, another at least a decade younger and the dark hair to prove it, stepped out of the library and struck up a conversation, inspired by the unusual, heavily loaded bike. June and Liz were extraordinarily friendly, and before long, June had offered me her place for the night. She put in a call to her husband, no doubt a chance to have this tall, strange cyclist properly vetted. As we chatted, I saw a thick-bellied, bandy-legged runner pounding across the wet pavement towards the library. Short grey hair, a white t-shirt pulled up to expose his round middle, thick glasses, a firm handshake and easy smile, Gene was the man, seventy and training for his first marathon. People who crack our expectations, step, jog, and run outside the confines of the status quo always inspire me. I liked Gene immediately. The would-be marathoner continued on his training run while I followed through the tree-lined streets. Gene pointed down the road where I would find their large log home surrounded by corn, the rain gone for now, shadows long on the damp ground. He had more miles to run.

June revealed the strange truth soon enough. After I was settled in, she said Gene didn't live at the house but kept an apartment in town. They still spent time together, but after decades of marriage and no obvious problems, he needed his space. There was a clear sadness and dismay in her voice as she explained the situation. She didn't seem uncomfortable explaining this personal problem to a virtual stranger—more resigned and saddened. No doubt because he wouldn't be staying at the house, she felt a need to explain. There was a lot to like about June, too, and I hoped they would resolve their differences. Before long, showered and dressed, Gene pulled up and we talked around the kitchen table as June made plans for dinner.

For years, Gene had lived in southern California, working as an engineer on the Cruise missile program. In retirement, he'd taken up small scale farming and, now, marathon running. He also had a love of the desert and had done some exploring in the sere ranges above the Salton Sea. We had a lot in common.

That night, I was stuffed at an outdoor dinner hosted by Liz and her family. The hospitality rolled out thick: mashed potatoes, barbequed chicken, baked beans, jello salad. All food was fair game on this ride. We talked and laughed and I filled two empty legs with heavy calories for the road. Liz's son was back from a stay in California. "Were you in school there?" I asked.

"No, just hanging out and partying too much," he said. "I hated the dry weather. Everything dried out, skin, bread—everything!" This dislike of the arid West was amazing to me given my struggles with humidity. We grow to love what we know. He was happy to be home. I told my best story about the hard-bitten couple in Ashtabula, Ohio, and everyone was astonished, but later, the son thanked me in a particularly earnest way. "I needed to hear that," he said. "Thank you." The implied struggle with alcohol was clear enough and none had been served at dinner, only a sugary, berry-flavored drink.

The next morning I joined in on a classic American event: A firemen's breakfast. There I endured spongiform pancakes, rubbery square mystery sausage, and a synthetic "orange" breakfast drink. The trials of the trail are many. Fortunately, I was able to score a pound of Starbuck's Sumatran at the grocery store, so all was not lost. I bid my hosts farewell, and rolled off into the maize maze, navigating once more the astonishing grid of the American heartland.

The Encounter
Sept. 10th: 1,660 miles

A rough patch of road marked the arbitrary division between Indiana and Illinois. A band of trees, a field of corn next to a field of soy, a warm, sticky afternoon. The miles fell under my wheels, a coarse patch of chip seal—Satan's favored pavement—a glassy run of blacktop, a rare curve around a home set back against the trees. The lawns were awesome to behold—acres of deep green fed by the soggy air and regular summer rains, expanses of grass that, save for golf courses, would be unthinkable in the West. A nearly constant feature of the middle of the country is the afternoon drone of lawn mowers, usually driven across the land like miniature tanks waging battle against the armies of fescue. Even the edges of cornfields were deep in grass and trimmed to military standards. Hour upon hour of sitting on noisy, spewing machines, all to keep the grass in check—not a life I could imagine. I had a hard enough time controlling the 900 sq. ft. patch of green at home. These were mutant lawns on steroids requiring superhuman maintenance. It struck me a bit strange, in the grand scheme of things, to wage war against grass. Really, what's the point? For that matter, what's the point in pedaling this hunk of German engineering across the continent? Did the farmer mowing his lawn muse on the *why* of his mowing? Or was there only the dull acceptance, the sleepy rumble of the machines, the toil of the task to be done? Did Sisyphus ride a lawnmower?

Another town rose out of the corn, a rank of silos, a line of rail, home for the night in the late afternoon sun. Curses, library closed. I checked with the city office and got permission to camp in the park, the usual pavilion, playground toys, wide patches of grass. I parked Mojo amongst the picnic tables, performed bandana ablutions in the restroom, and sat in the heat while mosquitoes closed in. It was going to be a long evening.

In retrospect, the insistent repetitions of an opportunity to "relax" should have been a warning or a clue, but I was an innocent abroad, a weary athlete besieged by tiny flying vampires. I was about to put on long pants when I was greeted by a fellow walking by with a soda he'd purchased from a machine in the park. Ron was nice enough, and before long he'd offered me his place to cool off, "relax" and escape the bugs. He stood close to six feet tall with closely cut hair but going bald, a thin mustache, heavy in the belly with thick fleshy arms and soft round hands. It was fairly clear from his speech that he was probably a homosexual, but this did not concern me. To each his own, I say. Ron seemed particularly lonely and made a point of emphasizing that he lived by himself.

I moved my gear over to his house only twenty yards or so from the edge of the park and went in to escape the insects. His home was small, just one bathroom, and paneled in dark wood. In the front room, images and busts of John F. Kennedy and Lincoln were everywhere--pencil drawings, a rug draped over a chair, two dead presidents on display. Wall units with numerous cubbyholes held tiny toys and old products from early in the previous century--bars of soap, figurines of dogs, barnyard animals, antiques of every sort. A candle burned on a chest used as a coffee table, and a Cubs game played on the TV in the corner. Some of his displays were dusty, but the overall effect was orderly if cluttered.

We called out for pizza that we had to pick up and got some beer on the way back. He graciously paid for the food. We talked about my travels. He had an odd pronunciation of "wow," drawing out the "o" into an "ahh" to round out the sound: "waahhow," again and again. He would punctuate many of his statements: "Do ya hear what I'm saying?" a tag expression I came to expect throughout the evening. I told him about my life in California, and he related some details about life as a traveling in-home caregiver to the elderly, a job he said he liked.

After dinner, we watched TV, a rerun of *Law and Order*. In the middle of a scene where the heroes were interrogating a witness, I caught a swift movement out of the corner of my right eye. Suddenly, Ron was beside me, his hand caressing my bare leg. He was quite impressed by my physique, it seemed, and needed some closer inspection. I was startled, particularly since he knew two key pieces of information about me: One, I'm straight, and two, I'm happily married. His touch, which lasted but a moment, spoke to me on levels he never intended, more of sadness and loneliness than sex. One man, fifty years old, one house, three televisions. A solitary gay man in a tiny Midwestern town, he wandered the countryside helping people but had not much life of his own. He spoke earlier of a cherished visit with a friend in Colorado but made it clear that he hadn't contacted her in over four years, "Do ya hear what I'm saying?" He was a man without real goals, no motivation to travel, nothing but his closed house with piped-in images of the outside world. He seemed to be devoid of ambition but for the short term objective of bedding a world-class recumbent cyclo-tourist.

In rapid fire, he said, hand on my thigh: "This doesn't offend you, does it? This doesn't offend you?" That, however, was one thing he could be sure of. I said in clear, measured tones: "You need to back off"—the law *and* the order.

As quickly as he arrived, he was back in his chair, staring at the screen as if nothing had happened. Later I imagined some snappy speech or comment I might have made, but I sat there, too, processing the strange, sad encounter. I couldn't imagine how hard his life must be in this place. I was, however, certain about my desires and how they did not coincide with his. For some reason, I stayed, thinking, on the whole, that I had judged his character correctly. When I lay down on the floor to sleep, however, I began to have second thoughts. The darkness of the house closed around me. He'd spoken of his ill mother, but I imagined a desiccated Mommy Dearest in the next room, rocking her dusty way into eternity with a mummified toothy grin. What if he were armed and loaded? What if he came storming into the living room, .45 at the ready, and demanded what he so clearly wanted? On top of these troublesome images, a wall clock clicked down the seconds of the night, chiming obnoxiously every hour. I slept little and was up at 4AM to get packing.

Nothing happened. I had my coffee and cereal, shook Ron's soft, limp hand, and pushed off into the chill September dawn. A melancholy mist hung over the land and my spirits as I wheeled westward. Feeling much as I had after leaving the faded glory of Buffalo, I found that the best antidote is movement, the straining and striving for the next town, the heart and lungs and muscles clearing my head and soul until only the effort remained, pushing back the darkness and loneliness.

Life on the Mississippi
Sept. 12th: 1,802 miles

The huge, wet crease of the continent dominated my thinking over the last few days. Although still the Midwest, it was a jumping off point for *The West*. Louis and Clark began on this river down in St. Louis. From its damp, forested banks, I would climb the gentle tilted mass of the earth, day by day working towards Colorado and the Rockies. But not right away. For over two hundred miles I would trace its flow downstream to drink in one of the greatest waterways in the world. Huck Finn clipped to flying pedals and a westward dream, I pushed on, hungry for my first glimpse of the mighty river.

A supernaturally clear, warm day inspired my churning legs. Inwardly, I still smarted from the knowledge of my incredible stupidity of the day before. Somehow, absorbed in the life of the tour, I had lost track of my wedding anniversary—stereotypically male forgetfulness made all the more glaring by the date: 9/11. How does one forget such a date? Extraordinary talent and dedication, I tell you, a flair for achieving the impossible. I sat hunched over my cell phone that night and felt miserable talking to Jodi after she'd hinted at my forgetfulness. In contrast, I had already purchased before leaving California a special birthday card, and I had decided on a gift, but this was not all due until November. Well played, Scotty.

Low hills and a slot through a band of trees led out to a bluff overlooking, at last, the Mississippi River and, on the far side, Iowa. A floodplain stretched to thick forest bordering the water. To the north, arching under a crystalline sky, a bridge crossed over to Muscatine. A smoke stack dominated the skyline, a plume of white trailing lazily in the late morning light—a perfect day to meet the river for the first time.

Draining thirty-one states and two Canadian provinces, the Mississippi extends its reach to make the third largest basin and, including the Missouri and Jefferson, the fourth longest river in the world. For 3,900 miles, this massive artery of the continent pumps life into the middle of the country, emptying out broad and slow below New Orleans and into the Gulf of Mexico at an average rate of 450,000 cubic feet per second. A highway to the natives for untold centuries and a place to work and dream for a young Samuel Langhorn Clemens, the river is central not only to American geography but to our history and literature as well. We cannot imagine the United States without it. The Louisiana Purchase was one of the sharper moves of the Jefferson administration and the best $15,000,000 this country ever spent. Apparently, Napoleon, besides getting some cash, thought the deal increased American power to establish a counterforce to the British, to eventually "humble her pride," as he put it.

The river, however, seems to have little trouble humbling Americans. We are a powerful, creative people, sometimes too sure of ourselves and the control of our destiny. Nature, however, cares little for such attitudes, and time and again, the river rises to put us back in our place. Looking down on it as I did that clear September day, I couldn't imagine its darker moods, the raw crushing power of all those tributaries joining the main line, the relentless heavy rains. Twice in the 20th Century, the Old Man River rose angrily from his bed, 1927 and 1993. The earlier event is considered the greatest flood in recorded North American history. All across the Midwest, the rains fell to flood the world. Fifteen inches drenched New Orleans in 18 hours. Eventually 145 levees were breached and thousands of square miles flooded. South of Memphis, the river spread to an unbelievable sixty miles wide. Over two hundred people were killed.

The flood of 1993 was almost as bad. In the modern event, an elaborate series of levees, reservoirs and cut-offs designed to prevent a repeat of the 1927 disaster failed, inundating—again—thousands of square miles. St. Louis was spared because of a massive floodwall built following the 1927 deluge. This fifty-two foot high wall held back a fifty foot wall of water. We can imagine the emergency workers, perhaps the mayor, looking down over the wall at the raging dark flood only an arm's reach away. Would it hold? Of course, for thousands and thousands of people, the worst had already occurred.

Crossing the bridge, I parked the bike mid-span and looked down into the quiet, calmly rolling water, the sign for the river above. A huge grin broke across my weather-beaten face. The Mississippi. The Mississippi! Thirty six days of hard work had carried me far. Although I still had almost three thousand miles to go, there was no doubt I was in it now. This was the heart of the matter, the blood and water, the sweat bright on my hot skin—*goddammit*, the Mississippi. I kicked off and rolled down into Muscatine, Iowa, Button Capital of the World.

Located on the corner of a huge bend of the river where it changes course from almost due west to due south, the small city of about 23,000 came almost down to the water's edge but quickly rose above on pleasant slopes and commanding bluffs, sharp Victorian row structures and brick buildings flanking wide, inviting streets. Initially a trading post, it was incorporated as Bloomington in 1839. Later the name was changed to avoid confusion with the number of other towns of the same name. The town quickly grew, supported by river trade, a major stop for steamboats, and, for a time, Mark Twain worked as a reporter for the local paper owned by his brother, Orion Clemens. In *Life on the Mississippi*, Twain had this to say:

> And I remember Muscatine—still more pleasantly— for its summer sunsets. I have never seen any, on either side of the ocean, that equaled them. They used the broad smooth river as a canvas, and

painted on it every imaginable dream of color, from the mottled daintinesses and delicacies of the opal, all the way up, through cumulative intensities, to blinding purple and crimson conflagrations which were enchanting to the eye [...]. The sunrises are also said to be exceedingly fine. I do not know.

On the most commanding bluff above the town, the local captains of industry built palatial homes, Corinthian columns twenty feet high fronting a colonial monster, across the way, a three story brick Victorian masterpiece, faded now from its glory days when buttons manufactured here dominated the world market, three of every eight buttons coming from Muscatine. Countless freshwater clams provided the shells. Zippers and plastics finally put an end to the industry, but the legacy, the rich history was fascinating. I sensed there was much to like about this place as I eased on the brakes in front of the public library.

As I pulled my helmet off my sweaty head, a neatly dressed, middle-aged man in jeans and a button-down shirt stepped from the building and gave me a huge smile of surprise. "Wow! Look at that!" he said, gesturing towards Mojo. "You're on quite a trip." I filled him in on the basics. After only a few moments, I found that he, too, had done some touring, and then he said: "Do you need a place to stay?"

I smiled back in astonished gratitude: "Yeah, I sure do. I need to lay over for a couple of nights to rest. I've been pushing hard for a week, and I need some time off the bike." Dan had no problem with that. Less than five minutes in town, and the people of America had opened their homes once again. I felt lucky to be alive in this time and place. Dan went back into the library to talk to his wife who worked there, and I collected some things on the bike. As I was about to follow Dan, a young man approached me and admired my rig. He, too, was going to offer me a place to stay—such a wealth of kindness and generosity. The evening "news" would lead us to believe none but thugs, gangsters and the vain, preening rich lived in America. Day after day my experience put the truth to that cancerous lie.

Dan and Irene were my hosts for the two days and nights I put aside the bike. He showed me around the town and filled me in on its colorful history as well as pointing out where the force 3 tornado had cut through back in June, destroying a town park and twisting off huge trees as if they were straw. The massive splintered trunks were sobering. Long term residents had never seen a tornado in Muscatine and thought the area immune. I wondered how they would react if I told them Los Angeles had tornadoes, too. The classic downtown of Muscatine was suffering from development in the outskirts, the vital center bled dry by new businesses wanting bigger spaces and acres of parking—the Buffalo/rust-belt syndrome. Still, the historic district was far from dead, and Dan said there were signs of improvement. I hoped the best for this fine little town. I would likely never see it again, but it stands in my memory as a special place, an oasis of charm and rest in my lone-wolf roll across the country.

Southbound Again
Sept. 14th: 1,874 miles

We world-class recumbent cyclo-tourists can be vain about our exploits, emphasizing the strain and struggle, the heroic climbs, devil winds, heat and cold. When honesty creeps in, these challenges are more humbling than aggrandizing. The other truth of our journeys, however, comes from the joy of movement, the easy miles, the sweet rolling panorama of the earth revealed by movement touched by grace, a salvation available to everyone, the blessing of our bodies and the miraculous contrivance known as the bicycle. As I shook Dan's hand and thanked him and his wife for their generosity, I slipped into a day of wonder.

Cool bright air had pushed down from Canada, and for a few days at least, the heat and humidity I'd endured across Ohio and Illinois would retreat, leaving me to smile and ride and drop behind my northern leg for a southern swing along the great Mississippi. Snapping tailwinds and wide empty roads opened up and took me in, the fields turning yellow, the trees fading now in the last days of summer. I raced the wind and became air and pure movement, my senses singing. Joseph Campbell said that we are not looking for the meaning of life; we're looking for the feeling of being alive. Right he was.

In Dallas City, I stopped for the night, averaging what for me was a blistering 14 mph for the day. A park, about a mile shy of town, provided a place to throw the tent beside a still crook of the river, its banks covered in vines, the shallows paved in water lilies. The high winds whipped the trees and chopped the water out in mid-stream. The faucets in the park had been shut down, so I grabbed my containers and walked a couple of hundred yards to a home set thirty yards or so back from the river. A friendly woman came to the door and let me fill my containers while she talked of her life here and the awful fight they'd had with the river back in '93. A board nailed to a tree down by the shore marked the high point of the flood in these parts, higher than my head, it seemed. She, her family, and many volunteers from town had labored for days, stacking 15,000 sandbags, and, on the worst day, operating pumps and resetting bags for 18 hours straight to hold back the water. Somehow, they saved the house. Standing on the dry ground, I could hardly imagine what they went through. With all the hardships, it was a wonder anyone lived in the Midwest. I chewed on all this as I lugged the sloshing water bags back to camp. Cool, breezy, I pulled on a knit cap and smiled. A chill! Fantastic. I huddled in the lee of the picnic table and cooked my solitary meal as the long shadows of night pushed out the day.

Chasing Joseph Smith
Sept. 15th: 1948 miles

Women married young on the frontier, so perhaps his taste for adolescent girls wasn't the problem. That Joseph Smith acquired over two dozen wives certainly was. Between 1827 and 1843, Smith hitched up with 34 women ranging in age from 14 to 58, the majority in their teens and twenties. Also of note is that a number of these wives were already married. I imagine you could have cut the tension with a knife when the little wife came home with *that* news: "Oh, by the way, honey, some of the girls and I got married to Joseph Smith today." How does one start that conversation? Smith was a brave man, no doubt about it. How could he even begin to keep track of all the anniversaries? I shuddered at the task.

I'd pedaled through his childhood home of Palmyra, New York, where there is no Mormon temple to be found. Not far south of Dallas City, on a crisp Saturday morning spin, I pedaled into Nauvoo, Illinois, the Mormon Mecca and spiritual theme park where Joseph Smith made his last stand. I was enchanted by the light of the day and interested to see where Smith's luck had finally run out. I could have killed for a strong cup of Java, but the Mormon prohibition against coffee meant Starbucks was scarce indeed. The town was spotless and strangely quiet, hardly a soul stirring. I parked Mojo and snapped a few pictures of the town and the recently completed gigantic temple gleaming crystal white in the sun—huge, incongruous, a white whale of a building set against a low-slung modest village. The Mormons aren't shy about their architecture. A large sign proclaimed the coming of a new motel to house the Saints on their pilgrimages. But all was not as peaceful as it seemed in this sleepy little town.

Later, when I posted photos and my observations on the web for this portion of the journey, my blog elicited this exchange:

Helen said...

> I stood at my window today and watched you heading down Mulholland Street toward the Mormon Nauvoo temple.
> I have a suggestion for you. Why don't you take your adventure to Mountain Meadows in Utah? You will find Real History there, as your eyes look upon America's first 9/11...you can look across the killing field known as Mountain Meadows:
> The "Mountain Meadows Massacre" was committed by Mormon Priesthood Leaders on September 11, 1857, when they murderd [sic] 120 unarmed men, women and children over the age of 7 on the Fancher/Baker wagon train traveling to California from Arkansas. You might want to pay your respect, where it belongs to those that were murdered, by Mormons that still blindly follow the teachings of Joseph Smith today!
> Ask yourself this question where are the well dressed tour guides at that Mormon historical site??
>
> September 15, 2007 6:46 PM

Scott Wayland said...

> Hi, Helen: I've read all about that unsavory business. It's too bad that so many groups and movements have bad business in their histories. One has to hardly crack a book to get into the shadows of the Catholic Church. Tracing all the Mormon history would indeed be interesting. Unfortunately, I've got to head south, which is what brought me through Nauvoo in the first place. Lots of blind people everywhere, eh? I'm doing my best to keep my eyes

open.

Be well.

Scott

September 15, 2007 8:20 PM

Helen said...

> Hello Scott:
> I find it odd that you didn't bother to mention the name of even one book in which you've read all the unsavory business about "Mountain Meadows Massacre".
>
> Also two of your photos posted today were taken by you having to stand in front of the "Nauvoo Christian Visitors Center" that is odd too, since this Center is a real Historic building in Nauvoo, built in 1893.
>
> The Nauvoo temple is not a historic anything! It is a new building built in 2002.
>
> I would agree with your statement "Lots of blind people everywhere, eh?" There are 13 million of them in the Mormon Church today.
>
> Be safe on your journey from one Californian to another...
>
> Grace and Peace,
> Helen

Hmmmm...a little testy, Helen? Got a little chip on your Christian shoulder there, eh? A wee bit edgy? I felt what must be a strong undercurrent of resentment in the area, the Mormons moving in, the typical human tendency towards tribalism and rejection of the other. Grace and peace, indeed.

Oh, for the record, Helen: *Mormon Country* by Wallace Stegner and *Under the Banner of Heaven* by Jon Krakauer.

At one time Nauvoo with its multitude of Saints, rivaled Chicago as the biggest city in Illinois. The mild, sluggish streets I patrolled gave little hint of this history. Of course, that was back in 1844, and the Mississippi was the wilderness as far as most of the country was concerned. Still, there were outposts up and down the river and some dissention and jealousy in the town. Smith was mayor, university chancellor, justice of the peace, and commander of his own militia. Life in Nauvoo was structured along theological grounds, quite contrary in spirit to the careful separation of church and state spelled out in the Constitution. This might have ruffled some non-Mormon feathers, but the Saints' economic success was cause for friction, too. When a local paper published its first edition with a major story highly critical of Smith and encouraging rebellion against the Mormons, Smith had the press seized. The paper's owners filed charges against Smith for inciting a riot, and these fell on sympathetic ears. Smith and his brother Hyrum were temporarily locked up.

Towns to the south published angry screeds calling for an all-out purge of the Mormons. The governor decided that Smith needed controlling and so ordered him to be tried again on the original charges, but these were later changed to treason based on Smith's control of the militia in Nauvoo. The brothers considered making a run for it, but in the end they surrendered and were locked up with two other Saints in Carthage, twenty five miles to the south. Imagine Klansmen guarding a black suspect, and we get the picture of the brothers' circumstances that June over a century and a half ago. It wasn't long before a mob assembled and a few men with guns and blackened faces ran into the jail under virtually no resistance and shot down the brothers, Hyrum taking a shot to the face and Joseph four rounds to the body. The strange story of Smith ended with a cry of "O Lord, my God!" blood on the floorboards, and the acrid sting of black powder smoke hanging in the air.

Those who hoped that the death of Smith would end the Mormons did not understand the power of martyrs. Today there are over 12 million Mormons worldwide, my own sister among them.

Me? I believe in the wheel, the pedal, the spoke and the chain, kinetics, sweat, forward motion and the aching poetry of a receding horizon, a curving mountain road, muscle, bone and desire.

Among other things.

No musket-toting, pitchfork-wielding throng greeted me as I rolled down into the old Nauvoo town site with its putting-green lawns, log buildings, stone walls and quiet Saints in white shirts and ties tending the grounds. Bright September sun filtered down through the turning leaves, and I thought about history and time and the steady flow of the river.

To the north, about one hundred miles, Iowa City was the departure point for the Mormon handcart expeditions or "companies" as they were called, headed by captains who led hundreds of mostly Irish, Scottish and English faithful across the plains to Zion, Salt Lake City, Utah, the promised land, escape at last from the likes of the Governor of Missouri, Lilburn Boggs, who, in 1838, ordered the extermination of all the Mormons in the state. That fatwa meant about two dozen dead Mormons. The rest fled for Illinois. The cost of crossing the country by handcart was a good deal more serious, however. Most of the companies experienced fatalities. The road was long and hard but hard beyond imagining for the fourth and fifth companies that started too late in the year. Arriving on the high, cold, lonesome steppes of Wyoming in October, over two hundred Saints would die in the frozen sage as they trekked towards salvation. Today we can scarcely think about starting out on a trip with three hundred souls only to lose half of them before the journey was over, our friends and family members collapsing in the snow or never waking from their frigid slumbers.

To their credit, the Mormons learned from their mistakes and, on the whole, had good success for the few years of the program, and the last crossing had no fatalities at all.

My own "cart" was a good deal more comfortable—full suspension, disc brakes, and a little computer to tell me how far and how fast. In a fistful of hours I covered more ground than a handcart pioneer could manage in days. Whatever toughness I'd cultivated seemed soft in comparison—not that I was complaining. Indeed, as most Americans can tell you, the Mormons were quick to adopt the bicycle for their missionaries, white shirts and dark ties flying, knapsacks loaded with sacred texts, the antithesis of the DUI cyclists with the cigarettes, plastic grocery bags, scruffy beards and defeated eyes. If only we had an army of the velo-faithful to proselytize this good news, the way, the truth and the light of the most efficient machine ever built. They'd pedal from door to door, bike maintenance and safe cycling manuals in hand, and say: "Have you accepted human powered transport as your personal salvation?" And it is, too! Practical, affordable, happy and healthy making, what's not to like? All that is required is a little sweat equity.

South, south, ever south, I lost sight of the river now and again as I followed vacant roads through farmland, an occasional weathered barn for company. I was bound for Quincy, which, in addition to supporting the fleeing Mormons in the 1830's, had another interesting story to tell.

When he was thirteen, he burned his elementary school to the ground.

So began the life of crime for James Robert Scott. By the time he reached his twenties, he'd spent time in six prisons for many crimes, including another case of arson. As the great flood waters of 1993 climbed higher and higher, Scott, now a full-blown alcoholic, was married and working at a local Burger King, slinging ground beef and fries during the day, softening his brain and pickling his liver each night. All that mattered was the next party, and, after helping with the sandbags for a couple of days, he was ready to flood his own system with good hard drink. There was one fly in his beery ointment, however: his wife. She was sure to put a crimp in his style. Then, this genius from Missouri dreamed the perfect dream: Break the levy and trap his wife on the other side of the river.

Many levies had failed. All were stressed to the limit. With millions of gallons of water surging by in the dark, it would take only one small break, a tiny crack in the dike to unleash the monster. Scott later bragged of his tour de idiocy to friends who would testify against him. That night, he walked the levy, found a couple of choice bags and began pulling. Once the breach was made, the hemorrhaging began, a great powerful surge of water breaking, splitting the levy, rushing in. The suction of the flow pulled in a barge that slammed into a gas station. A fireball burst into the air and flaming gasoline spread across the rushing water with liquid speed until burning itself out. Dozens of buildings were destroyed, bridges damaged and closed, and, ultimately, 14,000 acres submerged. Because of the bridge problems, a two hundred mile stretch of the river could not be crossed except by boat or by air. One bridge was unusable for over two months. Only dumb luck kept anyone from being killed.

No person before or since has been tried and convicted under a Missouri law making it a felony to "cause a catastrophe," but Scott was convicted—twice—for intentionally breaking the levy. His term enhanced by another conviction for robbery in 1994, he is currently serving a twenty year to life sentence. He will be in his fifties before he has a chance to walk the streets again.

Beer sounded like a good idea to me, too, as I rolled into Quincy, Illinois, after seventy miles of steady work. I passed the campground just before town, but I needed to find a grocery store. I hit the library but found that the nearest place to get something to eat was miles to the south, away from the campground. I pedaled on, mile after mile, realizing quickly that there was no way I was going back. Once again I'd have to scrounge for a spot to throw down for the night. As I pulled up to a nice looking grocery store, I espied a small park across the street—*maybe*. That familiar little dose of stress eased into my veins.

I ran the aisles, loading up with broccoli, more pasta, peanut butter, a load of food that required repackaging once I was outside. Cut stalks from the vegetables, pour boxed goods into bags, all to fit everything into my panniers—a little production for sure. A fresh reload of supplies was always disheartening, the added bulk in the bags, the added pounds to the load. I didn't know it at the time, but I was headed for some hard climbing further south. I would pay for every pound.

As I packed, a rather low-I.Q. sort bellied up to my personal space—fleshy folds in a strained and stained t-shirt pouring over his belt, ratty jeans, thick glasses, a few weeks' worth of shrubbery on his cheeks. He began firing question after question at me, hardly waiting for an answer— "Where're you goin? What's that bike? What'll you do in California?" I braced myself and shot back quick answers, hoping he'd get bored and walk away. I seem to be a magnet for these types. I was saved by a middle-aged angel in paint spattered jeans and a t-shirt. He made a brief comment on his way into the store but stopped to talk as he headed out. Dark hair, a round face and friendly smile, he was impressed by my load.

Within a minute or two, he looked at me earnestly and said, "Would you like a hot, home-cooked meal?" *Oh, mister, you don't even know.* I looked quickly at the fresh food I'd just purchased. It would hold a day.

"That would be fantastic!"

The road provides.

Pushing hard, I followed Mike "not far" to his home. Strung out from the miles, I strained to keep up behind his truck, my legs yelping at the effort. I laughed and carried on. He and his wife, Shelley, lived in a fine old neighborhood of classic homes thick with brick and overhung by huge leafy trees, such a contrast to the sparse oaks and grasses of home. Always feeling a bit awkward when I first stepped into a stranger's home, I gave them all my best smile as Mike introduced me to his family—James, the quiet high school junior, a bit pale and stoop-shouldered; Dan and his friend Tom, ninja skate punks of the best sort. A daughter, Allison, was away at college to the south, her first time away from home. Shelley was a warm and welcoming friend. The young guns took their boards out for a round of thrashing while the rest of us dug into a huge pot of jambalaya with a fresh apple pie chaser. After eating, we relaxed on couches in the living room.

"I was in the Marines at 29 Palms," said Mike when he heard I was from California. "I used to hitchhike to Palm Springs to catch flights home to Illinois to visit Shelley for the weekend." Now that's commitment. He painted houses, drove a cement truck, did what work there was to make ends meet. I was struck by how frequently and how easily he laughed about himself, always the mark of a good man.

Shelley worked for a podiatrist and knew well the town I was headed to the next day—Louisiana, Missouri, although she called it "Loser-ana" for all the down-and-out types she encountered there. The doctor she worked for sometimes made trips to see patients in these outlying areas. "One woman," said Shelley, "came into the clinic and for some reason had to talk about her medical history to everyone in the office. She hoisted up her dress: 'See! They done cut me open, mountain tops to glory hole!'" But that wasn't the only time the foot doctor and Shelley had a colorful patient: "With an attitude of *I'm-at-a-doctor's-office-so-better-ask-about-this,* another woman lifted up her dress to show us a bulging hernia the size of a small pony! Yeah, the people of Louisiana are special."

That night as I tried to sleep in a spare bedroom, I thought of my kind hosts, the arc of my life, the educated people I worked and lived with. Rural Missouri was almost a different country, certainly a different world from the one I lived in, yet it was all the United States. The next day I'd pass through Hannibal, a mandatory stop for any lover of literature and American history. I would also encounter some of the hardest cycling in the Midwest, although I was ignorant of this as I slowly drifted off. It's usually best not to see the punch coming. There was no dodging it anyway.

Huck Finn Camp
Sept. 16th: 2003 miles

Damp pavement and low grey skies framed the ride out of Quincy. Early dawn, little traffic, a satisfying zip of firm tires on the road, my last day along the Mississippi. I mused on Twain, his hometown a kind of Mecca for those in love with books and one of our greatest writers. America without Twain is unthinkable. He helped create what it means to be an American, so in this journey to find the essence of the place for myself, I needed to stop and pay my respects to the bristly old curmudgeon. He would understand my journey, my lust to "light out for the territories." He speaks to me still from the volumes in my library. In one passage from "Taming the Bicycle," he spoke of marking his age by putting on reading glasses for the first time and in the same day reclaiming his youth by getting on a bike. Yeah, Sam Clemens knew what this was all about: "Get a bicycle. You will not regret it. If you live."

The clouds burned away, and twenty miles later I was crossing to the west and over the river into Missouri, Hannibal a sling shot's distance away. Greeting me was a rather cheesy portrait of the crusty goat laid out in painted rocks along the side of the highway. *Let the kitsch begin.*

In town, Twain junk on crack. Don't miss Tom Sawyer's Cave! Becky Thatcher's House! *THE* White Picket Fence! You couldn't swing a dead aardvark without smacking some tourist trap or other. I ogled the fence and eyed the house, and, me the sucker, paid hard cash to get into the Twain Museum, complete with ghostly white statues of the Grand Old Man Himself and figures of Tom and Huck, fictional characters modeled after...? I did enjoy looking over original copies of Twain's articles from the local papers, and the collection of photographs from the whole span of his life was fascinating. I was struck by how our perceptions of famous figures are set by whatever image the media, artists, writers, and the press have selected for us. Twain, Einstein and others will *always* be the older man with wild white hair. But Twain was a boy, a vigorous young man, as much those as the sardonic sage mired in debt and loss at the end of his life.

Then, the punishment. The "Show-me" state showed me. The road out of town climbed in a dizzying ramp into the glaring sun, my lowest gear mocking my thrutching legs. Missouri would be the most beautiful Midwestern state, but it would also be the most painful in terms of sheer muscular effort. Short, brutal climbs dropped down into narrow valleys and draws only to smack me once more with another stinging ascent. It was like stepping into the ring with George Forman, and I soon adopted the technique of zigzagging to cut the grade. The heaving terrain led south, one slow grunting climb after another.

Then, midway up another slog, I crossed the 2,000 mile mark. I'd been glancing down at the cyclometer through my sweaty daze and stopped just as the numbers rolled over. A self-portrait—thumbs up, savage grin, a hard-fought milestone—was my only trophy. What I wanted most was a cold beer, camp, a place to spend the night. Louisiana, Missouri, was going to be it for the day.

A flurry of growling Harleys and a strange, dead-eyed clerk greeted my arrival in town. The woman behind the register at the gas station gave me the strangest stare, as if she operated only on a brainstem. Spooky. I smiled and took my orange juice outside. The motorcyclists, as always, were talkative and friendly, recognizing a fellow two-wheeled traveler. No one knew where I might stay. A police officer gassing up his cruiser understood my plight and knew just the place. My day ended on the shores of the Mississippi at an old fisherman's hangout. A set of tracks cut through the woods behind me in the trees, and a train bridge spanned the river to the south. Fortunately, rail traffic was light, though the ground did rumble when one of the diesel spewing dragons squealed by into the night. Mostly I watched the slow, dark water ease by the overhanging maples. A heron perched on submerged snags and watched for prey, looking like a grim undertaker from a Dickens tale with its hunched shoulders and dark cloak of feathers. Heavy-bodied fish jumped in the shallows. Night fell on my Huck Finn camp as I cooked on the shore, happy to spend a night by myself, just me and the river.

Killing Katy
Sept. 20th: 2248 miles

I am not part of the solution. I am part of the problem, a sinner sinning before a seriously sizzling small steak that quivers and smokes in a tiny titanium pan. Not organic. Not free range. Not blessed by the Dali Lama. Commercial, wrapped-in-cellophane beef. I swoon at the scent of it, the solid red protein singing a primordial song first heard when a heavy-browed troglodyte klutz fumbled a tossed hunk of mammoth and dropped it into the fire. *Hmmmm, smell good.* Hunched in the shade of a mastodon-sized RV, I lean down over the flesh and watch my West Coast pseudo-liberal credentials evaporate with the aromatic smoke.

Days of riding carried me far from the Mississippi. I cut west from my river hideout, decamped in fabled Troy, the Trojans happy to accept the credit card of a pedal powered Odysseus at the Holiday Inn, and continued south, free from the worst of the sharp climbs and cyclist-eating Cyclops, bound for a blessed route across the great state of Missouri, the Katy Trail. Once the Missouri, Kansas and Texas railroad, MKT or "Katy," trains ceased using it over twenty years ago. As part of a nation-wide effort to utilize abandoned rail lines, the "rails to trails" movement came to Missouri and converted virtually the entire length of the line in that state to a dedicated pedestrian and bicycle path, over two-hundred miles of blissfully car-free travel through the heart of Missouri. The trail marked the last of my south-bound jog and signified my second big westward leg, the long, long push for Colorado, the Rocky Mountains, and my final escape from the Midwest.

Thick with history, humidity, and deep, overhanging trees, the first half of the trail held close to the Missouri River, the Big Muddy, the trail of Lewis and Clark over two hundred years before. Life was hard for the Corps of Discovery. Sleeping on the job and getting drunk would get you one hundred lashes, and as Clark wrote: "Mosquetors verry troublesom"! Fortunately, the insects weren't bad for me, and any flagellation was self-induced lashing of the cranks as I crunched down the crushed limestone path at a steady ten to thirteen miles per hour, a fine plume of gray dust settling on my bike and bags. Whatever cool air I'd enjoyed on my run down the Mississippi was long gone, replaced by oppressive heat. The green tunnel of the trail often blocked the worst of the sun, but whenever I stopped moving, the damp blotter of the atmosphere settled down over my sticky frame. In the shade of the periodic trailheads—covered benches and interpretive signs and maps made to resemble railroad stations—I recovered and pushed on. Four AM became my preferred wake up time, on the trail for an hour of dark riding, a strange, illicit pleasure. Obscure, cat-like shadows rushed from my tiny light. No cars, no street lamps, nothing but random thoughts and anxious fingers on the brakes.

I crossed paths with many cyclists, although none on a cross country trek. I fantasized now and then on a world where most travel was like this, quiet, healthy, clean. How much road rage can we have upon the seat of a bicycle? Would so many Americans be obese if they had to ride everywhere? Go to Holland and count the number of overweight riders and you'll have your answer. A couple of Katy riders inspired my own efforts. While sagging in the afternoon heat, stretched out in the shade of a trail station, I gathered my nerve to move on when another cyclist pulled up, a thick man, sweaty and smiling. We soon fell into conversation. He was determined to get fit, and, riding regularly over the last two years, he'd already shed eighty pounds. I took in a deep breath—*impressive*. He still had some pounds to lose, but a man so deep into a change in lifestyle seemed bound to continue. Riding across the country was easy in comparison. I wished him well.

Perhaps twenty years older, another rider helped me to envision a fit old age—and the need for better dental hygiene. Most of his upper teeth conspicuous by their absence, he lisped gently when he spoke, a thin, energetic man with grey hair protruding from a sweaty ball cap. A loose fitting t-shirt and mountain bike shorts completed his ensemble. He was out for a sixty mile run on the trail, from Sedalia almost to Clinton and back at a brisk clip. We talked weather and the trail, riding out West where I ached to roll my wheels. As his contemporaries were sinking into diabetic debilitation and fat lethargy, this toothless man was refusing to go gently into that sick night.

At the scene of the meat crime, one day from the end of the trail in Clinton, I masticated happily with my full set of teeth and wandered off to find the showers located in the fairgrounds' labyrinth nearby. Removing the ready-mix of lime dust, sweat and sun screen was suddenly the most important duty in the world. Later, as I settled into my bag, I did battle with the ring of klieg lights circling the compound. What is it with this culture's addiction to high-wattage illumination? This was small-town America, so why all the floods? Fear of vandals? *Of death*? The lights suddenly struck me as a metaphysical battle against darkness. Illuminate or die. Or appear morally weak. Politicians who opposed extensive lighting could be chastised, said to be "soft" on darkness. Here, now, for all to see, I proclaim my love of the shadows, my allegiance to the dark side. A pox on all the houses of incandescence! Give me darkness, deep, black, inky night wherein dwell creatures unknown, the realm of nightmares and dreams, of danger and joy, sweet sleep and rest divine. As the sun banishes the day, so must the night take its turn. I pulled a cap down hard over my eyes and drifted off amidst a village of RV's, their doors closed, shutters drawn, owners retracted like turtles into their shells, my tiny tent and bike conspicuous against the beastly machines.

At Clinton, trail's end, I did laundry and camped under a looming water tower, a planet on a stick soaring into the night. I was bound for Kansas and, *again*, some of the hardest riding of the tour. The continent had many lessons yet to teach.

A Cretin Creeps across the Craton
Sept. 23rd: 2,423 miles

Two in the morning nature called, whispering at first, then pinching, waking me up. I staggered groggily from the tent and lurched over to the outhouse under a clear canopy of moon and stars. Back in the tent I lay for long moments, listening to the wind in the trees and, for the first time, coyotes, God's dogs. Symbols of the West, they are the guardians of the broad threshold I was crossing, canine singers of a moonlit night for a solitary traveler. The undercurrent of the wind, the quavering melody of the coyotes floating faintly in the background, and the primordial sky all left me in a state of profound wonder and gratitude. What a strange and beautiful place is the world. For all our complaints and grievances, we cannot deny this gift.

A few hours later, I climbed and descended on gradual hills, many times ripping into the darkness at unknown speeds, over-driving my meager light, flying on trust, hope and adrenaline. Still in the dark, I began to encounter tule fog in the valley bottoms. The weird mists clung to trees and obscured the farm houses. Like smoky rivers, the moisture flowed along the depressions, one after another, as my morning effort unfolded. Could such a damp dawn give way to an afternoon in the high 80's? Oh, yes, it can. You're not in California anymore, Dorothy.

And so went my first days in Kansas. Smooth roads, long, gradual climbs and descents, a rising sun that burned away the fog then burned away at me. My left leg was bothering me some but not as severely as the day before.

Periodically, my body had been rebelling, balking at the effort, the long hours of moving, pushing. Tight calves, an aching knee. *Tough luck, boys. You've got work to do.* I was not going to fail, although I was more conscious of taking breaks.

After midday I arrived at Osage City, end of the line for this Sunday. After some calls made by the helpful crew at a Casey's mini-mart, I was clear to camp behind the store next to the police station. Okay, no late-night drunken ne'er-do-wells here.

What followed was a challenging slice of camping. First, and perhaps most horrifically, I was reduced to drinking *Coors Light.* Scandalous, redundant, I know, but there it is. Actually, with the intense heat and humidity, it was more refreshing than I expected. Even so, I think this qualified as a new low for me, this tour, and adult malt beverages as a whole, but one never knows what rigors the road will impose. We can only be flexible and endure. The town had some quaint blue laws, only allowing the sale of beer between 12 and 8 pm on Sundays, although the clerk said that regulations were in the works to keep the mini-mart from selling any beer at all on the Lord's Day. The religious-based motivations for these laws are clear enough. I wondered, however, if they had actually done any good. Do the alcoholics forget to stock up on Saturday for their early Sunday binging? Certainly, I should not be able to buy a can of suds to pour over my Wheaties on the Sabbath.

I frighten myself. I'm bad, very bad, out...of...control bad. Dinner: 8 oz. salad mix with gobs of Emiril dressing; 9 oz BBQ kettle chips chased down with 48 oz. LITE! beer—a "silver bullet" for your beer snob credentials; 6 oz. sirloin steak; peanut butter and chocolate chip Clif Bar for dessert. And I wasn't too full. That was dinner. Over the course of the day, I guzzled three tall coffees and one 16 oz. orange juice, many handfuls of peanuts, an apple. A brimming cup of Grape Nuts with raisins and half and half, a big sandwich of Swiss cheese on whole wheat with cucumber and onion, some other chips and a Tollhouse Cookie Ice Cream Bar.

Huge calories, questionable food value. I wondered what Jodi with her master's in holistic nutrition would say.

No I didn't.

Besides the limp lager, the roughest part was the incredible humidity and heat. It's hard to get over what it's like to be sealed up in a tight space under these circumstances, sweat oozing from every pore, gasping for breath like a beached sturgeon, begging for release like a tortured sinner locked in a nylon sarcophagus—GET...ME...OUT...OF...HERE! But you can't get out. You've got to fight for sleep and keep a wall between you and the snarling insects eager for fresh meat. A breeze picked up, and at last I got some sleep.

Then the rain started.

Once I climbed back in after setting the fly over the tent, the misery index climbed back into the stratosphere. Worse, in my haste, and undetected for some time, was the handful of "mosquetors" that followed me in, "verry troublesom." Morning couldn't come soon enough.

For all the discomfort, each morning found me eager to move on, put shoe to pedal and find what lay around the next corner. I cycled into an unexpected treasure, the "Flint Hills" of eastern Kansas, a land not flat but cut by sharp, narrow valleys topped by "native stone," wide stout bands of grey limestone that give the region its name and flavor. More West than Midwest, the grassy mesas and narrow tree-filled valleys led me west then north, Manhattan bound, Kansas not New York, the university town and my nephew's home, a refuge after eleven days and almost 700 miles of continuous riding since my last break. Steep climbs and fast curving descents tested me again. Long sinuous stone walls stretched like backbones across the land, miles of hand-built fences that attested to the nature of the rock and the people who settled this country. I stopped for my first lunch along one of these walls, impressed by the unimaginable back-breaking labor they represented. Thousands upon thousands of limestone plates collected, hauled into position and lifted into place. No hydraulic-swing-arm-fork-lift-diesel-powered assist here. Muscle, bone and determination built these walls. I sat on the stacked rock, munched my sandwich and contemplated my good luck at missing *that* work party.

Nearly eighty miles on the day, sweat soaked, insect bitten, strung out and ready to stop, I rolled into Manhattan and the loving embrace of air conditioning at my nephew's home. Clint and his wife Jen would harbor this world class recumbent cyclo-tourist fugitive. I needed a safe-house, and this was it.

Denizens of the Heartland
Sept. 28th: 2582 miles

Three full days of rest, only five miles of biking, all the AC and cortisone ointment my itching hide could handle. I relaxed in the comfort of my nephew's home and toured the fabulous veterinary school at the university—corridor upon corridor of operating rooms, lecture halls, dog cadavers, snakes under glass. We had pizza on the town. I updated my blog, slept in, cleaned the bike from top to bottom, including a thorough scrubbing of the chain. This fine German horse needed some TLC. But good company and luxurious rest must be renounced for the demands of the road, so one early morning, I slipped from the house and rolled into the dawn, determined to beat down my last Midwestern state, put Kansas in my rear view mirror. Little did I understand the diabolical delights Dorothy had in mind. "As big as you think" goes the new state slogan? *Please*, on a bike, it's bigger, badderer and brutaler.

My fresh legs attacked the road, eating miles like miniature marshmallows, popping one after another, inhaled like air and left behind without a thought. The road was mine, and I was Colorado bound. I pushed south and west, heading for the way, the truth, and the light: Route 96, an arrow, a bullet, a laser beam aimed at the Rocky Mountains that seared the heart of Kansas. My trail of tears. I landed for the night over seventy five miles from Manhattan in a marginal small town, a necrotic burg adrift in the corn sea, half the buildings boarded up. After talking to someone in the city office, I set up camp in the small town park and stabled Mojo under the shade of a pleasant wooden pavilion. Across the street, a young couple sat in the shade and followed me with their eyes. The only place to buy food was Scanlan Hardware and Groceries, the usual mix of lag bolts and Wonder bread. I wasn't alone for long.

Obscenity was his religion, vulgarity his sacrament. He was a dark angel, a crude, friendly helping hand who left me grateful and aghast. He was a tangle of contradictions, not unlike Kansas itself.

A fat, red canister of Folger's coffee bulged from his left hand. Thinning, scraggly red hair and mustache, a face creased through years of service, a blue, paint-spattered t-shirt, ragged corduroy jeans, he called out as he came down the sidewalk: "Yer work done for the day?" I told him I'd had enough. He offered me coffee and a gap-toothed, tobacco-stained grin. "C'mon over here," he said in a loud voice and proceeded down the street to the weathered café, a notorious den the city employee had told me about. A tattooed dagger rippled over my host's sinuous right forearm as he swung along. I was here to meet the inhabitants, so true to my credo, I followed. Before we'd covered thirty yards, he invited me to biscuits and gravy the next morning. He was the town's social glue, there was no doubting it.

Outside, the careful styling of the café consisted of three black half-barrel grills, rusted metal benches and the seat from a car sitting on the stained concrete slab in front. "I figure you're gonna need a bathroom. Some people gotta take a shit in the middle of the night. Hey, we all got our problems!" I laughed. "That door over there?" he said. "I'll leave it unlocked so you can use it if you have to."

The interior of the café was a chaos of scattered newspapers, dirty dishes, ashtrays, beer cans, a debris field covering a long countertop on the left side of the narrow room and most of the tables to the right. At one of the tables, a heavy-set woman with short straight black hair and small, dark narrow eyes played solitaire and smoked indolently. I asked where a thirsty man might get a cold beer, and before I could finish speaking, my host was striding towards the back, yelling: "How many?!"

"You been workin'?" the woman called after the beer angel.

"Hell yes, I been workin'!" he cried. "Done got me a big fat nigger, been workin' all day long!" He reached forward at waist level as if to grab a set of massive hips and thrust into the wide, empty space, laughing.

The only other person was a man in his sixties, plaid shirt and faded blue jeans, and when I asked him about the town, he offered up that they had a crazy mayor who got into a conflict with someone in the city office and threatened to throw a punch. The mayor called the sheriff but then was hauled away. "Looks like he's gonna be forced to resign," he said.

"Seems like I rolled into a tough town," I said.

"Yeah, well, things happen here."

Hank, the impresario of all this grandeur, came back with a couple of sweating Keystone Lights. What did the wag from England say? American beer is like having sex in a canoe—*fucking close to water*. It was cold and free and I drank it gratefully as the heat and miles settled into my bones. Hank was of Swedish descent, he said; his wife, she of the big t-shirt, was from German stock. He rattled off a few expressions in both languages. "Yeah, I can say a few things." Just then, a young woman, short, stringy blond hair, stout through the neck and hips, sporting thick-rimmed glasses, swung through the front door. Hank, talking loudly about his daughter as she passed down the aisle, said she should go to the military, "get her head out of her ass!" and pay for college. A proud Army Ranger and Vietnam vet, Hank thought the military would set her straight. I cringed inwardly for the girl as another man came in, built like a football, narrow at both ends but bloated in the middle like a python after swallowing a goat. Without missing a beat, Hank roared to shake the windows: "Look at that sorry sonofabitch!"

Back at my camp in the park, I settled into cooking dinner as night came down, a steady breeze cutting in from the southeast. One by one, the street lights burned into life, and I scratched in my journal by headlamp until I fell asleep over the battered pages.

In the dark hours the next morning, Hank introduced me to the farmers in ball caps and a few women sporting long sheath knives on their belts. To the assembled crowd holding paper plates awash in pale doughy biscuits and beige, chunky gravy, Hank boomed at the top of his voice as I passed towards the back of the café: "Y'all can get yerselves educated. Scott is a college professor from California, and the mother fucker is riding his bicycle!"

Let the Lynching Begin
Sept. 30th: 2692 miles

The wind knows. It has intelligence and rejoices in spite and cruelty. The miles come dearly, torn from the turbulent atmosphere inch by inch. Battered, sneezing, gasping, I spend hours on the road bitch-slapped by God. Crosswinds from the south, headwinds, crosswinds from the north gusting thirty, forty miles per hour, I tilt Mojo left and right and struggle to hold my course, wobbling down the highway like a stoned armadillo. And then come the trucks, harvest time now on the "bigger than you think!" plains of Kansas. I curse the sloganeers and boosters, laugh with grim knowledge at the signs offering free land to any who would come and stay. Who would have thought, homesteading land in 21st Century America? The catch: You have to live in central Kansas. With each corn-laden tractor-trailer rig, the raging winds are amplified tenfold into a blasting vortex that leaves me wide-eyed and fighting for control, a blast that only lasts a moment but leaves me frightened and bracing for the next attack.

The wind knows. It anticipates and plays, leads you on as if to say, *Now, at last, I'll give you a break....* In a fit of wild optimism I increase my speed and right at the moment of shifting into a higher gear, the hurricane picks up again and knocks down any intemperate fantasies of going nine or ten miles per hour. On the slightest hill, I am pushed down to walking speed—a drunken, unstable stagger. As Odysseus said: "[S]hould I leap over the side [...] or grit my teeth and bear it, stay among the living?" Pounded skin, grit in the eyes, the constant noise of the wind slices through my aching head and burning sinuses, nothing but hundreds of miles ahead on a road that never turns, never ends. Minutes expand into ages. Sometimes I make progress in a rage-filled push, but I can't sustain anger for long. A few miles fall to this technique until I'm worn out and back off, drop once more into single-digit speeds, weave and wobble. Many times I can look fore and aft *for miles* and see no another vehicle. All points of the compass speak of emptiness save for a distant silo or spinning windmill, exclamation marks in the void. Now and again, green locusts pop up from the road to fly across my path, caught in the gale as I am, and bounce off my legs, my chest, my face and then vanish into the vast fields of chopped corn stalks or milo or plowed earth. This is pure, raw, animal struggle. I tell myself that this is why I came, to dig deep and face my own weakness and uncertainty. This is the marrow of the journey. *Crack the bone and see it ooze onto your shaking hands. Who are you to be out here on your own, miles from nowhere? Are you mad? Take it and like it. Choke on the bone. Rejoice in the struggle, for it is all you have.*

The effort, the elements, the black grinding mirror of the road pull emotions from deep within and suddenly something breaks. I start laughing, a deep genuine laughter born of the absurdity of life, of my crazy joust with the continent. For a few minutes, I'm the happiest man on earth. But it's a happiness that can't last. The battle wears me down, whittles away at everything until only a stupefied, lurching shell remains. I pedal in a fog of effort engulfed in the roaring din, always the roar.

Late morning, I crouched in the lee of a scraggly bush and contemplated a mile of riding straight into the maw of the wind-beast. I'd been seeing signs for a motorcycle museum, but now the effort hardly seemed worth it. But when was the next time I'd be in Marquette, Kansas? Oh, that's right, never. So I saddled up and cranked into town.

Streets paved in brick, restored 19th century buildings, the place had a certain charm. Established in 1874, the town has never had more than 600 people and is now one of the communities offering homesteading land. Of these few families, back in 1928, one Stan Engdahl was born, a boy destined to be one of the greatest motorcycle racers the

United States has ever seen. In a career that spanned an unbelievable sixty years, he won five national and sixteen Kansas state dirt track championships and accumulated over 600 trophies. I was shocked by this record of talent and hard work crowding one entire wall as I stepped through the door of the museum. Dozens of fine machines covered every possible space on the floor. Astounding. Vintage Indians, Harleys, strange scooters, bike after bike, some glowing like a sunrise, polished chrome and enamel. Before I could walk ten feet, I was greeted by Stan "The Man" Engdahl himself. Easy smile, stoop-shouldered and shuffling with a cane, he looked old and frail, but there was a fire in his eyes and a honest joy at seeing a stranger in weird cycling garb come through his door. LaVonna, his wife of over fifty years, sat behind the counter. Day after day, all year long, they greeted visitors from all over the world, even errant world-class recumbent cyclo-tourists.   I was the only visitor that morning, and Stan gave me the grand tour, pointing out that perhaps a million dollars or more of motorbikes filled the two display rooms. His favorite story was the time he raced in a national championship with a broken leg.   His doctor told him to stay off the leg, but Stan complained that he had a hard time getting around, so could the doctor please cut off the cast so he could bend the knee? His doctor yelled like crazy when he saw his patient racing with the modified cast soon after, a piece of wood strapped to the side for extra support. Stan won the race, of course.

I snapped many pictures, and as I left, Stan and LaVonna came out to see my strange bicycle and insisted on getting my picture, too.   Such a warm, interesting, unexpected encounter, I was glad the small, quiet voice urging me to see the museum was stronger than the bellowing wind.

Late the next day, punch-drunk and wrung out, I rolled into Otis, the image of a town shortly after the Andromeda Strain came through—vacant streets, wind moaning between boarded up shops, only a single car turning down a side street. Who would administer Last Rights? I didn't even bother trying to stay in town. I loaded up with water and pushed on, the sun now low in the sky. At the edge of development, I came upon some sort of industrial facility, and there, beyond the last fence, a dirt track led past a stand of trees and out to a corrugated tin utility shed. On a hunch, I took the road and found shelter, a hidden spot behind the building—home for the night. Out of the wind, I had only enough room for my bike and tent, but it was enough. Then, as I cooked my meal and rested, grateful for these simple pleasures, a miracle happened: The wind stopped. I smiled up at the cobalt sky and on-coming stars. I would survive, somehow. I would make it. And many days on, before I could finish my bicycle exploration of these United States, Stan "The Man" Engdahl would die of a massive heart attack less than two weeks before his 79th birthday. The winds of Kansas blow for us all.

Darwin's Delight
Oct. 2ⁿᵈ: 2801 miles

"They teach we came from monkeys," he said with a simian grin.

"No, they don't," I countered.

"That's what I heard!" he persisted.

Ceremonial wheel soaking in the Atlantic:

First camp by the tidewater:

Steep roads in New England:

First state line:

Steam-powered car in Vermont:

Misery, Upstate New York style:

Angels of Sodus Point: Edi (left) and her friend:

Erie Canal lock:

Morning coffee ritual (note the Pepsi can stove):

Brewski the arborist:

Ride this over Niagara Falls:

Disney by the falls, Canadian style:

One of the empty high-rises in Buffalo:

Dutch in Buffalo:

Ocean or Lake Erie? You decide:

Gehry weirdness in Cleveland:

Art guitar:

Museum rock and roll style:

Camp life at the dead mall:

Hottie cheerleaders in Freemont, Ohio:

Sailing the corn seas:

A young fan at the Ohio tractor show:

Tractor action:

Steve Kraft, free Marine extraordinaire:

Heroic Midwestern lawn (note tree growing from old silo):

The fabulous Pitts family in Quincy, IL:

Huck Finn camp on the Mississippi:

Missouri shack:

Escaping the sun on the Katy Trail:

The long tunnel of the Katy Trail:

My general attitude riding western Kansas:

Guerrilla camp in the Kansas wilds:

Hundreds of miles of *this* :

Getting ready for the 'hoods of Pueblo:

Milestone:

Pueblo, CO, street sculpture:

Classic Southwest:

Camp above Chimayo, NM:

Jesus in wood, Chimayo, NM:

Steve in Sante Fe, NM:

Sculpture in Madrid, NM:

Headed south towards Mountainair, NM:

The ruins of Abo, NM, (note the Kiva):

Radio telescopes on the Plains of St. Agustin:

My reaction to finding a 9,200 ft. pass in Arizona unknown to Forest Service personnel:

Cranking for glory in the Arizona wide open:

On the road to Kingman, AZ:

Frank of the desert:

From my last wild camp in Arizona:

The big day to Oatman, AZ:

Oatman, AZ, first citizen:

The Mother Road:

Camp in the big lonesome, CA:

My stealthy night visitor:

Alternate transportation modes—The Unimog:

Hiding from the wind all day:

The great Mojave desert:

My first view of the Pacific ocean:

Jodi—at last:

Into the Pacific:

It's good to be home:

Part III: The West

"There were dark pines against a lemon sky, grey peaks reddening and etherealizing, gorges of deep and infinite blue, floods of golden glory pouring through canyons of enormous depth..."

Isabella Bird—1879
A Lady's Life in the Rocky Mountains

"Pretty soon he would be hundreds and hundreds of miles away on the great plains and deserts, and among the mountains of the Far West and would see buffaloes and Indians, and prairie dogs, and antelopes, and have all kinds of adventures, and maybe get hanged or scalped, and have ever such a fine time, and write home and tell us all about it...."

Mark Twain
Roughing It

Horny Goats
Oct. 4th: 2911 miles

It was out there, waiting. An arbitrary line, an abstract construct, a chimera of politics, history, and accident: The Colorado/Kansas border. I'd sworn an oath to start well before dawn to beat the wind, so in the clinging dark at the edge of a town park, I crawled from my tent at 4AM, certain of my virtue and the promise of easy miles.

Humidity 10%; dew point 23 deg. F.

Astonishing. How could such things be? This, and a new time zone thrown onto the stack of gold medals I'd already achieved? Now if I could only beat the wind. *Roll, pack, stuff, eat, drink, move it, pardner.* "I" becomes "we" in the deep solitude of the road. Chores done, I saddled up and...What the...? Strange, uncertain power transfer. No grip or support. I looked down: Not one, but two flaccid lovelies splayed out beneath once proud rims. Muttering different sorts of oaths, I rolled the lame Mojo to a picnic table under a glaring light. My first flats of the trip, a serious double header. Several thorny goat heads protruded from my limp tires. The locals call them "Texas tacks." Cursing again, I lay my wounded steed on his side, pulled the wheels and with my Leatherman pliers got down to the serious business of these devilish thorns, scrutinizing the inside of the tires for any possible points I might have missed, my virtuous early start fading with the stars. Karma for tempting the Road Gods, no doubt. My cavalier shortcut to the campsite had doomed me the night before.

My mood improved once I was rolling again—straight into a fog bank. What the...? Heat, sun, sweat yesterday was now dank, close fog, a ground-cloud cloaking the land. I wiped fingers over my glasses to see through the distorting condensation as I pedaled in a soft, silent room, no edges, just a shifting uncertain floor and pliant gaseous grey walls. I plunged onward, wary of creatures that might lurk in the mist. Momentarily, the sun tentatively pushed through only to be driven back. Then, a blurred "fog-bow," a prism of color smudged through the fog miraculously framing the sign, THE sign, the clarion signal of my escape from the Midwest: "Welcome to Colorful Colorado." Somewhere beyond this soupy atmosphere, two or three days' riding hence, the Rocky Mountains waited. Two months of riding had paid off. I was coming home.

A short distance later, I broke through the weird, foggy threshold and out into brilliant Colorado sun. Reborn, as happy as a cyclist can ever be, I rejoiced in the cool sun, the wind, for once, a mellow friend. In my rearview mirror, the strange border phenomenon retreated like a bad memory, a lingering hangover that might still leave scars—too soon to tell. Now, even the corn retreated and the plains began to undulate, a gentle ripple or two foreshadowing the great upheaval to the west, mountains still over the horizon. I had only to keep the pedals moving, trust in my course, and hope maps don't lie. Range land, cattle country, Rawhide! Cowboys and coyotes, the winning West pulled me in, cottonwoods blazing golden yellow down in the ravines. Under a High Noon sun, I was greeted by a member of the clan, a devotee of the saddle and the chain, my first long-distance cyclist since Steve in Ohio. In the middle of the day, in the middle of the country, in the middle of my life, I talked with Theodore like we were old friends, swapping war stories, sharing information about the road ahead. I gave him a section of map and recommended the Katy Trail. He told me of his battle with long days, slipping somehow into consecutive hundred mile pulls, finishing every ride after dark. "I don't know how I'd get through this without alcohol," he sighed. The endless plank of the Midwest would not lessen his days, I thought, with little to shake a cyclist from the numbing daze of the road. We could have talked forever, reluctant to leave this brief kinship. Who else really understood? It takes an addict to counsel an addict, but the road calls, Theodore's home in Illinois, the Rockies and roads with turns for me, the unknown outside and within that whispers and tempts. While my young friend seemed destined to fight his way across, I resolved to ease up, linger when I could. This ride, this life would end soon enough.

Dawn Patrol
Oct. 5th: 2975 miles

The forecasters had been alarmingly accurate: Wind, wind, and more wind. It appeared that a serious blast was brewing to the southwest, and a rest day in Eads—as I'd planned—would leave me eating headwinds for hours. I'd already supped my fill at that banquet, thank you. Time to go lean and mean. Rig for battle and race the sun. The winds tended to be quiet in the early morning, so I would rise earlier than early and push for the next town, Ordway, where I could layover.

At first I planned to sleep in the open, but as I finished dinner, I could see across the lawn sprinklers coming on, water cannons on spinning turrets. Pitch tent or get drenched. As I was setting up the fly on the tent, a sprinkler erupted from the ground right in front of me, its ugly head bursting out like an alien from an unsuspecting space traveler's belly. Water blasted directly into the tent. I quickly grabbed my pot and tried to cover the spewing head. Bucking and shaking, determined to bust free, the high-pressure water poured out from the shuddering pan as I held it firmly and realized that other streams of water from the next battery were bearing down upon me. If I wanted to protect my tent and gear, I had to move. I ripped my tent from the grass and scrambled to get everything clear of the converging crossfire. Exhausted, angry, frustrated, gear scattered over the parking lot, I just wanted to lay my sorry ass down and sleep. With a sigh of resignation, I began picking up all my equipment and transporting it behind a small building where I could see no freshly irrigated grass--

just dry dirt and leaves. I threw my pad on the ground and worked on getting a little sleep.

Up and packing shortly before 3AM. This wasn't cycling. This was war. I was going to escape the advancing armies in the south or know the reason why. Riding by 3:35AM. *Good grief, man. Have you completely lost it?* I left the pools of light in town and quickly became engulfed by the vast emptiness and darkness of the high plains, my headlight casting a feeble beam. Only a few distant homes and a cell tower miles away broke the perfection of the night. Overhead, Orion burned its skeletal form in the velvet black of the sky. A crescent moon glowed through a high thin cloud, to the south, flashes of lightning. Mojo and I made our way towards the mountains we could not see. Such a strange and solitary life!

Shortly before sunrise, I pulled into a dirt lot to use a restroom, and before I knew exactly what surface I was on, I saw the telltale grass of vicious thorns. *Damn double crap.* I swung away, looked down and found the tools of detumescence protruding from the rear tire. I pulled out the biggest one to hear the song of my frustration whistling shrilly from the tiny puncture. On fixing this flat I discovered the folly of throwing out that other tube back in Kansas: The remaining spare was, in fact, for the smaller diameter front wheel. Running low on patches and tubes, I was starting to get worried. The nearest bike shop was still about 90 miles away in Pueblo. I fixed the flat and tried to be as careful as I could.

The dawn was a magical ride into immense grassy expanses turned to gold in the early light. This was fine compensation for my brutally early start. Then, at precisely 7:19AM, I saw the Rocky Mountains for the first time, a peak off to my right--Pike's? I couldn't say. But the mountains were still there. I would reach them somehow, and these trying high plains would fall into my wake to become a good story rather than these present trials.

After a short break, I started up Mojo only to feel that uncertainty on the road that only meant one thing: *another* flat. This one, however, was of the slow leak variety, and I decided to ride on, pausing occasionally to re-inflate until I got to Ordway, about 25 miles away. It was obviously a small puncture and would likely require placing the tube under water to detect, but I did not have sufficient water to do the job in the wilds where I found myself. Every twenty minutes I would dismount, pump until my arms started to ache, then ride another twenty. This went on until I encountered another cyclist, Matt, on his way to Philadelphia. A fine young lad, he gave me a spare patch kit. I gave a map to Theodore only to receive this. We cyclists must look out for each other, pay it forward. With renewed repair supplies, I pushed on into the rising wind and heat. Ordway seemed to be a long way off.

The town was guarded by a feed lot with the wind cutting right across my path. Fine particulate matter and raunchy odors assaulted me as I pedaled resolutely to clear the zone. I pumped up the tire one more time and rolled into town. Matt had told me of a hotel across from the park with excellent rates for cyclists. I'd stay for two nights and make a real rest of it. The Hotel Ordway was temporarily missing a clerk, and check in wasn't until 2PM anyway, so I went to the park to work on my bike in the shade.

I was right away approached by a squad of young boys. Eli, lean and blond, was the oldest at fourteen and a freshman in high school. He and his friends quickly became my Ordway Posse, and we spent the afternoon talking as I worked on my bike. They liked this little town and made a definite point about how much safer it was than Pueblo, which was known for gangs. I asked them about what they were reading in school, and one boy said, "Not much. We don't have to read much of anything. We don't really like it around here." Nice kids, but I feared for their future. Later, we did a tour of the town, I riding along at about 3 mph with Eli walking on one side and his cousin, Chris, on a BMX bike on the other. Eli narrated: "There's our saloon. That's the bakery. The library's down there, way at the end of the street." He checked with his cousin to confirm that the street was almost exactly a mile long. The electronic bank sign listed the temperature as 93 deg. F. Only about one thousand people lived here, and Eli explained that it was "an old person's town." What *exactly* that meant in his mind was unclear as I might be quite old to him. Perhaps affordable real estate meant retirees. The average income was about half the national level.

After our tour, I checked into my room and bid the young men good day. As I settled in, the winds picked up and lashed the trees into a frenzy, an absolute flying rage. I planned to sleep in, read, write, and do as little as possible. The mountains would come, but the winds must have their day.

A beer in Ordway meant one thing: brave the saloon. No Western worth a damn skipped the scene when the strange rider pulls in for a drink, pushes through those swingin' doors and gives a squinty-eyed look at the local ruffians, rounders and scoundrels. Clean shaven, baggy shorts, t-shirt, river sandals, I hardly looked the part as I crossed the darkening, empty streets into the den of adult beverages.

Empty—almost. The long bar on the left faced rows of bottles and glasses and a mirror, a looking glass to throw the drinker back onto himself. If one comes here to drink, to escape one's life, how does this help? I quickly took in the vinyl covered stools, scuffed and beaten concrete floor, a drum set, mic stands at the far end, Bud Lite banners along the ceiling. A lone drinker on the other side of middle age sat at the far end of the bar. He looked up with a smile as I stepped tentatively across the threshold. I could not recall the last time I had been in such a place. In my early twenties I made a few feeble attempts at the bar scene in my home town, but I had no skill at meeting women, and I was left with a feeling of desperate sadness from those around me. But this place looked safe enough, the night hardly begun.

Mostly, I was taken by the striking woman behind the counter. Slim, tight, low-slung jeans, black tank, a tattoo on her lower back in the idiom of the day, straight dark hair, even the multiple piercings of her ears and eye brows could not diminish her beauty, a more refined Juliette Lewis. Although this was the only bar in town, she was sure to make it the most popular. She seemed an unlikely bartender in this rough little corner of the state, a character out of Steinbeck perhaps.

I took a place at the bar down from the other patron who was working on lite beer and shots. He recognized me as a cyclist right away. No doubt because of my rippling quads and—"It's the purse and the book," he said. "They all got 'em!"

"Hey," I replied, laughing, "you never know what the scene's going to be. You've got to be prepared."

He talked too much about the weather, snow on the passes, but he was a friendly face, an old rancher who'd spent his life on these wind-blasted plains. Finally, he asked, "Why do you do this, besides the athletics?"

Without irony, I said: "To see *you*! Really, to meet people and see the country, to feel the land and invest myself in it in some way."

I asked the bartender about her life here, how she ended up in Ordway. Brief details of her two-year-old son and mother in town explained much. And what about the people? "The people here are ignorant, stupid and angry," she said without hesitation. "We have fights here all the time. We had one earlier tonight. My first night in town, I was jumped."

I looked around the quiet, empty bar and tried to imagine the chaos. When I left, I walked out into the dark, windy night. The six cars that lined the street had dwindled to three. I half expected a lone tumbleweed to roll by. The band, the drinkers and the fights? I had a date with a pillow, a bed, and dreams of the Rocky Mountains.

No Problemo, Pueblo
Oct. 8th: 3035 miles

"I pedaled from Maine," I said to the young man as I parked Mojo in front of the Loaf 'n' Jug.
"Is that far?" he replied.

The hood, edgy, taggers, graffiti, cholo and cholita, my ride into Pueblo seemed to confirm what Eli and the crew had told me back in Ordway. I was careful not to give any hard looks or inadvertently flash gang signs from my dorky bike. Elite cyclo-tourists know when to play it cool. Drawn and quartered by highways 50 and 25, Pueblo occupied a lower, grittier station in Colorado's municipal hierarchy. Without the power and pull of the capital, none of the glitz and glam of Boulder, little of the mega-church Christian shine of Colorado Springs, Pueblo was a hard-working steel town, one of the biggest in the country. Fat, wide and spreading, it reminded me of home: Pueblo was the Bakersfield of Colorado. The crime rate was a bit high, the average income a bit low, the two locked in a miserable cage match. The city fathers and boosters had plans for big growth, especially to the north. With time and persistence, all the cities of the Front Range will merge, forming a seething moat of development between the plains and the mountains. If the Pueblo developers are smart, they'll avoid the fate of Trinidad to the south. An Ordway local told me it had the best weather in the state, a prime slice of Rocky Mountain banana belt, but Trinidad suffered from one horrible, deal-killing flaw: A clinic in town performed sex-change operations. *For real.*

Gunshot splatter. Machine gun fire. *Water?* Up, man! Up! Go! Go! Go! Sprinkler Howitzers loosed a fusillade upon my dreaming bulk.   Panic, middle-of-the-night-what-the-hell-is-going-on scramble. Zipper jam. *Damn it! Get this fucker open—now!*   Out, away, clear from the soaking bastards.   Gasping, socked feet in the dust, pad and bag askew in the dirt, clear now of the water cannons, I cursed, reset my bedding and quickly crawled back in.   Nearly freezing temperatures and a damp down sleeping bag make poor bed partners, but elite reflexes had spared me the worst.   My pounding heart took some time to settle, but before long, the rumble of the Arkansas River below sang me to sleep in the dirt lot beside the ball field. Some old mules take repeated beatings before they learn the lesson.

Hard frost, 28 deg. F. In less than a week, morning temperatures had fallen by *forty degrees*. Wonderful and shocking. Today was a big day, the ride that would take me, at long, long last, into the mountains. I could see my error in placing camp the night before. Although outside the edge of the baseball diamond and the chain link fence, there was still green grass. Axiom for urban campers: In the West, green means irrigation—*always*. I draped my bag over a railing post to dry in the chill air. At over 4,000 ft., I was now higher than at any point of the tour in the East.

Freedom and joy of movement sang in my bones as I escaped the urban creep and crud of Pueblo.   Rocky Mountain high and getting higher, Cañon City bound, my freedom felt dearer still as on the horizon I could see prison after prison after prison. Freemont County had staked its economic fortunes on the fortunes to be made by locking up bad guys—thirteen state and federal penitentiaries. Mini-max, Maxi-max, *Supermax!*—The Alcatraz of the Rockies— opened in 1994. What one former warden called "a clean version of hell," the facility sits up on a bare, wind-blown mesa.   High double fencing and mountains of razor wire, huge, angry bristling accordions of cutting steel glinted in the bright sun. Grim gun towers marked the perimeter.

Reporters are not allowed in.   When a family member does get in to see an inmate, the prisoner is chained and restrained. At first, each prisoner must spend twenty three hours a day in his cell, a seven by twelve foot crypt—the bed, table and stool of poured concrete, immovable. The sink, toilet, and water fountain are of one stainless steel unit firmly bolted to the wall. If the toilet is clogged, it shuts down to avoid flooding. The shower unit is on a timer, so even there the inmate cannot flood his cell. A twelve inch black and white television beams down educational and religious programming—no *South Park*, *Family Guy* or *Gunsmoke* to incite the resident criminal minds. Each cell does have a fine panoramic window: a four inch wide by four foot vertical slot that reveals nothing but a piece of adjacent wall and a thin slice of sky. Everything is designed to keep the prisoner isolated and uncertain as to his place in the facility. After a history of good behavior, the criminal might get some exercise time in a room described as a "swimming pool" because there is no view out. A very few get the freedom to socialize in a small walled yard, but on at least one occasion, inmates got into a fight and two were killed by guards. One inmate who spent time at this *United States Penitentiary Administrative Maximum Facility* called it the "perfection of isolation," a soul-killing, mind-warping lockdown. Ted Kaczynski, the "Unabomber"; Richard "I'm gonna blow up my shoes" Reid; Zacarias Moussaoui, 9/11 sicko; and Anthony "Gaspipe" Casso of the Lucchese crime family are among the happy residents of the Supermax Hilton. For a time before his death, murderer Charles Harrelson, actor Woody Harrelson's father, was an inmate. Timothy McVeigh and Co., the Oklahoma City bombers, enjoyed the amenities, although McVeigh has since ridden the hot needle to oblivion. Terrorist inmates are sometimes fond of low-calorie diets. Like any good high-end establishment, the employees at Supermax take care of their clients: When on hunger strike, inmates are force fed, strapped to a bench, tubing jammed up their noses, liquid calories pumped in. Many hundreds of these feedings have taken place.

The ring of prisons served as a strong reminder not to go on a sociopathic crime spree. I was content to turn

Mojo's pedals and observe from a safe distance. Elite, high-end, long distance Ninja recumbent cycling is not a crime—yet.

As I rolled westward, the walls started closing in—the titanic tectonic tilting of the Great Divide, my promised land. The maples and cottonwoods of Cañon City blazed hot gold and flame yellow. A blue cloudless sky blessed my passage. I was in the mountains at last, over 5,000 ft. high. First things first: Recaffeinate. As I surveyed the locals coming and going from the café, one fellow stopped to ask about my journey. In no time, I had a place to stay, but I politely turned him down. I wanted to camp in the wilds, throw down in some obscure corner with mountains and trees and an unobstructed view of the stars. After a round of the usual chores—library for blog and intel gathering, laundromat to right the wrongs of my soggy bivouac, and resupply for meals—I headed for the hills and lightly regulated public lands, something lacking to a wide degree in the East and Midwest.

I rolled past the prison museum set against a rocky wall at the end of town, crossed the happy rolling Arkansas River, and climbed steadily. Where should I go? A painful grunt took me to a crest of the road and the gates of heaven: a walking/riding trail, no motor vehicles allowed. Blowing golden grasses, dark stout junipers, high ridges fringed in craggy stone, a view out over the Great Plains to the east—Hallelujah chorus, praise the Lord and pass the brewskis. All at once, the effort and strain of the Midwest, the heat, humidity and bugs and never-turning roads lifted from my soul. As the afternoon deepened, two cowboys rode by on horseback, black hats, handlebar mustaches, jeans, leather chaps, every classic, clichéd accoutrement imaginable. In the background, juxtaposed against these 19th Century throwbacks, two cell towers bristled with microwave antennae. Me? I danced with the junipers in the long evening sun, pitched camp, and watched the dark ocean of the mountain shadows spread over the curved, cooling earth. My only wish at that moment was that Jodi could be here, feeling this same joy.

High on this solitary ridge, the chill of night settling around me, I pulled the sleeping bag up tight around my chin. Below, the lights of town seemed to mirror the stars, the swirling constellations of autumn. The eastern reach of the continent was lost in blackness and distance, the stars feeling closer. On a different October evening, thirty four years before, the jewels of the night were ill at ease, discontented with their lot in the airless void. From 60 million miles away, an orphan asteroid had lost its way, and on that night it seared the mountain air and blasted through the garage roof of a house in town, ripping a six inch wide hole and exploding into fragments on the concrete floor, leaving a two inch deep crater and Misty the cat cowering behind an old piece of furniture. Weighing almost three pounds, the crystalline space traveler was one of only thirty-five meteorites to impact manmade structures in the United States. No one was home at the time. For those obsessed with adding a true space alien to their menagerie, an Internet entrepreneur will sell you a chunk of the Cañon City Meteorite: .352 grams for $350, PayPal, Visa, MasterCard accepted.

For as long as I could hold open my eyes, I let the wonders of the night sky dream in, lost for a time in more than I could ever grasp, hungry for this feeling of unknowing. Lame Deer, a Lakota medicine man, once said: "If all was told, supposing there lived a person who could tell all, there would be no mysteries left, and that would be very bad. Man cannot live without mystery. He has a great need of it."

Rocky Mountain Touring
Oct 9th: 3140 miles

The blood of Christ stains these mountains, in metaphor if not fact. The story goes that early European travelers were struck by the sanguine glow of sunrise and sunset on the many peaks rising thousands of feet into the thin air. Being Christians—and Spanish—the immense mountain wall was called Sangre de Cristo. A better story lets blood do the talking: A Conquistador ranged too far from his compatriots and found himself surrounded by a squad of restive locals. These natives, more than a little angered at the arrogant Spaniards, decided this one had to go, perhaps an inducement for the rest to go back to their flamenco and sangria on the Iberian Peninsula. The lost soldier, finding himself amply skewered by a quiver load of arrows, clutched his bleeding chest, cried "Sangre de Cristo!" and died.

My 21st Century bike carried me into these storied peaks, my own blood pounding in my veins. A too breezy survey of the map the night before convinced me I faced a moderate day in the saddle—forty five miles. The facts proved otherwise: Sixty miles, climbing, stiff headwinds, a long, draining battle into the heart of the mountains. My first pass, too small by Rockies' standards to warrant a name or mention on the map, gained over a thousand feet from Cañon City. The wind. The wind. As I climbed, it pushed back, allied with gravity to weaken me while the landscape compensated and compelled me to keep moving. The sparkling river coiled through craggy canyons, pink granite and rusty red sandstone. River, rock, and sky graced every turn. If I had to take a beating, this was the place to do it. Push, pull, pedal, pound and pump, round that bend and crank for the next. Persistence, relentless, everlasting, undying, keep-those-legs-moving-you-grinning-idiot effort was the only currency for this transaction. Traffic was sporadic and light, although too many trucks for my taste. I imagined the horrors of full tourist season, the countless river rafting company buses, the RV's. This Tuesday in October made the route reasonable. The summer holiday season was long gone, and I was free to roam. Down in the river, low now after all the high snows had drained, fly fishermen in hip waders worked the shallows, their rods arcing in the sun.

Twenty miles out from Salida, my objective for the day, I stopped for ice cream. I'd grown addicted to Blue Bunny ice cream sandwiches—huge thick fatty sugary hockey pucks of ice creamy goodness. I craved a sweet counterpoint to the soul-killing work of fighting the wind. In front of the store, a flag snapped in the wind, snappy snap snappity snap snap! A happy snapping flag! I cursed it, scowled, and bit down on the Blue Bunny. *Dark mood, Scotty, gotta* snap! *out of it.* I shook my head, sighed. *Don't think, don't dread, don't worry. Do.* At least Mojo didn't complain. I saddled up and cast off, upstream once again. I had a place to stay, compliments of a road god, Trey, who took in errant cyclists. A meal out in Salida, a shower, a bed, I had good motivation to keep moving.

Maybe it was the Blue Bunny. Maybe the gods, for some reason, took pity on my lonely straining self, but minutes after retaking the road, the wind stopped. Oh, the joy, the simply animal joy of movement. My average speed jumped five miles per hour. The mountains were beautiful again, the autumn trees resplendent! Twelve, thirteen, fourteen thousand feet, the peaks heaved their mighty bulks into the clear October sky. Wind-scoured, barren-topped, the summits were only exposed stone, far above the region where trees could take hold. Happy chemicals flushed the sour and I pedaled into Salida a new man.   Grass-fed buffalo burger, fresh salad, "adult malt beverage recovery drink"—as the bike shop boys called it—and I was fully recovered.   Salida welcomed this long-distance rider with open arms. Originally a 19th Century railroad town, it now subsisted on tourism—rafting, fishing, skiing, backcountry hunting. Fewer than six thousand souls called it home. Lacking a world class ski resort, the town also lacked world class phoniness and overly slick development. A friendly, solid little place, it spoke to me immediately. The Arkansas River ran along the eastern edge of town, kayaking gates hanging low. And mountains, mountains everywhere. Yeah, I could live here. Once again I did battle with that restless spirit of mine, the core that emerged too often, looking always for the "perfect place," something new, different, better. I had yet to fully make peace with who I was, where I was. This longing for the perfect home in the mountains came in waves, but I resolved to simply enjoy what was, to see and smell and taste these Colorado mountains and meet the people.

I cleaned every crumb and drop of food from my plates and stepped out into the chill of the early evening. Autumn was coming on strong, and I needed to find Trey's home across the valley. I pedaled through the deepening shadows as the last rays of the sun glowed on the Sawatch range seven thousand feet above.

Intergalactic Cattle Manglers
Oct. 11th: 3225 miles

Perhaps the Cañon City meteorite knew something. Or maybe it wasn't a rock at all. A vehicle? Anything can happen in the mountains of southern Colorado. The San Luis Valley, over 130 miles long and 45 miles wide, is one of the largest mountain basins in the world. It is also a desert, receiving hardly six inches of moisture each year. There must be something in the water, however, for few places have generated such intense interest from the UFO community and late night radio shows. Events strange and inexplicable plague this remote recess in the Rockies. "Flying saucers killed my horse," Nellie Lewis said back in 1967. "They'll come out in force one day."

I left Salida with some reluctance, although not because I feared paranormal threats. I had been bewitched by the warm spirit of the town and its people. As with my other stops across the country, I'd been taken in, made to feel at home, like I belonged here. The solitude of the road both beckoned and repelled. However shallow and tenuous, I'd put down a root or two. These places and brief relationships create a gravitational pull that requires a bit of effort to escape. But the remaining 1,500 miles to the Pacific would not pedal themselves. An icy dawn, shadows pooled in still, cold pockets, I pushed off carrying the warmer gear Jodi had shipped, praise to my enduring Penelope. My toes were soon numb, but I didn't care. They would warm eventually. What mattered was this sensation of moving, of life and living, a sunrise over these Rocky Mountains and the gold up high to mark the place of my striving.

Before long, I stood on the crest of Poncha Pass, 9,010 ft. above the sea, watershed for the Rio Grande to the south and the Arkansas to the north. Under a glaring sun and down a black ribbon I descended into the San Luis Valley, vacation destination for transient space aliens, cattle mutilators, and El Diablo himself. On my weirdo couch bike, I fit right in.

According to an article by Christopher O'Brian, Nellie Lewis was the first. Her mare, Lady, was nicknamed "Snippy" by the press after Lewis reported a strange death and disfiguration of the horse, its tissues seemingly laser cut, vital organs removed. Who—*or what*—could do such a thing? To Whoa Nellie Lewis, there was only one explanation: Intergalactic butchers. Snippy had to have been subjected to alien experiments. How else explain the strange circumstances? Since then, thousands of domestic animal mutilations have been recorded across the country—lips and eyes removed, among other horrors—each report more evidence to the believers that *we are not alone*. Many of these have occurred in the San Luis Valley framed by the majestic mountains of Christ's Blood. Coupled with hundreds of UFO sightings, these UAD's (unusual animal deaths) made this lonely Colorado valley ground zero for the next close encounter of the creepy kind.

Equally disturbing, as O'Brian puts it, is the recurring appearance of Satan himself beguiling the local hotties. It is told that a tall, devilishly good-looking stranger decked out in a white tuxedo saunters into dance halls and hits on the finest filly in the place, sweet talking her with his evil, reptilian skill until in a daze of lust and abandon, the beautiful young thing is dirty dancing and grinding most licentiously! Lost in his own hell-dance, "Old Scratch," as the locals dubbed him, kicks off a shoe to reveal a cloven hoof or lets his impish tail fly freakishly. The villagers give chase, and Beelzebub vanishes without a trace. Was there a lingering odor of sulfurous cologne? The reports are inconclusive.

These tales took on a certain currency as I pedaled by an alien viewing center, a metal cutout of a bug-eyed visitor hailing passersby. And on closer inspection of one of my own photographs, I noted a smudgy object in the sky. Plane, bird, saucer, Jimmy Hoffa, Elvis? I'll never know. A great flurry of these sightings took place in the late '60s, a point worth considering given the rise of American drug culture.

For most of us, the story of mutilated animals ("mutes" to the cognoscenti) finds its conclusion in the interesting although less fantastic inquiries of Kenneth Rommel, retired FBI agent with almost thirty years' experience.   In 1979, after accepting a grant of over $44,000 from New Mexican authorities, Rommel applied his considerable sleuthing skills to solving the mute problem.   Wading through the foul rancid muck of twenty five carcasses, interviewing dozens of ranchers, consulting with numerous experts, Rommel determined that, alas, there was no need to result to fantasies of aliens and Satanists or Satan himself: Lack of blood was explained by the natural pooling and congealing that occurs with downed animals; the lack of lips and eyes and other organs is easily explained by scavenger insects' taste for soft flesh. The "laser" cuts are the result of natural bloating and splitting of hides—prosaic and stinky but hardly otherworldly.

My legs fresh after a day off in Salida, I lay into the long straight miles due south, New Mexico somewhere down the road, and put scorching flamenco on the mp3 player to ignite my cadence and burn the day, 200 proof cycling straight up.   Villa Grove, Moffat, Hooper, rolling to the slashing guitars, I stitched the little towns together, the turquoise and stucco, the braids of dried peppers swaying in the bright sun. To the east, a broad expanse of sand dunes spread incongruously against the mountains, Great Sand Dunes National Monument. The road did not turn for a full fifty miles, but the music, my burgeoning energy, and the wide open road kept my pace in the mid to high teens for mile after mile. I was a cycling superstar! Elite, refined, leading the peloton for the yellow jersey, I was untouchable, high above everyone and everything.

A small gallery and need for water pulled me out of cruising mode. I looked over the usual Southwest kitsch—

turquoise, paintings of mesas, Kokopellis everywhere. The clerk was a man ten or fifteen years my senior, a face creased by experience, blue jeans, plaid long sleeve shirt. A prominent nose and slight southern accent gave him an unusual air for the mountain West. Before long, he spilled his story, how he came to live in such a remote place. He'd picked up the accent during a long but faded music career in Nashville. "For some reason," he said, "I tried carving in stone, some sculpture, and loved it. I tried to make a living selling my art. At some point, I found myself almost homeless, living in a warehouse, hardly making enough to eat. I was living on the edge for years. Then a friend told me about this job. I'd kind of hit bottom and knew I had to change. I love it here."

I looked out the front window of the shop at the serrated panorama of the Cristo's and understood. A man could spend a lifetime looking at those mountains and feel like he had only begun.

In the afternoon, I crossed the Rio Grand, the archetypal Western river, here a living, moving body of water, far removed from the damp, fetid channel it would become in the south. More Rio than Grand, it was remarkable for existing at all in this arid basin. The Rockies runoff made life possible here, a carotid artery for high plains drifters. Alamosa marked the end of the day's riding. I had to be efficient as the afternoon was getting away from me. The shorter days would make big miles more of a challenge, and over 80 miles this day had kept me busy. My body hummed from the effort as I settled into a seat in front of a computer in the town's library. A quick blog update, then I had to be finding a camp. To my right I found my informant. He was an aging hippie, grey hair tied back in a ponytail, red bandana around the forehead, a beard. In shorts and bare feet, his legs wrapped like a double-helix and tucked under his chair, he curled over the keyboard and pecked at the keys with his index fingers, bespectacled eyes focused on the screen.

"Hey," I asked, "are you from around here?"

"Only since 1968," he replied—with an air more of pride than irony.

"Do you know where I might camp around here, not too far from town?" I told him about my situation and need to economize, my dislike of campgrounds.

"Sure, I have friends who've had to sleep out. Head through the park here behind the library, cross the footbridge, and head down the levee. You'll find places."

I thanked him sincerely and headed out. Once again, I couldn't believe my luck. My Higher Touring Power had placed me beside exactly the right person. The whole country seemed to conspire in my success. In no time I was crossing the river and riding a dirt path curving along the water, the sun almost setting. *Camp, camp, gotta camp.* At the last moment, I found a flat spot off the main path, my bedroom walled in by iridescent autumn colors with a view across the dark, silent river. I cooked my meal in the last light of the day and listened to geese honking overhead and jumping fish breaking the river's surface. Yes, this camp would do quite nicely, thank you. I had no worries of "Old Scratch" luring me into an illicit dirty dance, for I had "[danced] on the pedals in an immodest way," as Phil Leggett put it, and the guardians of the road were looking out for me.

Dreamtime New Mexico
Oct. 13th: 3322 miles

A coyote's alto bark cut through the thin fabric wall of the tent followed by the gallop of quick paws on hard dry earth. A raven's squawk echoed in the narrow rocky canyon. My first morning in New Mexico, the last new state of the tour.

I'd risen early the day before beside the liquid black opal waters and fought a long, wind-blasted battle to cross the state line below the horizon-filling dome of Mt. San Antonio. I'd wondered at the blighted, empty town of Romeo, and found the only secluded camp between Tres Piedras and Taos. Sun and sky, wind and distance, the constant churning of my legs carried me onward. This cycling life is simple but often difficult. A single day carries me across the range of emotions. In the morning, I am strong, upbeat, ready for anything. By late afternoon, energies fading, I struggle for the next mile and lament the wind that punishes my progress. It could not be otherwise, nor would I change it. The range of experience is the point.

Late, late, late in the day, rolling across exposed, mostly private land, I saw a dirt track dropping into a gorge before a bridge. Below was the old, abandoned crossing, steep, rutted, half overgrown...maybe.... I slid and bounced down, grateful for Mojo's full suspension. In a moment I was below a vertical embankment on a perfectly flat bench on the far side of the decaying bridge, rebar, crumbling blacktop. Out of sight of the road, quiet, my camp was better than any motel. I looked out over the chaparral and basalt walls of the canyon.

In the morning, a thin grey veil covered the western sky. To the east, clouds broke into drifting ragged islands of mist shot through with pale early light. I was bound for Taos, home of the ancient Pueblos, Georgia O'Keefe, D.H. Lawrence, Julia Roberts, Donald Rumsfeld, and countless tourists. Breakfast and coffee finished the last of my water, so I rolled on, anxious to refill. I was gifted with light to trailing winds and a rolling, downhill run, long easy miles at last. On the gentle slope to yet another crossing of the Rio Grande, I slalomed around one hairy beast after another. A huge migration of tarantulas was afoot, and I, Indiana Jones on a recumbent bicycle, dodged the palm-sized hirsute monsters for miles.

Across the Grand Canyon of the Rio Grande, a tenuous bridge reaching over the abyss, down and down at last to the fabled town, the mountains above awash in luminous Aspen, Mojo and I, old friends and confidants, smiled at our good fortune. We had a perfect day to land in this remarkable place, notable for its long, violent history. Conquered by Conquistadors in the early 17th Century, by 1640 the Pueblos had had enough and killed their priest and a few settlers for good measure. It wasn't long before the natives joined in a remarkable and unique event in American history: For the first, last, and only time, the native population succeeded in defeating and driving out the European invaders.

Although some degree of peace had existed between the Spanish and Pueblos, the outsiders' attempt to squelch the native religion was too much. All religious instruments and icons were to be collected and burned—masks, Kachina dolls, everything. Then the Catholic forces rounded up over forty medicine men, torturing, humiliating, ultimately hanging three of them. A fourth committed suicide before he could swing from a Spanish rope. Pope', a mysterious leader in Taos, organized the revolt, sending runners with knotted cords to all the other Pueblos. Each knot signified a day: Untie one knot a day until one remained, the day of the attack. Two runners were intercepted and forced to give up the plan, but Popé was able to start the day before. Over four hundred Spaniards died, stabbed, hacked, impaled, smashed—Padres, men, women and children. The remaining survivors fled to Santa Fe and held up in the mission while Pope´ and his forces laid siege, cutting off water and waiting. Ultimately, the Spanish agreed to leave and marched for many days to the south and out of Pueblo territory, following a route that I, too, would follow through rugged mountains and bald, harsh plains. The Spaniards returned after a twelve year break and retook the territory. Conflict among the Pueblos, lack of a common language, and other problems kept them from maintaining a unified, consistent resistance. Still, the severity of their resistance meant the Catholics took a gentler, less dogmatic approach the second time around, and the Pueblos have maintained their native religion to this day.

Hindus and the Goddess

I had no idea where I would camp, but the road provides. First things first: The Dragonfly Café for huge chicken burrito and Sante Fe Pale Ale, overpriced and wonderful. Then, to the library. I suspected that finding a suitable bivouac in a tourist town was going to be a challenge.

The road turns. Faces appear and vanish. Winds drift through the sage and sing across whirling spokes. I turn, someone smiles, exclaims at my bicycle and the nature of my pilgrimage, and I've found a new friend, a guide, the right person at the right time. And so it transpired in Taos.

A post-modern goddess, the shock of blond hair, two nose piercings, bangles, movie star sunglasses, she had no trouble identifying me as the cyclist belonging to the heavily laden Mojo out in front of the library. Kayla had done a long tour herself and was thrilled to see me and hear of my travels. This was the person I needed to meet. I asked her about where I might camp for the night. Without hesitation she said, "Yes! The Hanuman temple has people camp out all the time. I live next door to the ashram. They have food and

I'm sure they'd let you stay there." She gave me a big, warm hug—who was I to refuse?

Sometimes the magical guide is an aging hippie twisted up in front of a computer. Sometimes she's a pierced young woman in dark glasses. Sometimes he's a truck driver in paint-spattered work clothes, sometimes a grey-bearded farmer in Ohio. From one to the next, they help me along. When people ask if I'm alone, how should I respond? I am by myself for the long miles, working the passes, but am I alone? Everywhere I am greeted with such warmth, openness, offers of help. People say I inspire them, but I suspect they do not fully understand that they inspire me in equal measure, perhaps more.

So I would dwell amongst the Hindus.

Neem Karoli Baba Ashram. I crunched down a gravel drive and found myself in another world. A web of stone paths branched out from a loose fence of weathered vertical poles. A pair of young, very dark men stood beside a Jeep and spoke in accents heavy with the sounds of Africa, or so it sounded to me. A young boy of East-Indian descent exclaimed at my bike as did his mother. I asked her about the person in charge and eventually found Chris, one of the caretakers. Enthusiastic, himself a veteran of a trans-American peace walk, I received an offer of food and his blessing to camp behind the main building. I thanked him profusely and looked around the place.

The ashram and temple were of classic Southwest design: ringed with aspens, heavy wooden beams (vigas) above windows set in deep, earth-tone plaster, ramadas covered in parallel branches, gravel and sandstone walkways leading to different corners of the property. Behind, where I would camp, stretched an expansive grassy area. A cool, late afternoon sun cast long shadows through the trees, the air lightly scented with incense. I pitched my tent and quickly returned for food.

Chris had said that the temple was in the middle of a weeklong series of ceremonies for a string of nine goddesses, a gathering for one each night. This was a "low-key" event, he said, and for some ceremonies there could be hundreds of people in attendance. I passed only a few of the devout and picked up my savory dahl and spicy vegetarian masala. With loaded plate and bowl, I made my way outside to the long wooden tables. Simple food to be eaten in a plain, rustic setting—no linen or crystal, no fawning waiter hustling for a gratuity. Good food in the open air—what else did I need? That question was answered as I sat down.

I had met her only in passing as I first came in. "Chooch," as she called herself, called out from across the gravel and walked toward me with her own bowl of food. Short, grey hair tucked under a warm knit cap, down jacket over a thick sweater, her eyes flashing with a quick intelligence, she said, "So what made you want to do it?" referring to my tour. I told her about my desire to see the country, meet people, invest myself in the journey in a more meaningful way. She seemed to like this response. What followed was a wide-ranging talk about life, my interests, the way physicists and mystics are finding common ground.

Chooch called herself an "intuitive" and a reader of hands. She said I had the hands of a musician and a good "writer's fork." I told her of my choice of the high road to Sante Fe. At this, she fished a coin out of her pocket, flipped it in the air, closed her eyes, then looked at the side facing up in her palm. "The high road can be dangerous," she said. "I wanted to make sure you would be safe. You'll be fine."

So I was. From the prayers of Midwestern fundamentalists to the insights of palm-reading, coin-tossing aficionados of the link between physics and metaphysics, I couldn't go wrong. I even had the Mormon angle covered. My diversified portfolio of spiritual support rewarded me with deep dividends.

It didn't seem proper to attend a ritual that I did not understand, and I had not come here as an official member of the ashram and felt like something of an interloper. I retreated to my nylon shelter and listened to the chanting and music from across the field, the darkling sky grey and close. In the morning, I would take the high road to Chimayo, the Lourdes of the Southwest, and beyond that, Santa Fe.

Two Little Inches
Oct. 14th: 3365 miles

That's all it was on the map, a couple of inches, fifty millimeters, give or take. So much beauty and wonder, sweat and strain packed into the length of my thumb. Beware the innocent map, pilgrim, beware.

Frost lay heavy on the ground, inside and outside the tent. I gingerly reached out through the mesh to check the temperature on my altimeter watch: 25 deg. F., coldest morning so far, but the sun was rising and so should I. These long nights were starting to remind me of winter tours in the desert. I thought of Jodi and home with a sharp sense of separation and got to work packing. Although I could not rush our reunion, I could take another step in that direction by getting this day on the road. I shook the heavy icing from the tent, resolving to dry it out later.

Before leaving, I needed to use the restroom. Next door was an open room with broad windows facing the glassed-in veranda. Inside, Chris, looking a bit pale, bearded and sitting cross-legged on the floor, carefully pumped a harmonium with one arm and sang a haunting song in a clear, melodious voice, all in a language utterly foreign to me. The sounds floated through the room, and for a moment, I stood enchanted. There was warmth in the building, but there was warmth, too, in his song. I stepped out into the freezing dawn and bid the Hindus farewell.

Later, while out on the road, toes numb, I thought about my experience at the ashram. The quiet lane, the forest, and my rhythmic movement were good motivators to my own style of meditation. I thought how strange and wonderful it is—sometimes terrible, too—that human beings have found so many different ways to fill their days. Several of the non-East Indian Hindus I saw were rather grimly serious young white males who did not seem to speak and hardly cracked a smile—or any expression, one bearded fellow in particular spending his time walking to and fro, a shawl draped over his head and shoulders, spinning a prayer drum. With a wooden handle and weighted beads on strings extending from the center of a blue cylinder, the faithful could keep the prayers written on the drum in constant motion by wiggling his wrist, a sort of fully automatic prayer gun. Walking, spinning, walking, spinning...not unlike an elite cyclo-tourist. Like me, did this peripatetic acolyte sometimes curse the wheel? Did he cry out in joy upon some new revelation it had bestowed upon him? To what places did his rotating supplications take him?

So I filled my days with musings, a cycling mendicant, a seeker bound for a vision out of reach. My Sunday, my day of worship led me into the mountains, higher and higher above Taos, juniper and cypress giving way to tall pines and huge stands of glowing aspens. Great pools of gold washed over the slopes. I could not keep my eyes off them. The wind in their quivering leaves was all the prayer I needed. Indeed, their Latin name, *Populus tremuloides,* rings like a poem and speaks of their gentle dance on the wind. These were the jewels in the heart of the lotus. What else? Higher and higher still, the mountain tested me, probed for weakness. Would I be found worthy? Little did I know that the pass was only the first of many to come. Time and again I would push for the crest only to plunge and climb again these enormous waves of a topographical sea.

The small villages followed one upon another-- Vadito, Penasco, Las Trampas. The last, Chimayo, was feeling too far off, the day rapidly reaching retirement age. My left knee was giving me some sharp pains, pulling down my spirits and raising my anxiety. I dreaded some terrible tendon injury, a failing of my body that would end my dream. *No, stop it. You've come this far, over 3,000 miles through terrible winds, heat, ferocious climbs. You'll make it. This is only a temporary complaint brought on by too much climbing.*

Yeah, that's it. But my physical complaints could not diminish the beauty of the day, the glowing white clouds and sky of pure blue. On with it, then.

Later, atop yet another climb, I had the brilliant idea of stretching. I'd taken an anti-inflammatory with my noon meal, but I'd not done much stretching. What an idiot. Right away I felt better—a lot better. I resumed climbing with little discomfort.

After a while, I had to laugh at the relentless nature of the hills, cresting one after another between 7,000 and 8,000 ft. Perhaps I'd have my yellow jersey taken away because of a doping scandal, but I was determined to continue. To the east, high peaks broke free of the trees in grey pyramids draped with storm clouds and curtains of rain. Clouds, blue sky, storms, a full day on the high road to Sante Fe.

At last I topped what I believed to be the last major climb and pedaled into Truchas, a wind-bitten settlement on the edge of the mountains. Thousands of feet below lay Chimayo, lost in the folded foothills. A dark cloud hung over the town, and a chill breeze came off the high peaks and cut through the main street. I stepped into a tiny market and looked around to get my bearings. Weathered and worn bare wood floors stretched back into dark corners. Most of the shop was unlit. I could barely make out the cans on the shelves, and none of the refrigerated cases had light either. Next to the beer case, a cardboard cutout of a sexy young brunette in a tight bikini promised hot sex if only I'd drink Bud Lite. I peered into the murky depths of the case, pulled out two Coronas, and waded back through the darkness to the counter.

Dark skin, dark eyes, feeble dark goatee under his dark chin, the clerk of the dark shadows looked up as I approached. I asked him where I might camp for the night. He stared at me like an iguana drunk on Valium. After an incredibly long pause, he said, "You mean, like camp out?"

"Yeah," I said," I'm on a bike. Where could I go and not bother anyone?"

Another...very...long...pause...

"Maybe up on the mountain?"

This was going nowhere and getting there quickly. I dropped the first line of inquiry and tried something simpler: "I need some water. Do you have a sink or a faucet I could use?" This was an easy one, a problem with a solution served on a platter. No differential calculus here, no sir. *Of course* he had a sink, all buildings like this do.

He stared at me, looked out the window. *C'mon, man, you can do it. REALLY, this is a no-brainer.* I briefly considered another question for him: *Would you like to have sex with an armadillo?* At last, eleven years later, he said, "You can try across the street. He's got some water."

I almost lunged across the counter to slap him into a coma. I paid for my beer and stepped outside. The gallery across the street was closed. Then the stupefied reptile came out of the store, locked the door, hopped on an ATV and roared out of sight. I looked up and down the street, felt the cold wind on my face and wondered where I was going to spend the night. This place was *dead*. Rigor mortis had set in. The coroner was on his way. Time of death? I didn't care. Of course, there was a charming rental available down the street, complete with cracked windows, split and sagging dull orange stucco, peeling paint and rank weeds on the march to reclaim lost territory. Reasonable rates, no doubt. We needed to leave this carcass behind. *C'mon, Mojo, let's get out of here.*

We started down the long ridge that would take us back to the desert. Going slowly, we paused here and there, eyes sharp for a possible camp. *Scotty boy, you can solve this problem. There's a place somewhere to camp on this ridge.* A cemetery was too exposed, the land lumpy and sloping. Down, down, down—*there.*   At points along the ridge telephone poles were placed in flat areas with dirt access from the main road. The first I explored was so thoroughly trashed that Mojo and I backed out in disgust. Every pull out we'd seen recently had the same treatment, locals dumping trash all over the place. The second pull out was trashed as well, but there was one possibility. To the east and below I discovered the decayed remains of an old paved road, a now disused section of the main route. The black top was broken, cracked, run through with grasses and turning to sand, the center yellow line almost gone. The top section of the road ended in a berm and a flat, sandy area. Only a few plastic bottles sullied the scene. The site was below the level of the road with a mind-blowing panoramic view of the mountains in full sunset glory. Home sweet home. *Mojo, let's do it.*

My lodgings assured, dinner was hard on my mind and stomach. Fortunately, I had just enough water for the task. I cracked one of the beers and got to work. My recipe: Potato, broccoli, chicken sausage--into the pot with the lot of you. Gawk at the mountains while the pot simmers. Add olive oil, garlic, salt, pepper, onion flakes, top with grated Parmesan—*food, oh my God, food*—the great, deep pleasure of eating after a day of mountain climbing on a fully loaded bicycle. Animal joy, sustenance, calories, sweet, salty, savory, bite after bite I worked through the big pot and scraped it clean—twice—with pieces of sourdough bread (the carbs! the carbs!). I finished off my last piece of Dagoba dark chocolate spiced with chili. And I had an apple. I knew no shame, no limits.

All around the sky bruised and flamed, poured tears from October's heavy clouds and swallowed the sun in a final gluttony of raging orange.

The Needle and the Crucifix
Oct. 15th: 3,410 miles

All day long, the Padre had been seeing the glinting light coming off the hillside. Finally, his curiosity could stand it no longer, and the Spaniard climbed the juniper studded, sandy slope. He dropped to his knees and began digging with his hands. There, radiating holy energy, was a crucifix in the Guatemalan style of Esquipulas, far, far to the south. No one could explain how it had come to be in this place of northern New Mexico, but the luminous object held a strange and wonderful power. Three times in processions to other villages, the crucifix had vanished only to reappear once more on the hillside in Chimayo. It wasn't long before the miracles began, the healings of body and spirit. To honor this power and the spirit of Christ, a man built a modest adobe church modeled on the grand Cathedral found in Guatemala. Here, in the cool, earthen church, in a small room lit by candles, can be found El Pocito, the "little well" containing tierra bendita, the "sacred earth." Word spread of the earth's healing powers, and the faithful began to come. Or so one legend tells the story.

Another tale mentions the finding of the crucifix, but in this version, there is no miraculous light. Still, the healings follow, and the church was built on the very spot where the cross was discovered, giving us the sacred, healing earth of El Pocito. Whatever inspired the builder, the church was completed in its present form in 1816. Not many years later, the Catholic Church took over administration of the site, which continues to this day. The Santuario de Chimayo is now the "Lourdes of America," and perhaps the most popular destination for traveling Catholics in the United States. Each year during Easter, thirty to forty thousand faithful descend on the small village set at 6,000 ft. in the dry, sun-drenched mountains. These pilgrims walk for miles, some from as far away as Albuquerque, 90 miles, as a demonstration of their faith, praying for insight and healing. Tables of free food and drink provided by volunteers line the route. Portable outhouses are placed at key intervals over the dozen or so miles that most choose to walk, following the circuitous road through sandstone hoodoos, juniper lined washes, and sere, climbing ridges.

Once at the Santuario de Chimayo, the masses file in to give their prayers. Many will touch the sacred earth, some taking small bags, others rubbing wounded limbs, still others marking their bodies with stigmata from El Pocito. So many dip their hands into the well that fresh earth must be brought from the hillside regularly, 25 to 30 tons a year. For two hundred years, the Santuario has stood, its smooth earthen walls reaching into the painfully blue sky.

But the villagers of Chimayo have experienced two kinds of stigmata, the soft, red earth from El Pocito, and the relentless needle tracks from a deep and destructive addiction to heroin reaching back to the 1950's, a curse on this blessed place that runs through families and poisons the whole of the Espanola Valley, community after community in northern New Mexico having fallen to "black tar" or "chiva" as the locals call it. A culture of heroin use developed over time, in some cases grandparents shooting up with grandchildren. Like going to the park on Sundays or having a barbeque on the back porch, shooting up was simply what people did. The epidemic swept through like polio, leading to the highest per capita death from heroin overdose in the entire United States—not blighted Detroit 'hoods, not run-down LA slums—rural northern New Mexico. Ground zero for this plague was Chimayo, and the people had had enough.

One June morning, hundreds of citizens, religious leaders of many faiths—native, Catholic, Hindu, and more—gathered to walk, to shout and pray for release, to show that the community and its supporters were united in driving out the drug dealers, the culture of death and loss, the chiva that clouded their lives. Their prayers seemed to go unanswered. The politicians were silent. What could they do?

Then one day a helicopter pounded the dry desert air. Truck load after truck load of armed officers, DEA agents, converged on the tiny village. At the end of September 1999, one of the largest drug raids in New Mexican history went down, over 150 troops blazing in to arrest members of five notorious drug-dealing families. Vicious pit bulls were gunned down, the shots echoing in the tight canyons radiating like spokes from the center of town. Houses were surrounded, and, when the operation was over, thirty four criminals were hauled out of the valley.

Eight years after the big raid, I descended from the High Road, slipping under glowing cottonwoods and a warm, clear sky. The scattering of homes, the old adobe church, the white-washed walls pulled me in. I felt as if I'd discovered a small piece of heaven. Trim, quiet, removed from the chaos of urbanization, Chimayo revealed nothing of its troubled history. The drug trade had moved to other towns, although the effects lingered in Chimayo, addicted locals taking clean needles from a treatment program. Now that the locals had been locked up, Narcotraficantes Mexicanos, the Mexican drug gangs, had taken over the business in the Espanola region. I could only hope that my impressive legs and strange bicycle would throw off any would-be attackers. In Chimayo on that morning, I had nothing to fear—except the appeals from an attractive shopkeeper.

As I pulled to a stop, a slim, dark-haired woman came striding out of a white-washed building, saying, "Oh, you must have one of my shirts!" She held a Day of the Dead-themed t-shirt featuring grinning, laughing, howling skeletons astride all manner of bicycles, teeth and bones a-clacking, wind-blown hair and mustachios. One even appeared to be riding a recumbent. The shopkeeper was correct: I did need to have this t-shirt. I threw down Mojo's kickstand in the dusty earth and followed the woman back into the Vigil Shop—"Santos, Woodcarving, Popsicles"—a room packed with Catholic curios, saints and candles, racks of fantastic t-shirts. If the dirt from El Pocito could fill the wounded souls of the pilgrims, the knickknack shack could empty their pockets. I was happy to play along and purchased the shirt and a small bag of the dried local hot peppers, an industry here for over three hundred years and only recently revived. These became my sacred "Chimayo Peppers," and I would sprinkle them on all my evening meals as proof against the dangers and rigors of the trail, my own satchel of special spicy powder to see me through. The flaky red magic would last almost to the Pacific, over 1,000 miles away.

Back out in the glaring sun, the fabulous high-altitude photons pushing into every nook and cranny, banishing any possible dark thoughts, I strolled down to the Santuario. As a product of the ever-changing *Nouveau West*, I felt a pleasant sense of grounding as I stepped across the threshold. For two hundred years, these heavy wooden doors had welcomed the seekers and the needy. Unique, organic and authentic to this place, there is only one Santuario de Chimayo. Unlike the synthetic replicating plague of fast food joints, Walmarts, and Starbucks across the land, this building and place could never be duplicated. The Santuario will always be itself for as long as it stands. I got much the same hallowed feeling when I strolled through cemeteries in the East with markers dating back to Revolutionary times. The modern age is about change and ever increasing rate of change. Engineered obsolescence. But the spirit of Chimayo speaks to that which never changes, the longing of the human heart and the truth of suffering.

Compared to modern cathedrals, the main room was small, the ceiling composed of log beams, low and dark. Primitive but colorful paintings of saints and the Crucifixion lined the walls. The altar at the end covered floor to ceiling, bright panels of gold, copper and red. I have often been uncomfortable with the brutal nature of Catholic iconography, but few depictions of Christ have unnerved me as much as the wooden figure near the front doors. As tall as a man, this fisher of men stood in gaunt, horrifying detail, the polished wood stained dark, the form skeletal, the bony fingers seeming to ache. The black, sunken cheeks and eyes spoke painfully of the Buddhist insight that all life is suffering. For a moment, gazing into those wells of agony, I believed it. I was relieved to step back into the sun. Santa Fe was waiting, and I still had many miles to go.

Although I'd collected no tierra bendita from El Pocito, I had my holy chili peppers and the dust from Chimayo's streets on Mojo's tires as I climbed the short, steep grade out of town and dropped into the hoodoo wonderland beyond. Like the Catholics in their thousands who trudged this path every Easter, I too was a pilgrim, and I found a stretch of the Holy Land, a few miles of empty New Mexican blacktop meandering through twisted sandstone towers and sparse junipers under a perfect dome of blue.

Too soon I was out in the main valley south of Espanola, although I did have a wide-open deserted road that paralleled the main highway. Days Inn! Hilton Santa Fe Golf Resort Spa at Buffalo Thunder! Cities of Gold Casino Hotel! Executives and natives coaxing ducats and doubloons from pale faced tourists who come by the busload. The truth behind the shiny development was darker and more complex, the river of heroin flowing north from Mexico, the sea of poverty making New Mexico one of the poorest states in the union. Ranked 43rd in per capita income, the state received over two dollars in federal assistance for each dollar it paid in federal taxes, the highest ratio in the country. I was headed for the richest region of the state, the capital and home to artists and movie stars, captains of industry and real estate speculators. How different this all was from the days of the Pueblo revolt. Not far from where I rode, a tough band of natives had held out against the Spaniards. High on a mesa, they threw rocks down on the invaders. But muskets and modern military trump stone throwing every time, and the Pueblos ultimately surrendered.

Like the road from Taos to Chimayo, this line on the map concealed the rigors of the cycling. A long, rolling climb chewed away at my energy. When at last I cut off the main line to pick up Bishops Lodge Rd., I was faced with a hard, steep, punishing grade. Santa Fe would not give up its secrets without a fight. Any cyclist that would make it this far has had the lessons of persistence carved into his legs, and I was no different. Burning pistons slowed me down, but the climb relented, for now lactic acid would defeat gravity, and I crested the rise to fall, at last, into the arms of Cibola. The Spaniards should have waited. Four hundred years after their arrival, the streets were paved with gold. Here it was called *real estate*.

Adobe style palaces lined my route, so many up here with outrageous views of the broad high altitude basin. At 7,000 ft. above the sea, it must be one of the biggest towns at this altitude in the United States. The sky was absolutely clear, not a smudge or cloud or blemish to besmirch the heavens. I relaxed into a long, gradual descent aimed at the heart, the old Plaza and center of town. Traffic increased but gave me room, and before long I rolled to a stop on the brick pavement of the town square, walls hundreds of years old closing me off from the rest of the city. Tourists in sweaters, cameras slung around their necks, wandered along the shops and studied jewelry and, no doubt, some Chinese made curios spread on blankets. The bright, autumn-dimmed sun washed over us all like a prayer. I parked the bike and felt keenly Jodi's absence. She should be here. I sat on the steps of a gazebo and called, but we both felt the strain of miles between us. The phone was so inadequate. We needed it, relied on it, but, at last, it was only two tin cans and a very long string. I hung up, feeling adrift.

I rallied, though, as I walked among the crowds and soaked up history, these walls centuries ago protecting the terrified padres and their flock, government functionaries, a few natives gone Catholic. Outside stood the raging Pueblo hordes, Popé's soldiers who killed hundreds of the invaders. Here the Spanish occupiers gave up the fight and agreed to leave Pueblo land. A ragged, defeated and frightened company collected what belongings they could carry and headed south, bound for Mexico, following the route that I, too, would follow. In less than twenty years the Spaniards would return and, without a shot fired, retake this lost territory. But the initial defeat set a tone for the return of

Catholicism, and never again would the Pueblos lose their old ways. And, as I was to find farther south, the two traditions would blend in some surprising ways.

Lunch took the form of a huge spreading burrito awash in a flood of cheese at a café just off the square where I placed a call to Uncle Steve. We'd been in touch via email and another call from my unlikely camp on the ridge below Truchas. Now, weeks and weeks after we had set up the meeting in Cleveland, Ohio, I was to stay with the fabled Steve at his unique community, Rainbow Vision. I saddled up and headed south again. I was due for a couple of rest days. I could not recall my last shower and feared I might drive off the natives. It was time to stop.

Perhaps unique in the country, in 1912 the city of Sante Fe determined to limit new development to the rather specific architectural style called "Pueblo Revival"—stucco and plaster walls, vigas, parapets. The goal was to maintain a certain look and attract tourism. Rainbow Vision hewed close to the requirements with lines of condo's and a few apartments looking like modern iterations of the Pueblo style, sandstone colored walls, rounded corners and flat roofs. Although the style of the development was typical of the region, the motivation and spiritual center tilted to the left. Rainbow Vision in Santa Fe was one of three such developments in the country, all specializing in catering to the gay and lesbian community. From the lonely gay man's home in the wilds of Illinois, I'd landed in an extensive community devoted to supporting people with a different take on relationships. It sounded like an excellent idea. We all strive for places where we can feel safe, accepted. I was to be so energetically pulled into this little community and made to feel at home. There was even a fitness center called—what else?—the Billy Jean King Fitness Center. Classic. They were, however, as one fellow said, "straight friendly," and they proved it during my stay.

Steve was the perfect host, bringing me into his home and showing me around the area. In his seventies, a cyclist, he was a retired librarian working part time as...a librarian. Fit, engaged, he proved a good role model for my own life only a few decades away. I showered, relaxed in my own room, updated the blog, and put on the new tires I had shipped to Steve's. After thousands of miles of hard riding, the rubber was getting thin. I moved little. That evening, we ate at Garbo's, the fine restaurant in the development where I supped on dark, tender flesh, roasted vegetables, and a blood-red wine—Sangre de Christo! I also met Jerry, who would feature in the next evening's adventures.

Sunday night, Steve had plans, so he set me loose with his account to eat on my own and suggested the café menu from the bar. I strolled over in the cool evening light. As with the saloon in Ordway, I carried a book, uncertain as to whom I might encounter, if anyone. My worries of a solitary meal were unfounded. I had barely occupied a seat when Jerry recognized me and I was invited to join their table. Slim build, flashing eyes, semi-flat topped grey hair trimmed to perfection, Jerry held court with his outsized personality and totally charming Tennessee accent. Steve had told me of a terrible attack Jerry had suffered, leaving him with some short-term memory loss, but I could detect nothing in his demeanor but enthusiasm. He introduced me to the others—Jack, his partner, about forty, looking like a model with a smooth dark complexion and open v-neck shirt, and Buddy, who staggered up with a cane, a man easily in his late seventies or older with thick glasses, hard of hearing: "Everyone," said Jerry, "this is Scott, and he is pedaling a bicycle across the whole country. Isn't that *fucked up*? I think that is *so* fucked up. I tell you, though, if I tried to ride a bike around the block? Now *that* would be fucked up!" We all couldn't help but laugh at his outrageousness. Jerry beamed. We were his happy audience.

Buddy, slumped in his chair, cane under old weathered hands, turned his fish-eye lenses to me, his gruff voice seeming to quiver in anticipation: "So, Scott, I'm totally addicted to sex, and I must know about your string of sexual adventures as you ride across the country. What did you do as you got into each town?"

I laughed at the lunacy, the boldness of this stately, grandfatherly figure asking such a question. "Oh, no," I said,

"I'm married and far too tired at the end of the day for that. I'm just a crazy cyclist."

Buddy would not be put off: "But I'm fascinated by the sexual habits of crazy people!"

Separation Anxiety
Oct. 18th –19th: 3,518 miles

It's always harder than you think.

I had my last meal at Rainbow Vision with Steve and Jack at the clubhouse. Yogurt, granola, coffee, orange juice, a toasted bagel and cream cheese. A banana. My figure wasn't in danger. Jack killed me when he said he was a "fully recovered Mormon." I didn't suppose the local Bishop would look too kindly on this gay community, but here I was, taken in, supported as surely as I was by Hindus in Taos, Mormons in Kansas, and Christians everywhere. Somehow we made a country, a people, and I felt the sting of parting as I said my good-byes. Steve and I walked back to his place in the chilly mountain air. It had rained a little the night before, stray pools on the blacktop. Jerry stood with a cup of coffee in hand on a balcony overlooking the parking lot. He waved and wished me luck. I was leaving? Again? The wonderer's curse. A blessing, too. The usual separation anxiety settled in as I set sail, tracking west then south, struggling with an icy westerly, the right side of my body numbing in the wind.

Once again I was a free agent, the lone cyclist on a strange road. I missed my new friends and felt the gravity of companionship pulling against me, dragging each turn of Mojo's steady wheels. I longed for the familiar and realized that for all its fascination and romance and gifts, I could not be the perpetual wanderer, not in this solitary fashion. I missed Jodi and home sharply just then. So I pedaled hard and stretched the threads of connection to Sante Fe until they snapped twenty miles out. I needed to be forward thinking. The goal, the next camp. This was my life. But I felt cut off, adrift, too far from everything—the friends I'd just made, the coast for which I strove, my wife, my life. Who was I? Why was I doing this? Wind beaten, anxious about camp and the miles to come, I slipped into a wanderer's funk, pushed up hard against the Odysseus Paradox: The closer I got in distance to my destination the further away in time was my separation. The remaining time grew shorter, but the accumulated hours, days, weeks—now months—grew longer, deeper, sharper. Still weeks of riding and the fickle winds of Aeolus lay between me and the shores of Ithaca. And what of a house full of suitors bleeding my coffers dry? *Don't think. Pedal. Focus on what is good and grand. You'll never be here again even if you return.*

Broad, barren plains of tawny whipped grasses gave way to hills and then mountains, high, scruffy and steep against my October sky. Hot yellow cottonwoods in the draws, a deep blue sky of forgetting, the black twisting road taking me into unknown mountain folds. *Ride, love, breathe in this day, pilgrim. We get too few like it.* I rode the Turquoise Trail, named for the mineral dug from the nearby mountains by the local tribes long ago. Now, the turquoise filled the sky. Mid-morning, port of call: Madrid. For some reason, the locals pronounce the name MAD-rid, first syllable emphasis. This was an unexpected gem of the road, a place utterly unknown to me and appearing like a dream out of this empty corner of the state. Drawn by gold and silver, Conquistadores enslaved the locals but finally moved on to be replaced by coal miners, whose numbers swelled the population to 3,000 or more in the late 1920's and '30's. Eventually the town and mine were owned outright by a man named Huber, known for honest dealing and giving the workers a hospital, the first lighted baseball field west of the Mississippi, and even a secret place to crank out homebrew during prohibition. In classic boom-bust fashion, the market for coal dried up and so did the town, the miners and shop owners, doctors and bartenders blowing away in the dry desert wind. In the 1970's Huber's son began renting buildings to artists and others, and so began the town's rebirth. Cheap, beautiful, remote from the noisome hustle of Sante Fe, in Madrid the aesthetes of the Southwest found a home. Galleries, cafés, and shops now occupy the old town, each restored to a heartening degree. I was greeted on one side by a welded tin, larger-than-life Don Quixote strumming a guitar. There was the Ghost Town Kitchen aka No Pity Café. A huge grey snag of a tree loomed in front of one establishment, sign hung from the top: "Java." All right then. Below, another sign: "Bad Coffee Sucks." Indeed, that is true. *Must stop and recaffeinate.*

I was in danger of never leaving this enchanting village when I met a beautiful young girl. Lithe, smooth, joyful, she ran about like a lovely vision. Oh, that bitch was everyone's favorite. I was bewitched, and her name was Trouble, a coyote mix I considered stuffing into my over-stuffed panniers. I gazed longingly, grabbed my coffee mug, and went in for the promised non-sucking liquid black life. Although not the best coffee of my addiction, it did not suck, so a mug of happiness was mine all mine. I sat under that perfect sun and watched the scene, travelers hitting the long string of galleries, locals at the café. It seemed the perfect life, a quiet backwater with just enough contact with the outside world to keep the roughly two hundred residents afloat. That's it. I'd call Jodi, get her to pack up a truck with the basics—bikes, books, hiking gear and dog—and meet me. We'd spend the rest of our lives sipping coffee on this quiet main street and exploring the mountains. As I seemed to do in most places, I tried to imagine a life here. Not unthinkable. Romeo, Colorado, or Otis, Kansas? Unthinkable. Madrid, New Mexico? Not bad...

Sooner or later, long bike rides are about the riding, and I had much more ahead of me, long climbs through the cantankerous cartography of this most Southwesty state. Slowly, up and up past the Kickin' Ass ranch—a collapsing shack—miles of steady work, lunch beside the cholla, more and more work, long ramps, always up or down. Late in the afternoon, cruising along through dense pinyon forests, expensive houses appeared on the slopes. I was headed toward Hwy 40 and the cutoff for Albuquerque. Here were the exclusive estates of the wealthy urban refugees. I wondered how they would fare in a wildfire. Late in the day,

I crossed under the highway, fumbled around until I picked up Rt. 14 again, and started climbing—again. My simple AAA map was deeply inadequate. I had no idea how high, how far, but I knew I had entered National Forest land, so camping would be reasonable—or would it? I'd expected to have this road to myself, but steady traffic rumbled by in the fading light. Huh? At least a good shoulder lined the route. Steep, craggy escarpments, narrow draws and canyons. Hardly a place to sleep for a weary wheelman. The shadows drew dark and cold across the road. Hard, steady climbing. Must. Find. Camp. Getting frustrated. Exhausted. Late. Late. Late. At long last, the daylight almost gone, I pulled into a day-use rest area, camping prohibited. Yeah, right. This was home for the night one way or the other. Ranger Gestapo would have to drag me away in irons, by God!

In the deepening grey of evening, the last of the sun draining from the chill pines overhead, I leaned Mojo up against a picnic table and surveyed my lonely corner of the planet. Restroom? Check. Flat place for a tent? Check. No other people? Check. I quickly changed into polar fleece pants and fresh, dry top, my sweat-soaked frame cooling rapidly. Fleece hat, gloves on, off with the cycling shoes, on with the runners. I frowned. An out-and-proud campsite didn't sit well with my stealth ethos, and the last thing I needed or wanted was an unsympathetic ranger or obnoxious drunk pulling in. I scouted about. Down a slope, around a corner, beneath a short vertical wall of limestone...perfection. Mojo didn't complain as I muscled him down to my hidden canyon and set camp. Out of sight, out of mind. As I cooked dinner, the temperatures were already in the 30's. At almost 7,000 ft. in October, I was in for a cold one, and it wasn't long before the refuge of down and sweet slumber pulled me into the tent. The wind moaned a forlorn song in the trees overhead as night fell around me. Fatigue, warmth...gone.

As I packed in the morning, having slept in to an unthinkable 8AM, I looked up to see a galloping herd of three golden retrievers descend on my camp. Wild, bouncing, goofy beasts, wet noses, flying paws, unbridled doggie energy all around, everywhere at once. Suddenly, a woman appeared over the ridge and yelled out: "Hold it! Hey, do you have a dog?"

"No, only at home."

"One of mine likes to pick fights!" she gasped and ran down the loose, sandy soil. The dogs where flying about, noses into panniers and stuff sacks, one licking my breakfast bowl as another grabbed my spoon firmly in his mouth, a silly lexan lollipop. I lunged for the utensils as the woman managed to call off the hounds.

"I'm sorry. They go for anything related to food."

"Yeah," I laughed, "I noticed." She asked about my trip, wished me luck, and hiked steadily up into the trees, the three stooges bounding after in a lurching wave of golden fur. After this hit-and-run encounter, I was ready for the road to see what else the day would bring.

Pulling away from my illegal camp, I quickly realized I'd made the best choice the night before. No other suitable option appeared as I finished the climb into the brilliant dawn and leveled off amidst the pines of the Cibola National Forest. As suspected, however, I encountered a substantial semi-rural subdivision, ranchettes in the trees, the source of all the traffic the night before. By the looks of them, these were the somewhat lower-end counterparts to the palatial homes north of Highway 40. Needing a mid-morning break, I stopped at a small market and purchased an orange juice. To my surprise at all the development, the friendly clerk was philosophical: "Hey, people got to live somewhere, and this is a hell of a lot nicer than some gang banger 'hood in Albuquerque." Irrefutable logic, that. It didn't take long in the weak sunlight to leave this woody 'hood in my rearview mirrors, rolling, climbing, descending through a day etched in crystal. Eventually, I cleared the forest and gained broad vistas across limitless grasslands to the east.

Chilili, Tajique, Torreon, Manzano, I strung the beads one after another. A combination of Spanish land grants and Pueblos, these hardly qualified as towns. Tajique, however, was flat out depressing, mountains of rotting junk and run-down buildings and a big sign promising big fines for taking pictures. Hardly a question of national security, but I couldn't blame them. Would I want tourists taking photos of my dirty closet? I was tempted, however, to take a picture of the sign prohibiting the taking of pictures, but momentum carried me through before my impish impulses could get me in trouble—not that I could see anyone about to object. I strained in solitude.

The crest of the Manzano Mountains came into view in the afternoon, the summit over 10,000 ft. high. Wilderness and National Forest, it seemed a pristine playground, but few things are as they seem. Research told me otherwise the story of these mountains. Of course, I should not have been surprised. Besides the "Land of Enchantment," New Mexico was also the birth place of the Atomic Age, and my ride took me through regions traversed by ancient natives, conquering Spaniards, and fat-bellied airships pregnant with radioactive cargo. To the north, Oppenheimer's crew designed and built the doomsday machine. To the south, he became "death, the destroyer of worlds." On the west side of the Manzano Mtns., the government constructed deep bunkers for the storage of our burgeoning atomic stockpile, and in April of 1950, with nuclear weapon and detonators aboard, a B-29 lifted off from Kirtland Air Force Base in Albuquerque. Three minutes later it augured into Manzano base, exploding into a fireball visible fifteen miles away, killing all thirteen crew members. Although they could not save the flight crew, safety measures were followed in the packing of the bomb so the radioactive core was stowed separate from the high-explosive case. The fire and death were fearsome, the worlds of those airmen destroyed, but nuclear disaster was not to be.

My own worries were merely banal: Where would I camp? I passed a turnoff for a Sufi retreat center. Already an adept at spinning, should I whirl with the Dervishes? *No, keep rolling.* I stopped in the micro-burg of Manzano, a term given to this town and adjacent mountains meaning "apple" in the Spanish. One story has it an unexplained orchard was discovered in the area in the 18th Century. My aim was a campground indicated on the AAA map. A pleasant woman behind the counter of a small market said, "Oh, it's just about a mile up the road."

I should have known then I was doomed.

Like a stupid, foolish child, I munched my ice cream sandwich, content with my treat and camp soon to follow. I was tired, ready to put Mojo out to pasture for a while. We both needed the rest. So began the punishment, as much psychic as physical. One mile, two miles, three miles...painful, grinding ascent. *Where the freakin' hell is this freakin' campsite? And what the freakin' hell was that freakin' moron clerk freakin' talking about?! Why the hell can't freakin' locals know the first simple freakin' thing about where they freakin' live?!* I cursed and muttered in glorious tones, scripted lines of Pulitzer Prize-winning invective. I was, for a few moments, the Bard of Noxious Vulgarity.

At the three mile mark, I hit a turn with a sign indicating the campground was a further three miles up into the mountains, steep hard lactic-acid-burning miles all the way. My lovely informant was not off by 50% or, *the horror*, 100%. She was off by 600% in distance and thousands of feet of climbing.

I gave up.

We turned and rocketed down, in moments of breezy descent arriving back at the main road. After loading up with water to camp wherever we might land, we headed out of the mountains, the shadows reaching across the road, a warm sun fading, the wind at our back. Miles of fast easy joy cleaned the carbon buildup from my clogged spirit while Mojo and I surveyed the countryside for a break in the fencing, a lonely dirt road, anything. Time and again, we were disappointed. Before long, the hill bled out into dry, grassy plains and a minor congregation of buildings. Just beyond...what was this? A rest area? I pulled off the blacktop to see a stone gazebo set a few dozen yards back, a stone-lined path marking the way. Further on, a windmill stood against the late afternoon sky. A sandstone slab said this was built to honor Eden Romero, died 1990. In a prolonged fit of grief, someone had gone to great trouble to haul in the stone and mortar to build this santuario, which seemed ill-tended now, weeds growing up everywhere, but there was water, no one about, and the low walls of the building would provide shelter from the wind. I rolled Mojo up into the beautifully constructed sandstone refuge and called it camp. I brewed up a cup of tea, raised a toast to Eden Romero, and watched the evening fall over the low juniper hills to the west, the night blowing in off the darkening mountains.

Ancient Ruins and a Punch in the Mouth
Oct. 20th: 3,550 miles

That shocked expression is the gift to long-distance riders when they inform the curious about where the journey began, where it's headed. The man in the library shook his head in disbelief—or pity at the dim-witted fool in the strange clothing—and turned back to his computer. I hoped he was a little impressed. I'd worked hard for that expression and wanted to savor it. Certainly riches, fame, a ticker-tape parade were not awaiting me on the far end of this ride. Who even has tape for a ticker, anyway? What old-timey nonsense was knocking around in my touring-addled brain? Next I'd be looking for a telegraph office: Wayland, World-class recumbent cyclo-tourist in New Mexico—stop! Wayland picks up supplies—stop! Wayland can't stop—stop!

Outside, I sat on the curb in Mountainair, an obscure town in the plains, a wave of hard emotions pouring into my head and gut. I held the cell phone in my hand and listened to Jodi's tears cutting across the airwaves from a thousand miles away. What could I say? She felt abandoned, cut off, the solitude at home getting to her day after day. "Do you even think about me, Scott? Do you care?" I was never good on the phone, rarely connecting in a way that satisfied Jodi. Like so many men, my vocabulary for connection is often limited, and I feel so much better at doing than saying. I hated being the cause of her pain and told her so.

"I'll keep pedaling. I promise!" I felt ambushed, besieged not by hostile natives but the truth of our separation. These moments would come over such a long trek. I could only reassure her as best I could and keep working the pedals, which today would be more easily said than done.

The wind is a cagey boxer. Sentient, cruel, he knows your weakness and when to push. Whenever I mustered the temerity to shift up to a higher gear, the wind would redouble in force, mocking my optimism, forcing me back down. The roiling mass of invisible boxing gloves was my badass daddy, beating me into slowly crawling subservience. My one consolation was a shorter-than-average day. That, and the wide-open mesa country of central New Mexico. For reasons I couldn't quite discern, the wind thrashing didn't ruffle my spirit. I'd arrived at an emotional truce with the elements, whatever they were. Warm, sweating, I had ample time to study the meager beavertail cacti, dry grasses, and crumbling sandstone lining the highway. I was headed for Abo and another piece of history.

One of the only existing structures of medieval architecture in the United States, the mission was first established in the late sixteenth century. Charged with Christianizing the Godless natives, padres moved in, bringing new plants, animals, technology, a bleeding Kachina hung from crossed sticks. A grand mission was built, stone by stone, heavy plates of soft red rock pulled from the ground and nearby cliffs and placed into walls rising far above the scrub desert landscape. Thousands and thousands of rocks, dozens of rooms, three stories high. It was doubtless the grandest structure ever seen in this region, an area long inhabited by the Pueblos and, earlier, the Anasazi.

Happy to leave behind my blistering pace of 6.8 mph, I turned off the main road and descended to the ruins, a red serrated outline in the distance. The wind died as I parked Mojo and strolled into the past. Once thousands of natives called this area home, but the confluence of Apache invaders, drought, and belligerent Spaniards with communicable diseases finally cleared the territory. Now the mute stone ruins were the final testimony. Burnt umber, ocher, pale sand, vermillion and blood, the myriad tones of the rock pulled me into room after room, the ceilings long gone, the wide azure sky pouring in, the golden light. Only a handful of other tourists ambled about, so the old place was quiet. In front of the main building was the unmistakable circular pit of a Kiva, the Pueblo house of worship. These crumbling walls were the fading legacy of a dream of Spanish conquest. In four hundred years, what will remain of our modern desert cities, Las Vegas, Albuquerque, Phoenix, Tucson? In two thousand years, will a future archeologist unearth a singlewide trailer, Chevy truck on blocks, a midden of crushed beer cans? The wind and coyotes now sing where once the friars called the faithful and coerced the reluctant. How can we even imagine what the future will bring? A head full of such ramblings, I climbed back to the main road and struck out west once more.

Down the road I performed my Good Samaritan deed for the day. There, parked in a huge dusty pullout, sat the Mother of All Recreational Vehicles: Towing rig styled after a tractor-trailer, dual rear axles, massive diesel engine; a fifth wheel with six wheels, three axles, pop-out rooms, cathedral ceilings, atriums, golf courses, swimming pools, and equestrian center—and who knew what else. Behind the fifth wheel, four more wheels, a mid-sized Sport Utility Vehicle. This was a gawdawful road train. My chosen mode of travel could not have been a greater contrast. A thin, older man in blue jeans and white, button down short-sleeved shirt bent over a wheel in the dirt. He looked up as I pulled to a stop. "Hi," he said, "could you lend me a hand here?"

"Sure, what's the problem? Need to change a tire?"

"No, that's all done. I just need help getting this flat one into the bed."

Together, we hoisted the wheel and dropped it in behind the spacious double cab truck. As I rolled away, my water supply topped off by the friendly RVers, I wondered how long we would be able to travel like that, taking, virtually, *everything* with us. I could not imagine many would be able to afford it in the future. The oil supply won't last, but when it runs out is up to debate. My clothing had oil in it, many of the bike parts, the oil on the chain, the tires, the oil in the road surface that made my "easy" miles possible, all of it the fruit of slimy black fluid. On the road for so many days, the cyclist is confronted by the truth of the gasoline culture. When the final oil drought hits, our world will be changed in ways hard to imagine. For now I was glad for the good road and waved happily to the retired couple as their diesel locomotive chugged by and vanished up the grade. I was alone again with my thoughts and the wind and the search for a camp.

At last I found what I was looking for. The dirt track cut off the highway and wound up into the mountains. Washed out, rutted, rocky, the path fought back as I bounced and balanced, pedaled and pushed until I topped a pass in the late sun, the wind singing through tight branches and bunched needles. I pitched camp on the lee side of the pass and watched the alpenglow fade on the distant rugged mountains, not a soul about to disturb my meditations. A long way from home, from Jodi, but in the moment, where and when I needed to be, I pulled the sleeping bag tight and looked out at the stars, the tent packed away on this clear and cloudless night.

It toyed with me, seeming to leave and then return like a nagging memory, a bad beer, violence long forgotten. Like a murderer from a teen slasher movie, the wind could not be killed. It grew in the night, changed direction 180 degrees, tugging at my bag, the trees across the ridge. Annoyed, I burrowed deeper into my nylon retreat and drifted off.

Shock. An explosion of pain ripped across my face— *STINKING FUCKING HORSE FUCK! What the hell?!* The blasting shrieking, moaning wind had upended Mojo and flung a bar end and mirror into my face. In a disoriented panic, pegged and bleeding, I struggled to free myself from the confines of the mummy bag, yanking at the stuck zipper, thrusting a hand awkwardly through the small face opening to get Mojo off me. Gasping, holding my mouth, I righted the fallen bike, wedged in the kickstand deep into the soft earth, and dove back into the bag to lick my wounds. *Holy crap, what a way to wake up.*

I slept little and just hung on for the remaining dark hours. The wind screamed its discontent as I tensed for the next assault. An overloaded eighteen wheeler, my name tattooed on the grill, engine brakes failing, each ill-tempered gust started low on the mountain and roared up through the flailing trees, the sound breaking like a wave until my bag thrashed and shook. I covered my head, curled into a ball, and hung on. In the morning, I scrubbed the dried blood from my lips.

Pulsars, Saints, and Beer-Swilling Pedagogues
Oct. 22nd: 3,662 miles

In 1054 A.D., in a crabby galaxy far, far away, a portly star was faring poorly, bloated, dyspeptic, in need of a mega-dose of astrophysical nuclear Midol. Having spent its inheritance with a certain profligate flair, the star was on its last legs—at least that's how things looked from earth. No one knew it at the time, but the events transpiring in the sky took place millions of years before, the light of the big show only then reaching our puny orb. Perhaps ten times the size of our sun, itself a million times bigger than the Earth, the star wheezed and gasped, expanded, contracted, and finally collapsed in on itself, then in a final spasm exploding out into that most magnificent and fearsome of celestial tantrums: the super nova. The remains of the blast—besides the awesome cloud of hot gases and heavy elements that make planets and the life of this resplendent recumbent cyclist possible—resided in an ornery, hot, angry little ball, perhaps twenty kilometers across, spinning over 600 revolutions *per second* and throwing out an electromagnetic blast two thousand *billion* times stronger than the Earth's magnetic field. With their tiny size but truculent demeanor, pulsars are the Tasmanian devils, the wolverines of the galactic world. Until the late 1960's, astronomers didn't know they existed. It was the advent of radio astronomy that made the discovery and study of these and other mind-bending delights possible. Jocelyn Bell, a young Ph.D. student from Ireland studying at Cambridge, only missed getting the Nobel

Prize for her discovery of the first pulsar because she was a student, a turn of events that didn't seem to bother her. No doubt she possessed deep reservoirs of patience as the discovery was made possible by the minute study of *three miles* of printouts. The press, however, went a trifle loony when it found out *a woman* had done the discovering of this new and strange type of star. Reporters wanted to know if she was as tall as Princess Margaret and if she had many boyfriends—the 1960's. Forty years later in outback New Mexico, radio astronomy was the goal of the other-worldly structures spread out across the vast Plains of St. Agustin that I descended into after a long, moderate climb from Socorro to the east.

The winds at last abated, leaving me to stretch my legs and spirit across the wide open country and gentle grades of Highway 60 cutting due west towards the Arizona border. Traffic was light to nothing; sometimes for miles in both directions not a soul appeared. In general, I was finding New Mexico to be one of the best states for bicycle touring. In the early afternoon, I paused on a low summit and looked across at twenty miles of dead-straight road to the next mountain range and my camp in Datil—a solid afternoon's work. Out there, in the middle of that nowhere, stood white daisies, flowers sprouting from the dry grassy barrens, a scattering of huge radio telescopes that I knew nothing about until closing in and finding an information sign. The Very Large Array (VLA) was indeed an array and very large. Each dish measured 82 feet across and easily over 100 feet high. According to the National Radio Astronomy Observatory website, each of the twenty-seven telescopes weighs 230 tons. The basin is laid out with a series of rail tracks in the shape of a gigantic peace sign missing the middle leg— an outsized Mercedes Benz symbol, if you will—twenty-two miles across. Coordinated with atomic clocks and sophisticated computers, the dishes work together to create a virtual telescope of immense proportions. And as any grade school science nut can tell you, the bigger the telescope, the greater the sensitivity and the resolution.

When most of us think of astronomy, we imagine a nerdy fellow with unkempt hair in a white coat gazing into a small aperture attached to a giant cylinder aimed at the stars, some variation on a Gary Larson theme. While true in some cases, the science of astronomy is about much more than the "light" we can see. In fact, visible light is only a narrow band of the whole electromagnetic spectrum. Much of the information coming from the skies is beyond our ability to see and study unless we use radio telescopes and computers to process the information and put it into a form we can use—numbers, graphs, photographs of radio images, the information translated into colors in the visible range. The resulting pictures are like scenes from a psychedelic painting. With this fantastic array, astronomers can look into distant galaxies and plumb the origins of the universe, all delivered a year ahead of schedule, on budget, for a very reasonable $78 million and change.

I stood beneath these magnificent contraptions and felt intellectually inadequate and more than a little small. The Plains of St. Agustin are a strange, wonderful place, the broad sky overarching in a compelling clear dome. I wasn't bothered by the high technology in a place otherwise dominated by nature as it seemed a noble monument to our desire to know and explore. Strange, too, and perhaps fitting, the basin is known by UFO fanatics as a 1947 crash site of a spacecraft, a lesser-known parallel to the famous Roswell event to the southeast. The remains are a piece of tinfoil, the "proof" of the crash. I suspect the foil dropped from some bloke's hat as he staggered about under the blazing New Mexican sun. The obsession with UFO's seems a religion, the followers steeped in their "faith." What is this need, this compulsion for the supernatural? Isn't the natural "super" enough? Who needs UFO's when we have pulsars, quasars, black holes, various and sundry dark matter and nebulae? In *Abbey's Road*, Edward Abbey, the arch curmudgeon of the Southwest, wrote:

> [M]en like Democritus, Galileo, Copernicus, Kepler, Newton, Lyell, Darwin and Einstein [were]

liberators of the human consciousness, intellectual workers whose insight and intelligence have expanded our awareness of existence infinitely more than all the pronouncements of all the shamans, gurus, seers, and mystics of the earth, East and West combined. The simple telescope, for instance, has given us visions of a world far greater, lovelier, more awesome and full of wonder than that contained in an entire shipload of magic mushrooms, LSD capsules, and yoga textbooks.

Bring it, Mr. Abbey, bring it.

St. Agustin/Augustine/Augustine of Hippo (take your pick) was an interesting and important character. It turns out the late 4th and early 5th centuries were bad times for the Romans, if you haven't heard. Hoards of badass gangbangers known as the Visigoths were sacking Rome, bringing an end to eight hundred years of imperial rule. All good parties have to end, however, and the Romans were frightened and perplexed by this serious turn of events. Who wouldn't be? The decadence of Rome at The End—to be repeated by the French at The End—is legendary, and many at the time believed the collapse of the empire was a result of straying from the one true religion. Rather than tackle the geopolitical complications and societal decay that led to the break up and invasion of 'Goths with their body piercings, dark eyeliner, strange tongues and weird fashion sense, Santa Augustine did the sensible thing: bury his head in religion and philosophy. If the Romans couldn't have Rome, they could have *The City of God,* a long treatise on Christianity stressing the rewards of heaven. More of St. Augustine's writings survive than almost any other medieval writer, and he did a lot to bring Christianity into its modern condition, connected in many ways with the philosophy of Plato, influencing theologians, scholars, and philosophers into the 20th century. He was born and spent the majority of his life in North Africa and died in Hippo while the town was under siege by the Vandals, who were also to have their way with Rome not long after. The Dark Ages were pretty dark.

Growing up and living all my life in an isolated, rich, stable country, it's hard to imagine my home town being overrun by foreigners, the collapse of government and order. A surging multitude of hockey stick-wielding Canadians blasting through the gates? Unthinkable, eh? And I love Canada. I looked into the world of saints and their multi-tasking job descriptions. Among other things, St. Augustine excels at looking out for brewers and those with sore eyes. St. Gerard Majella is to be invoked against the forces of nature (where was he on that lonely hill in the wind?) and the pitch forkin' stinky imp, Satan himself. And of use to all lunatic, long distance, elite recumbent cyclists and any who would tilt at windmills and win, St. Rita Cascia, *Patron of the Impossible!*

Humbled and high, I pushed on towards the far side of the basin. As I chugged the final miles, a hefty RV pulled up alongside and a pleasant middle-aged woman leaned out to yell a greeting: "Hello, recumbent rider! On a long tour?"

"Yes," I replied, "coast to coast!"

We ended up camping next to each other that night. I pitched my tent in the cold shadows of early evening and set out my stove and gear to prepare dinner when a man from an RV across the way came down to talk—the driver of the vehicle I'd seen earlier. Satisfied that I wasn't a fruitcake, he invited me to dinner in their camper—barbequed ribs. I couldn't turn this down and strolled over after setting up camp. My own food was all dried and canned. It would hold. Leaning against the RV were two short wheelbase recumbents. Ah, members of my tribe. Jack was a retired college teacher (this was getting scary), and he and his wife, Betty, traveled for a few months late in the year to avoid some of the hardest weather in their home state of Alaska. Juicy ribs, baked potatoes, corn piled high and everlasting beer flowing like the Nile in flood. Hail, Augustine! I swilled Coronas while Jack displayed a penchant for light beer. I worked the food and beverage like a champ, but I was no match for Jack, who slammed can after can of the lite, a veritable spring-loaded beer-guzzling machine, the dead soldiers lining up like casualties at Verdun. His wife, growing clearly agitated at his drinking, said, "Honey, don't you think you should take it easy? You'll be up all night peeing." To this he shook his head, finished one beer, and got up to get another. We were men together and had manly things to talk about and manly beverages to consume in great quantities. Her civilizing influence was lost in a sudsy wave of conversation about the academic life, bikes, touring and travel. Finally, I could take it no more, my belly crammed to a fine bloat, my head groggy with flagons of grog. Time for bed. I thanked my hosts profusely and wandered through the icy forest to my bag and cozy oblivion. It was a difficult job, but *someone* had to do it.

That Border Crossing Feeling
Oct. 24th: 3,774 miles

The first sound was the beating of raven wings. Still, frigid air pooled icily around my bag, my refuge and prison for the last twelve hours. At 3AM, I had crawled out to irrigate the sage brush—24 deg. F. Not a soul about, my companions only the distant shimmering stars. My water bottle was freezing, so, slipping a glove over the finely chilled cylinder, I jammed it into the bag. Tough times, stern measures. I passed a good night nonetheless, but now I needed out, and it was a long wait for the sun on the pinyons. I would leave New Mexico and my last new state. Frozen gravel and rat turds—Grapenuts and raisins—the usual morning grub washed down with a steaming tumbler of smokin' java. I stomped and paced and packed as the golden sun slowly warmed the Earth, another perfect day. I would miss New Mexico.

Mesas and mountains, canyons, grassy steppes, my Southwest dream. I turn the pedals 70, 80, 90 times a minute for six hours a day. How is it possible? I ask and the body responds. Whirling legs, pounding heart and steady breathing merge with the pure line of black gold. I become movement and the road, the blessing of the mountains and sky. The soft, dry grasslands glow like a vast animal in the angular sun. Near midday, the moment finally comes. After a series of undulating false summits, I crest the last, the Continental Divide, the hydrologic frontier of my journey. Many mountains and deep valleys lie between me and the ocean, but whatever water survives to the west, its destination is the Pacific. We have that in common.

A crucial turn left me facing a blaring star bursting from the horizon, a sign, the official state emblem of Arizona, the border at last. As if to proclaim the transition, bands of deep red sandstone appeared, small cliffs jutting up through the pinyons and junipers, a sweet and welcoming landscape. In shorts and short-sleeve jersey now, I soaked up the warmth and pushed on for Springerville, Apache County, Arizona, and lunch out on the town to celebrate. A long, gradual ramp led downward off a high plateau into the Round Valley and Springerville. Grassy, wide-open, mostly surrounded by high forested mountains and ridges, the basin lay over six-thousand feet above sea level, the sky perfectly clear. Little did I know what a notorious region I was entering.

Banditos and gunfighters, criminals and pugilistic prosecutors, the Round Valley and nearby regions simmered and seethed with the ghosts of a turbulent Western history. Jack Becker, a fourth generation Arizonan and native son of original Springerville pioneers, spent much of his life hunting down the rich history of the region. At *Roundvalleyaz.com*, his wealth of research provides a window into a fascinating and violent place that was the Round Valley in the 19th century. Albert Banta, an early law maker in the area, said, "I am no angel and have seen most of the tough towns in the West, but Springerville was the worst of them all."

Conflicts with Navajos resulted in killings on both sides of the white/native divide. Becker unearthed accounts from the old papers detailing one particularly notable tragedy. Supposedly, a Navajo, Hostine Chee, had stolen a horse from John King. Deputy Sheriff George Lockhart took King and E. L. Palmer deep into the reservation to reclaim the horse. To say it didn't go well is to put it mildly. The three never returned, and when a rescue posse went out to investigate, the grisly truth lay rotting on the ground. At Chee's hogan, Lockhart lay outside, his head caved in with three hatchet blows, a bullet hole in his chest. Inside the building, a Navajo lay, shot through the head; beside the building, two horses, shot dead. A chaos of prints in the snow led away from the carnage, two men barefoot. The search party followed, no doubt resolved to finding the worst.   They weren't disappointed. Four miles from the hogan, the bodies of King and Palmer had bled out into the snow. In some sort of terrifying blood sport, the two were forced to run for their lives through the cold and finally collapsed. King was shot point blank in the back of the head. Palmer was shot in the same way, the flash from the muzzle burning his hair and skin, but apparently he had already died from two previous shots. Sheriff Commodore Perry Owens, thirty-four, lean, with a long mustache and hair well below his shoulders, wanted to invade immediately, with or without permission from the appropriate Indian agency, but the situation was complicated by an agency report that the killings were justified because, according to the *Cincinnati Inquirer,* it "was brought upon themselves by their abusive and threatening attitude. Col. Ben Grierson stated that the peace officers were drunk at the time and 'were clearly and grossly the aggressors.'" Becker doesn't report how the case was resolved, if ever, but Sheriff Owens emerges as one of the most colorful characters in the region, absolutely calm and deadly with his guns.

The historian found other chilling stories from Springerville's frontier heritage. A residue of the Butch Cassidy gang known as the Westbrooks, gunned down an innocent Mormon settler by the name of James Hale to "see if a bullet would go through a Mormon." These events occurred in the shadow of a long, miserable feud that would come to be known as the Pleasant Valley War.

In the early 1880's, the Tewksbury and Graham clans already had a dislike for each other, apparently a little bad blood over some cattle they had rustled together. When the Tewksburys started managing a substantial flock of sheep for the wealthy Daggs of Flagstaff, real blood would flow soon enough. The Grahams, along with other cattle ranchers, resented the competition for rangeland and claimed that sheep left little feed for the cattle. The first death was a particularly unlucky Navajo sheepherder gunned down by Tom Graham. He was the first of at least nineteen people who would die before the war ended, with some unconfirmed reports putting the number closer to thirty. The most notorious battle occurred when a group of Graham supporters, Andy Blevins among them, closed in on a remote cabin. In September of 1887, John Tewksbury and William Jacobs, no doubt looking forward to a pleasant fall day on the range, stepped from the cabin into a rain of lethal lead. Their bleeding, perforated bodies lay in the dirt as the Graham posse continued firing for hours, the survivors inside shooting back. One account of the battle has it that hogs began to feed on the corpses, and the battle only paused when Tewksbury's wife stepped out with a shovel to bury the dead. One can hardly imagine that grim task. The two men in shallow graves, the Tewksbury widow returned indoors and the shooting resumed. Perhaps bored or out of ammunition, the Graham gang finally left. Murder, death and reprisal, one following the other for years, ate away at the valley like a cancer. In the end, only one, Ed Tewksbury, would remain after he succeeded in killing the last Graham. Ed Tewksbury was tried—twice—for the murder, but the first trial ended in a hung jury, the second in a technical mistake, so even with supposed eye witnesses, Tewksbury walked away a free man. But at what cost? His declining years were spent with the knowledge that his entire family had been destroyed, a bitter victory indeed.

Commodore Perry Owens himself became entangled in the Pleasant Valley War. No stranger to death, he appears to have fully embraced the concept of "shoot first, ask questions later." Andy Blevins had been overheard boasting of his killings at the Tewksbury cabin. Owens happened to have a warrant for Blevins on horse stealing charges and took this as an opportunity to bring in the violent thug. In Halbrook, a town not far to the north of Springerville, the sheriff went to serve his warrant.

Rifle in his hands, Owens approached the Blevins' home not far outside the town. Owens had no way of knowing that a dozen people of the extended Blevins family were inside when he stepped in front of the door, the muzzle of his carbine pointed straight ahead. He told Andy he was there to arrest him for horse rustling. According to Becker,

Andy replied he'd be "ready in a few minutes." In no mood to wait, Owens replied, "No, right away!" and opened fire. He blasted through the front door with his Winchester, killing Andy Blevins with a shot through the abdomen and spine. John Blevins, Andy's half-brother, took a shot from a nearby window as Owens reloaded. Without hesitating, Owens turned and fired again, hitting John in the shoulder and again in the arm with a third shot. At this point, another suspect, Mose Roberts, scrambled from the back of the residence with a pistol in hand and rounded the building, right into a fourth round from Owens' Winchester. Roberts collapsed in a heap, a huge hole through his lungs. In this storm of gunfire and blood, a teenager, Sam Huston Blevins, his mother screaming and clutching after him to stop, grabbed Andy's gun and stepped over the body and fired at the sheriff. Owens shot again, killing the boy instantly in front of his mother's eyes. As Becker reports, Frank Reed, editor of the *Halbrook Critic*, summed up the scene:

> After firing his fifth and last shot, Sheriff Owens coolly threw his rifle across his left arm and calmly walked past, at a distance of twenty-five feet, going to Brown and Kinder's livery stable where he had left his saddle horse.
> As soon as the firing ceased, several civilians went to the house, where a horrible sight met their gaze. Dead and wounded in every room, and blood over the floors, doors and walls.
> One little child, seven years of age, was literally bespattered with clots of human gore.
> The agonizing groans of the wounded, the death-rattle of the dying, mingled with hysterical screams of the females made a sight that no one would care to see the second time.

Other government officials seemed to be similarly prone to violence, and once again the editor of the *Critic*, Frank Reed was there. After printing stories critical of the Apache County District Attorney Harris Baldwin's association with the railroads, Baldwin beat the hell out of Reed. Becker quotes the *El Paso Sun*: "Harris Baldwin, District Attorney of Apache County, attacked Frank Reed, editor of the Holbrook Critic, and gave him a severe pounding with brass knuckles which was very cowardly, to say the least." Reed had just recently recovered after a two month battle with rheumatic fever so could muster no defense. After the beating, according to Reed, Baldwin yelled, "That man does not know me yet. If he ever uses my name in his paper again, I'll blow his brains out."

One can surmise from these accounts that, elite cyclo-tourist or not, it would be wise to keep a low profile in Apache County.

A line of pines presented a dark edge to an expanse of pale, late season grasses that ascended in waves to some unknown summit above me. The afternoon sun banked off the road and into my eyes, sweat running down from under my helmet. My legs, by some incomprehensible miracle, kept turning and churning, muscles, bones, cartilage, tendons that have carried me across the continent and put up with too many ridiculous demands. Good legs. Can't forget to thank them. The White Mountains were my first test in Arizona. No snow yet, so they were shimmering gold and piney dark green. Route 260 was my path across some of the highest terrain in the state, a fact seemingly little known to National Forest Service employees I'd left behind. A wild-eyed bike rider flying high from the wide lonesome of New Mexico, I'd rolled into Springerville, needing food and information--in that order. An attractive Mexican place soon caught my eye. A huge celebratory Chimichanga with south-of-the-border brew had a very short life expectancy when I walked in. I cut an odd figure among the small town locals, a pair of police officers and their friends, others dressed in casual jeans, t-shirts. My Chernobyl-green jersey clashed with the Old West decor--replica lever action rifle, horse shoes, the usual iconography. For such a short period of history, the Western mythology has tremendous staying power and commercial value. I suppose my cycling togs and clacking shoes were no greater an affront to the "Old West" of the place than the ubiquitous Budweiser advertisements. After lunch, I headed out of town and stopped at the Forest Service for that much needed information...

Beware, cyclo-tourists, elite and otherwise, beware the women at the National Forest Service information center in Springerville, Arizona, for they know not of what they speak!

Let me preface this brief tirade with the comment that Rt. 260 from Springerville to Show Low is well worth riding. As indicated on state maps, the road is indeed "scenic"—lots of trees, open glades, the occasional view up to forested peaks or down into valleys. No quibbles there. She's scenic all right. I enjoyed the ride immensely although riders should know that traffic could be an issue during peak vacation periods in the summer.

But, and here it comes, I went into that office seeking not to confirm any aesthetic merits Rt. 260 might possess. No, dear readers, no. I wanted specific information concerning my chosen path. Consequently, I asked a few specific questions, such as 1) How far is it to the turn off to the campground that the attractive employee suggested I use? And 2) Do I need to be concerned about any major mountain passes? In other words, what kind of climbs was I going to face?

To the first question, the slim, blond one answered immediately, an indication of certainty and familiarity with the route in question: "Fifteen miles." To my second query she had the presence of mind to first ask if I were an experienced cyclist, implying that my fitness level would be an important consideration. That I had already told her I was cycling across the country should have been a clue here. Regardless, I replied in the affirmative. Then she paused, deep in thought, her eyes looking at some unspecific point over my right shoulder, scanning the interior of her mind like Data in *Star Trek: The Next Generation*. "I'm trying to visualize the road," she said. "No," she said, finally, "there isn't much climbing on Rt. 260. It rolls along, kind of up and down to Show Low." I then asked about Highway 60, the alternate. They were both emphatic that it was much, MUCH worse, with a huge climb mid-way. Thus reassured and assisted by these two helpful, friendly women, I set off confident I would reach camp before too long.

I did indeed reach camp, but it was not due to any overload of excellent information. Rest assured. These Forest Service employees were so utterly, totally, completely, amazingly, astoundingly, staggeringly, egregiously, mind-bogglingly wrong as to nearly defy my ability to apply a proper string of adverbs. *For crying out loud, ladies, what the hell were you thinking! Don't you ever get out of the office and actually **see** the forest you are supposed to know? Good God!*

First, this one in my favor, the turn-off was about ten miles out of town, not fifteen. No big deal. Pleasant surprise. But again, a clue, eh, Holmes? And the climb, you ask with white-knuckled anticipation, Biker Scotty, what about the climb? By the time I finally reached the summit, I had powered through a good twenty miles and ascended over 2,400 ft. to probably the **HIGHEST PAVED PASS IN THE STATE** (emphasis mine) at over 9,200 ft.—higher even than Ponchas Pass in the Colorado Rockies, a saddle ringed by 14,000 ft. peaks. Now, one can easily imagine higher passes—the Upper Saddle on the Grand Teton and the South Col of Mt. Everest come to mind—but give me a spoke-busting break. How is it possible that she, an employee charged with knowing key information about the National Forest visible from her back window, didn't know even this most basic, fundamental topographical fact? Simply amazing. Such ignorance should be criminally actionable, if you ask me. Maybe a civil suit? Her powers of visualization must be dim indeed. Harrumph.

Before the summit, I spent two nights in a deserted campground outside Greer, at 8,500 ft. After all the climbing from town and late in the day, I was feeling grumpy, ornery, feloniously inclined towards incompetent government employees. For the first time in weeks, some moron had honked at me in anger for being on the road. I descended from Rt. 260 toward the campground, and all I could think about was having to climb back out. My cranking was making me cranky. I'd come to recognize this end-of-the-hard-day condition. Worn down and strung out, ready for a camp that seems out of reach, I get short fused, impatient. Zen goes down the toilet.

I climbed again and at last found my campsite. I rolled through weakening, low-angled sun to my camp in tall pines next to a small lake and meadow of dry tawny grasses. Deserted, empty, not a solitary soul, no RV's, no host, just Mojo and me, the lone cyclist, castaway, the last camper on earth, Omega Biker. The cold, with its long, probing fingers, began to search out my weaknesses. The sun was already low in the trees to the west, so I could not linger in my chores. Get that tent pitched and dinner on the stove. Before long, I sat down to my solitary meal in the trees in the White Mountains.

So was I lonely sitting alone at my table in the cold on this late October evening? Indeed. I missed having Jodi to share my thoughts about the struggles of the day, compare notes. We would not be curling up in the tent together to ward off the high altitude chill. Django wouldn't be snuggled up at our feet, his sharp ears ready to detect any intruders. But I wasn't completely alone. A line of honking geese banked in from the north in tight formation, bound for the water beyond the trees. I could hear the beating of their wings as they passed over in the closing darkness. Somewhere, lost in the forest to the east, bull elk called out challenges in their other-worldly trumpet, a haunting sound of the wilderness strange to my ears. We made a congregation of sorts in this temple of the woods—my rattling thoughts, the scratch of my pen on the note pad, the fading sounds of wildlife. As I at last settled into my bag and prepared for the long night ahead, coyotes howled and yipped and picked up the song of the mountains in autumn. They understood the value of a rising moon and told me I was not alone.

Riding the Rim
Oct. 27th: 3895 miles

"Hey, that looks hard to balance!" the heavy one said, a big sagging belly drooping over his jeans, t-shirt straining mightily. "Can you do that after a sixer of beer?"

Oh my, these were special neighbors.

I'd struggled hard to get here, a campground at the edge of the Mogollon Rim, the start of a long, waterless stretch of dirt road that would take me through some beautiful, remote country. Aghast, I'd faced a steel toilet seat in sub-freezing temperatures. Appalled, I'd pedaled through what I had expected to be small towns in the National Forest, places like Show Low, only to find rampant development, strip malls, Home Despots, the usual suspects of *Genericus Americanus Developmentitus*. And then I encountered real estate kitsch on crack. It would be funny if it weren't so obscene: The (I kid you not) *Bison* developments. What I thought would be high, remote roads through the forest turned out to be access to resort homes, getaways, escape ranchettes and "Estates!" for the Phoenicians seeking to flee the molten pavement oozing in the valley below. Bison Ranch, Bison Ridge, and—you know it's got to be good because of all the high end phraseology—*The Retreat at Bison Crossing*. Prepositional phrases required for the best of the best. Big fat ugly bronzes of bulging bison. In front of one subdivision, a trio of bronze cowboys astride bronze horses, the men's bronze faces frozen into strange bronze grimaces. And the one good thing about riding through Show Low ended with the Bison puke: The shoulder vanished and I was left to battle for space on this narrow, heavily trafficked boring road, a rolling, tiring shot through a

289

tall slot of pines, no views, only effort, traffic and noise—my worst stretch of road since west Kansas. I waved my left arm regularly at the approaching and passing drivers to remind them a human being on a naked bicycle was sharing the road.

But now I had special neighbors.

The big one clearly had the alpha position, telling his thinner, shyer partner a string of jokes, all ending with the eloquent punch line: "Lick my balls!" Thin man, not to be outdone, composed a beautiful little song, right on the spot: "Blah, blah, blah—Lick my balls! Blah, blah, blah—Lick my balls!" Over and over again. With each lovely chorus, my heart sank another notch. No... can... not... deal... must... escape.... Being the master of my own ship, realizing I owed not the slightest thing to my silver-tongued friends, I picked up my gear and moved as far away as possible to the opposite end of the loop, if not out of sight, at least mostly out of hearing range. I was able to relax and strolled over for my first clear view of the rim.

Two hundred miles long, up to 2,000 feet high, cut by canyons, capped by ponderosa forests, the Mogollon Rim was named after Don Juan Ignacio Flores Mogollón, an early 18th century Spanish governor of New Mexico. Vertical walls, fins and towers of sandstone and limestone mark the boundary of the Colorado plateau. Below, lower, hotter, drier country fades into the scorching deserts, the creosote and Saguaro cacti most often associated with Arizona. Much of the state, however, is cut from a higher, cooler terrain, hence the rampant development fueled by people who don't enjoy deserts being deserts—bloody hot and miserable. I often pondered in the ponderosas how the West would have been won without air conditioning. More than barbed wire, railroads and Colt revolvers, it was the modern invention of manufactured cool air that changed the face of the Southwest. Sooner or later, however, one must step outside the climate controlled boxes, and the humid blasting heat of the Arizona desert in high summer is something to experience. Here, one cannot even find refuge in the cliché of "dry" heat. It's damn humid, beset with thunderstorms and hot soggy blankets of air streaming up from the Gulf of Mexico. Massive, anvil-headed super storms range across the land, splitting the sky with lightning and flooding the arroyos, bringing that most ironic of deaths to the desert: drowning. Yes, Arizona is an awful place. Everyone should stay away.

I pushed through the trees beyond the road to stand and gape at the dizzying gulf of air and golden light at the rim of the world at sunset. I selected a suitable sandstone bench, dangled my legs over the escarpment and for a moment or two thought of nothing at all. Not bad, pilgrim. Tomorrow, I would head out on the rim road, fifty miles of dirt and gravel track without water or services of any kind. A walk on the wild side was just what the touring doctor ordered.

Slow, loose-footed cycling dominated the next day's effort. Nine liters of water sloshed and swayed in bags, Mojo bloated and pregnant for two days without resupply. A few hundred yards off the pavement in the cool morning forest, I hit deep soft gravel and fell over, my speed so low that ego was the only casualty. Mr. Elite Cyclo-Tourist on his fine, high-tech Euro-steed blazing along at 3 mph fell over like a drunken sailor. Fortunately there was no troop of girl scouts to witness the event. I righted the heavy pony and pushed on, determined to pedal every inch of this road. A local had said the route was mostly flat, so I was not surprised to find significant brutal climbing. My new cycle-touring axiom: NEVER trust what the locals say about their roads.

Corner followed corner, elbow, hairpin, climb and descend, sometimes in deep forest, sometimes out on the edge of existence, air, sun and stone. Before long, I encountered evidence of a huge fire, a scar that stretched for miles along the rim, the once rich and majestic pines scorched down to black and grey ghosts, shadowy charred skeletons of a once rich forest. The perpetrators of the fire were the suspects usual: a criminal and a fool.

The criminal: Leonard Gregg, an Apache born on the White Mountain Reservation, did not begin life with many advantages. His mother was sucked into the prison of escape, a life of hard drinking, so Leonard was born with fetal alcohol syndrome, a condition recognized early in life. He muddled through, growing to adulthood with no viable skills to make a living, although he was well liked and considered a gentle soul.   By his late twenties, he had somehow managed to pass all the tests for seasonal, part-time firefighting work, the kind of man who would be called in only the worst circumstances when every last firefighter was needed.   Sometimes he would be shipped out to other areas when the need was great. But big fires cannot always be counted on, unless, of course, a particular firefighter is willing to help. At the time, wages amounted to about $8 an hour.

Leonard had found a girlfriend, who we hope was a comfort, but she came with a bonus: five children. They all lived together, and Leonard felt the pressure to help support his adopted family. He was not being called for work, and there were no fires to speak of in the state. Salvation was only a matchbook away. In mid-June, 2002, he set off into the dense high forest and got a blaze going, but a quick response team foiled his plans. Smoke and fury signifying nothing, the small fire was squelched along with Leonard's money making scheme. His mother, a drunk or not, taught him well the lesson of persistence. Leonard set out again, determined to get some money-making work. This time, he succeeded, and before long, in the hot, dry forest, a healthy blaze was cutting a fearsome swath through the trees. Leonard Gregg was finally called to action after the fire was first reported on June 18th. By the next morning, over 2,000 acres had been consumed. With increasing sharp winds and lots of fuel, by June 21st, the newly christened "Rodeo" fire had grown to 150,000 acres.

The fool: Valinda Jo Elliott's life could have been going more smoothly, too. A single mother employed by a vending machine company, struggling to make ends meet, she found herself with co-worker driving through the White Mountain Apache Reservation and looking for a way through the road blocks set because of the Rodeo fire. Like Gregg, she would not be deterred, so she and her companion set off down unknown dirt roads in search of a bypass. What they said to each other during the long drive is lost to history, but tense must have been the moments as the driver watched the gasoline gauge swing towards empty. The engine, bled dry, finally died, miles into strange, remote forests. They doubtless struggled with a rising feeling of dread, but rescue was only a cell phone call away. The American Automobile Association cannot be summoned, however, if it cannot be called. This was the wilds of northeastern Arizona not downtown Phoenix, and the cell reception was zero.

Plucky and determined, Valinda broke the first rule of being lost: Don't leave the vehicle. No worries. She'd hike to a high point. Perhaps that mountain over there, Chediski Peak, would get her into a line of cell towers—somewhere. Clad in shorts and tank top, flip-flops on her feet, a cell phone, cigarettes and lighter in her pockets, Valinda set out on her rendezvous with destiny. It wasn't long before two things were undeniably clear: One, no cell signal was to be had; two, she was totally lost. For two nights and three days, she wandered about, fear rising, shivering through the dark hours. She could see smoke from the Rodeo fire in the distance. This was getting desperate. Then, like an angel's song, she heard the "thump, thump, thump" of a helicopter closing in. Being down in the forest, she was understandably afraid of not being seen and so did the only thing she could think of: light a signal fire. Soon, a good head of smoke was pushing up through the canopy, and the television chopper, there to cover the other fire, swooped down and picked up the grateful castaway. Her partner had long since been found. As the helicopter lifted away, Valinda worried about the fire she had set. The pilot was certain the small smoldering spot would soon be put out. He was dead wrong.

In a few hours, the "Chediski" fire had covered 2,000 acres with no sign of letting up. The winds were high, the fuel abundant and dry. Stately ponderosas exploded like gasoline-soaked rags as the two blazes began to close in. Already 8,000 people had been evacuated because of the Rodeo fire, and by the time it was over, more than 30,000 would be at least temporarily displaced. At last the fires merged, blazing across the land for weeks unchecked. Almost half a million acres burned, nearly 500 homes destroyed, at least $27 million in damages and $43 million in firefighting costs. Most severely impacted were the Apache people who derived much of their income from the abundant forests. Sixty percent of their trees were lost, a terrible blow to a tribe where far too many already lived below the poverty level. As it was, the average annual income was only $14,000. The Rodeo-Chediski fire was at the time the largest wildfire in all of Arizona's recorded history.

Somehow, word got out that Leonard Gregg was the arsonist in the Rodeo fire. He ultimately confessed to starting the two blazes but not before his attorney argued diminished capacity because of his alcoholic mother. The judge didn't buy it. Gregg was sentenced to ten years in prison and fined $27 million, which I'm sure he will dutifully pay off once he gets out.

The conclusion to Valinda Jo Elliott's story is more complicated. After the fire was contained and residents with homes still standing could return, a meeting was held in the Mogollon High School gymnasium in the tiny village of Heber. The Cantor Law Group website tells the story:

> As Paul K. Charlton, the US attorney for Arizona, prepared to announce that he was not going to file criminal charges in the catastrophic "Chediski" fire, Overgaard resident Steve Lillie entered the gymnasium toting a charred pine log.
>
> "I had 12 acres I was building a resort on," Lillie said, "and this is what's left. ... There's no accountability. No remorse. Nothing."
>
> When Charlton took the microphone and said, "Our decision — my decision — is not to prosecute," Lillie, 44, stood and hurled the burned log near the half-court line, where it crashed and broke in two. "And there's my decision!" he yelled. "You want to take me? Go ahead. That's my life right there."

Criminal charges were never filed, although Lillie was hauled off the court in handcuffs. If the anger of the residents could not be cooled through a long prison term, the Apache tribe could seek civil satisfaction. Some members of the tribe felt racism was at play when one of their own was sent to prison while a white woman walked free, but as the district attorney made clear, no crime had been committed. Elliott had done what any reasonable person would do when faced with similar circumstances. But civil "remedies" are a different matter, and the Apache Tribal court pressed its case. The first legal contest was decided in the Apache's favor when a high court gave the tribe jurisdiction to try the case. This had been in doubt since Elliott is not of Apache descent. In 2009, the tribal court had the go ahead to sue. The outcome is uncertain, but the end result is obvious. If successful, the suit will be a protracted post-modern example of "counting coup," a Plains' Indian ritual of striking one's enemies on the battle field that illustrated bravery but caused no physical damage. Like Leonard Gregg, a single mother employed by a vending machine company is never going to pay much of anything. A month or so after the fire, residents finally got their apology from Elliott. Initially she had expressed no remorse in public and had even been featured on at least one television show. Unfortunately, apologies don't rebuild houses or reforest a devastated region that ecologists say will require 300 years to recover to pre-fire conditions.

Five years after the fires cooled and the displaced residents returned to clean up, rebuild, start over, I grunted, slipped and pedaled through the slowly recovering forest. Seedlings here and there and a lot of scruffy undergrowth were filling in the blank spots between the toasted husks of pine, the arboreal equivalent of a five o'clock shadow. An occasional truck or car gave way to virtually empty conditions, the solitary experience I was craving. Bright sun, clear sky, and some of the hardest riding of the tour filled my day. I had considered the possibility of two nights out on this stretch, but I covered distance more quickly than expected, so one would be plenty. As the afternoon wore on, my legs slowly turning to jelly, I turned off the main track and followed a secondary road into a clean stand of undamaged forest. Away from the ravages of the fire, I could pitch camp under spreading green arms, my bed on a thick layer of pine needles, the wind sighing mournfully in the canopy, as fine a camp as any on the tour. I drank herbal tea as the stars scattered across the sky and bats scrambled in frantic silhouettes. In two days' ride, I would land in Prescott, home to my best friend and his wife. Prescott, too, was a serious marker for my crossing. Once before, traveling east from California, I had pedaled to the town. Now, going in the opposite direction, I would cover some new ground, but with the exception of four days' riding, all the terrain to the coast would be familiar, roads already traversed. Although still weeks away, I could feel the beginning of the end.

Grinning Like an Idiot, Riding Like a Fool
Oct. 30th: 4,000 miles

Like smooth water, the fresh road surface carried me at startling speeds into the valley. Thirty, forty, fifty miles per hour, a gluttonous bounty of speed and gravity embraced, turn and bank, no margin for error, no yesterday, no tomorrow, the roar of a hurricane pounding in my head, the Verde Valley opening below as a gift, the distinct vermillion cliffs of Sedona to the north, a massive mountain wall to the west, tsunami surfing an arid anticline of kinetic dreaming. I became movement and release, the prize of speed honorably achieved. Peaks, buttes and ridges faded into a hazy autumn light to the south. Elite bicycle touring has its rewards.

Before this massive swan dive, I'd been stopped by my first flat since Kansas. Tight road, no shoulder, fortunately light traffic, I lay Mojo on his side and pulled the deflated shoe. Bent over the bike, I didn't notice the car that stopped until the driver called out his window: "Hey, are you okay? Where are you guys headed?" Huh? "Guys"? I looked over my shoulder to see another cyclist straddling his loaded mountain bike sporting huge slick tires, easily two inches across. Bulging black panniers hung off the back. Traffic was coming, so we waved on the driver. I never got his name, but my roadside companion was the first cycle tourist I'd seen since eastern Colorado. Ours is an exclusive club. Maniacs and malcontents only, please. This rider fit the profile all right: Young male, bearded, lean and sinewy, solo. A Canadian, he'd left his homeland and was bound for Tierra del Fuego, the Land of Flames, terminus of the Americas, and then off to Asia somewhere, a two and half year odyssey. I told him about the rim road, although he said he was headed for Payson. It was good to share a few moments with a like-minded traveller, but the road was narrow, and I wanted to get into the valley. I wished him well and pushed off, watching his form miniaturize in the distance, and looked down to see that I'd put the tire on backwards. Lovely. Stop, pull the wheel, deflate, pop the tire, pull the tube, replace, re-inflate, check the seal, replace the wheel—*back on the road, you bozo*. The rocket-sled ride into the valley sufficed to clear my head.

Although quiet now, the Verde Valley has been molded and folded by powerful forces. Tectonic action lifted the mountain walls and sank the valley bottom, what geologists call a "graben." Extensive volcanic activity baked and boiled the surface. Now real estate developers and highway engineers are having their way. Still, most of it is open space, and as the Spanish name indicates, rather green due to the river and rains during the winter and summer. I was excited at the prospect of a campsite at the base of the mountains.

Boosters speak of the "hospitable" climate. That is true, if you happen to be a Gila monster. Four months out of the year the *average* high is 90 deg. F. July, the average high is 100 deg. F. Historically, the months May through Oct. have seen record highs of 100 deg. F. This is desert, no mistaking it, but it is beautiful, and unlike many desert regions, it has water, the Verde River. For this reason, people have lived here for at least 11,000 years, and it is now one of the fastest growing areas of one of the fastest growing states in the union. We shall love it to death even if it kills us.

What of the denizens of this place? Little remains of the earliest inhabitants, but the Sinagua (Spanish: literally, "without water") were here by 600 AD. The Yavapai, perhaps descendants of the Sinagua, were the last native peoples to live here before the Europeans arrived with their Walmarts, mobile homes, and SUV's. General Crook, who got his start fighting truculent natives, made his impress on the area by handily rounding up many of the dark-skinned rebels, although it would take General Miles to bring Geronimo to heel. Crook was one of the first to use Apache guides against their own people. Crook, who graduated bottom of his class at the U.S. Military Academy, overcame handily any classroom deficiencies to eventually die as a Major General, advancing ahead of others in line. To his credit, Crook fought for the rights of the people he helped put onto reservations, in particular working to no avail to free the Apache guides who had helped capture Geronimo. Along with the few remaining members of Geronimo's band, the guides languished in Florida for twenty-six years. A Yavapai-Apache reservation now occupies a patch of land in the valley. Crook's name is pasted on the maps for the stretch of Highway 260 I pedaled down so enthusiastically.

A handful of communities dot the boundary of the valley. To the south, where I would spend the night, the oldest white settlement, Camp Verde, occupies perhaps the least hip, most plebian level of the hierarchy. Next up, Cottonwood, then Clarkdale. The cognoscenti gravitate towards Jerome while those who *think* they know end up in Sedona. Jerome is a wonder of mountainside development, a town coiled upon itself like a diamondback in repose. Street level is also rooftop, the hairpins of the road so steep. Built up in the 1880's with millions of dollars in copper, gold and silver flowing from nearby mines, the town ballooned to a population of 15,000. Perhaps the most dramatic event occurred in 1938 when a blast in one of the mines unhinged the foundations of the entire business district, which, following the dictates of gravity for a town perched on a mountainside, beat feet for lower ground. The town's jail slid an amazing 225 feet. But booms will bust, and after an estimated billion dollars had been yanked from the earth, the last mine closed in 1953. The pulsing multitude moved onto the next best thing. The population dwindled to a mere fifty souls hanging by fingernails to the Victorian era town in the sky; however, like its twin in New Mexico, Madrid, Jerome was discovered by artists and writers, creative folk looking for an inexpensive, off-beat place to call home. So the mining town was reborn an artists' colony and is now a mandatory stop for tourists, art buffs, and historians.

Across the valley and visible from almost anywhere in the area, the red cliffs of Sedona call out, entice, bewitch and beckon. The Mogollon Rim breaks into monumental walls of bright red sandstone, vertical towers and sinuous canyons. It is a place of extraordinary scenic power, and the developers, conmen, New Age Spiritualists, tourist agencies, and the Mafia have not failed to capitalize on it. The architecture is Pueblo Revival on crack, multi-million dollar resort homes, spas and golf courses. Don't want to use your legs? No problem: Pink Jeep Tours can take you where you need to go. Feeling down in the dumps, need a little spiritual tune-up? The Vortices of Sedona are there to put you in perfect harmony with the universe. Of course, you could do this same tune-up in your kitchen in Davenport, Iowa, but then you wouldn't spend money on the Chinese-made "Native-American" jewelry and knickknacks laid out like so many fishing lures.

The most notorious New Age goo-spreading guru connected with Sedona had already been disseminating his own brand of mind softening residue when I passed through the valley. James Arthur Ray learned the lessons well of his preacher father. According to Bob Ortega in *The Arizona Republic*, Ray cobbled together a salad of various mystical traditions with only superficial knowledge of any of them. Drawing on lessons learned as an AT&T salesman and observing how others made money selling self-transformation, Ray began peddling what he termed "practical mysticism" and "harmonic wealth," playing not only on people's emotional and spiritual needs but also their greed. Tell the right kind of people that they can get rich if they follow *your* plan—and do it convincingly—*you* will get rich. With the release of his book, *Harmonic Wealth*, an appearance in the movie, *The Secret*, and appearances on *Oprah* and other national TV shows, Ray began to realize his dreams, growing James Ray International into a multi-million dollar company. He became the truth incarnate of his teachings. As George Burns said, "Sincerity—if you can fake that, you've got it made." Charismatic, boyish, energetic, Ray could play a crowd, and people eager to give up their money and self-determination fell eagerly into his cult of personality.

His "Spiritual Warrior" retreats in Sedona and elsewhere became popular with well-heeled desperate types willing to give up themselves and their cash. For a week, participants would attend lectures, workshops, walk on broken glass and break boards (and hands) in poorly conducted "mind over matter" exercises. In the Sedona retreats, attendees would spend thirty-six hours alone in the backcountry—no sleeping bag, tent, or supplies—no food or water. If they didn't want to shiver too much, they could fork over $250 for an "authentic" poncho to huddle under. Throughout many phases of the week, warrior wannabees were encouraged to forgo sleep and water, to push themselves. One exercise involved a simulated suicide with Ray as some sort of robed "god" overseeing the "death" and "rebirth." Special to the week in Sedona was an extreme sweat lodge, and as early as 2005, at least one participant was hauled off to the hospital for heat-related problems. Ray was direct with his students: They would feel like they were going to die, that their skin would feel like it was melting off. In 2009, three warriors did achieve spiritual and physical transformation: They died. The good news is that these unfortunate souls got to die, gasping and vomiting in the dirt, for the perfectly reasonable sum of $10,000. James Arthur Ray, whose philosophy dealt with the "law of attraction" wherein we "attract" the good—and bad—in our lives, managed to "attract" not only three dead spiritual warriors but a conviction for negligent homicide.

From the high, cool pines, this warrior on wheels slipped into the arid regions below, spindly, heat-blasted vegetation, cottonwoods and sycamores in the creases. An especially green and thickly treed band running down valley indicated the line of the Verde River. As a perfect conclusion—too rare in bike touring—I finished the day's ride on a coast, rolling into a campground at the base of the mountains. At the far end, a picnic table close to a creek and blessed with a magnificent sycamore, I made camp, the low, thick air warm and welcoming—shorts, t-shirt, home. I pedaled to a nearby market to procure celebratory suds and settle into the early evening, the camp in deep shadow, night beginning to assert its dominance.

I sat alone at my table in the dark. Crickets chirped; the road groaned with distant traffic like a river, quiet; a skunk ambled by not thirty feet away. I contemplated the nature of my desires, the need to take this trip—or have this trip take me. Did I even have the choice? I have, as Jodi says of men generally, the ability to focus my energies, my consciousness on this one task, but thoughts of home would arise and play across my mind. Pangs of loneliness forced their way in when the day's challenges were over. *What can I do? I am lonely. I want to see Jodi and home. Yes, this is difficult. And?* People would often ask me, when they discovered that I was traveling alone, "Don't you get lonely?" Of course. This is a given, part of the challenge, something I have to face and overcome. There is, however, an interesting and important subtext to the question: *How can you possibly do something that will make you feel lonely? Are you a masochist? An anti-social curmudgeon?* This is the emotional counterpart to the physical struggle and discomfort human-powered travel demands. Is the pursuit of comfort the highest human value, the endpoint of all effort and evolution? While extolling the virtues of struggle, however, I establish myself a hypocrite. Mojo was selected for comfort—among other things. I carry lightweight gear, a tent, an air mattress that turns into a chair. In the muggy buggy heat of an Illinois afternoon, I sought the shelter of an air conditioned library. I strive in my tours for comfortable discomfort, the Zen koan of the elite cyclotourist. But I leave the climate controlled room, too. I crank into the blazing sun, through clouds of insects, up the tilted sides of mountains. The knowledge of the body, its delight in use and hard effort cannot be denied. The body is meant to move, and the cornucopia of modern diseases flowing from our addiction to comfort is grimly documented. The weakness of the spirit saps the vigor of the flesh, what it needs and wants.

We lose the sheer joy and exhilaration of movement and so forget the wisdom of muscle and bone. So I push on, deal with my struggles physical and spiritual. I get lonely. But I proceed, and on the other side of loneliness, I find solitude, self-knowledge, and insight. To cross a continent by yourself is to gain riches that cannot be gained by any other means. As Twain put it in *Tom Sawyer Abroad*: "[A] person that started in to carry a cat home by the tail was getting knowledge that was always going to be useful to him, and warn't ever going to grow dim or doubtful...."

Such were my musings that night alone at a table under the spreading sycamore.

Prescott, Arizona, is hard to approach from the southeast. Protected by mountainous ramparts, besieged by Phoenicians in vast columns of automobiles, encircled by spreading rings of development, the original state capitol would hardly seem worth visiting until you reach the old square and regal courthouse and walk through the pine forest and wilderness that spreads beyond the city limits. Like most everyone, I had a soft spot for this town a mile in the western sky. My friends Pete and Emily knew I was coming, and I keenly anticipated that warm welcome and a place to park for a few days. My arrival would mark a key moment in my quest since I'd already pedaled that remaining distance to my home a few years before. As I made a sharp turn in the climb, I looked down at the cyclometer: 4,000 miles. I was in Arizona, only a few miles from a familiar town, old friends. I had pedaled here from the coast of Maine. Damn. I dismounted, photographed the tiny screen with all the little zeros lined up, and looked around at the dry grasses, spreading low developments, the steady stream of noisy traffic. It was a private moment of triumph in a nondescript place that few would ever remember in their hurry to be elsewhere. I drank some water and began the punishing, headwind battering climbs into town. By the time I hit the square, I was a wreck, but a fine brew and chicken wrap at the Gurley Street Grill stabilized my condition so that I could, at last, climb the remaining hill to my refuge in the trees. Hot shower, a bed, my best friends, home for a few days. I was a wealthy man indeed.

What can I say about my idyll in the trees of Prescott? I slept in until a decadent 7AM. I sipped coffee slowly, late into the morning. I gave Mojo a well-earned cleaning, did laundry, updated my blog and drank in the clear autumn light. October drew to a close, and at long last the infernal regions of the desert below were becoming more friendly to the pedal powered folk. Late one afternoon, Pete, a Buddhist rock climber of considerable skill, and I hiked to the top of Thumb Butte, an imposing plug of volcanic rock commanding an impressive view over the town. After so many months apart, it was a fine, grounding experience to hear his voice, talk of our lives and friends. We shared a deep connection in the outdoors, a bond developed over many years climbing rocks and hiking peaks around the West. I had tried once, unsuccessfully, to get a job in Prescott. Our friendship now was a sporadic business, long periods tied into our separate lives punctuated by a few days, a week perhaps during the year when we might travel to the Sierras and continue where we had left off. As with the best of friends, the pauses didn't seem to matter. With the first handshake and warm embrace, we were brothers again, as if no years had passed. We looked out over the lengthening shadows, the high plateau leading east to the lofty cone of Humphrey's Peak above Flagstaff almost a hundred miles away. I stretched my imagination, kept reaching east across Colorado, Kansas, Missouri and on and on into the night and lands I had traversed so intensely. It was getting late. In comfortable silence, we crept down the summit rocks, regained the trail, and headed down to Pete's truck. It would be dinner out on the town, but first a fine ale at the brew pub. I was going to make this layover count.

Kicking 66
Nov. 3ʳᵈ– 4ᵗʰ : 4,166 miles

I was ready to go, but I didn't want to leave. I had settled into a comfortable, familiar place. In some ways, I was already home—but I wasn't. Six hundred miles of deserts and mountains still lay between me and the Pacific, two weeks of hard riding. With a deep reluctance confused with an eagerness to continue, I left town on an early Saturday morning, the steep roads cool, smooth and empty. This time I would take the high route, a few days of new terrain on the road home: North to Ashfork then west on old Route 66, the fabled highway from Chicago to California. I left Prescott with a few pangs of separation and settled into my accustomed cadence, the miles flowing easily on rested legs. It wasn't long before the craggy ramparts of Granite Mountain were receding in the distance, and to the north I could see the dense pinyon and juniper forests that blanket so much of northern Arizona. The riding was easy, a gift. In two hours I covered almost thirty miles and soon entered the spreading green sea of stubby trees washing up against the banks of Hwy 89.

By 1:30PM I was in Ashfork, resolved to push on beyond Seligman, farther than my initial estimates. The day was young, my legs hungry for more. For a few miles, I pedaled the shores of Interstate 40, a throbbing four lane scar across the northern part of the state, and, at last, slipped onto Route 66, leaving most of the traffic behind. I rolled down the center of the road, the big wide open embracing me like a friend. A long, steady climb led me back up to 5,700 ft., higher than Prescott, and from the summit, I could see Seligman. In the late afternoon, I cast off and raced the quick miles down.

Route 66 is one of the oldest highways in the U.S., at the time of its completion second only to the original Lincoln Highway in length, and its impact was arguably greater. Formally begun in 1926, it was termed "The Mother Road" by John Steinbeck and others. The Joads in *The Grapes of Wrath* were but fictionalized portraits of thousands of real immigrants who flooded the road to escape smothering dust, drought, and bankruptcy. When it was finally all paved, it linked Chicago and Los Angeles in a smooth, fast lane stretching almost 2,500 miles and gave birth to countless roadside attractions, the first motels, and, in Los Angeles, the first McDonald's. Fast moving people wanted fast moving food, and the McDonald brothers were happy to get rich serving that need. As high voltage boosterism and millions of dollars of federal money poured into southern California during WWII, the largest automobile migration in history would take place, turning Los Angeles from a dry, second-rate town into one of the biggest cities in America. The pavement these motorists enjoyed, was, ironically, the result of the "good roads movement" pushed by activist cyclists in the late 19th century, the League of American Wheelmen. Route 66 helped give rise to the modern American road trip, the constant movement and restlessness facilitated by the automobile. The highway was officially decommissioned in 1985 when a network of super highways finally made the storied road a quaint, crumbling anachronism. For the elite touring cyclists, however, this was a fortunate turn of events, for now the bulk of motorized traffic stays on the interstates, leaving long stretches of lonely road free and quiet, albeit with an often deteriorating surface. I pedaled with the ghosts of Okies, Jack Kerouac, and uncounted dreamers.

Fading light and miles from town, I hunted for a place to camp, some break in the continual fencing that bracketed the road in a solid, inhospitable wall: locked gates, barbed wire, "No Trespassing" signs. Beyond eighty miles for the day, I was looking forward to pitching camp, cracking that large Foster's lager rolled carefully in my fleece jacket, and watching the golden light fade on the juniper grasslands. Ultimately, I was forced to settle for a marginal strip of flat ground between the barbed wire fence to the north and the lonely highway to the south. A small congregation of junipers obscured my camp from the road, but they couldn't block the sound of the train. I'd made the tactical error of stopping near a crossing, so all night long, in addition to the diesel rumble of the engines, I was blessed with the wailing screams of the whistle, penetrating the silicone earplugs and vibrating my bones. At least I had ample opportunity to study the stars, the spinning wheel of the Milky Way arcing across the dome of night, Orion high and mighty.

It was a strange lump, a puzzle that stood on the shoulder of the highway in the distance. Much like the Plains of St. Agustin in New Mexico, the dense junipers had fanned out into broad, grassy flats. To the north, a miles-long volcanic ridge curved beside the plain like a rising wave frozen in the instant before it breaks, a North Shore bruiser rolling in geologic time. I worked the razor cut of the road, grateful to be fit and alive and cycling across the West on this best of all possible days. What was that lump? Legs? Two people?

A few minutes of cycling answered the question as I stopped beside another touring cyclist, but this fellow was cut from a different cloth. Fred, as he called himself, had a blue mountain bike with a huge sagging bedroll strapped to the handlebars. On the back, smallish panniers hung below an enormous Rubbermaid storage tub and other gear held to the rack with a heavy duty nylon ratcheting tie-down strap of the sort that would be used to hold down a motorcycle in the back of a pickup. Dressed in a dark blue t-shirt, baggy camouflage pants, running shoes and a sweaty, salt-encrusted green hat, Fred stood beside his massive load that reached almost to his shoulders. He took a drag from the stub of a cigarette wedged between the exposed grubby tips of his gloved hand and extended the other to me. "Hey," he said, "another one!" He smiled broadly, revealing a thick gap of missing teeth across his upper jaw. It took only moments for Fred to begin off-loading details about his wandering life.

"Yeah," he said, "I came from Truth or Consequences. Been on the road about two months. I worked there washin' dishes for seven months. I was only going to stay for a couple of weeks but ended up stayin' seven months!" He let out a husky laugh. "Yeah, some of my gear wore out, so I had to save up some money and resupply." Graying hair, some miles on his weathered face, it was clear he was in his fifties, but despite the smoking habit and missing teeth, he looked strong. He pedaled when he could, pushed when he had to. "That other life?" he said, waving his hands as if pushing away a bothersome fly. "You can take it. This is it for me," gesturing towards the bike. "I'm livin' like this from now on."

I pondered his life as I sped down the road. Fred was going to push for a while, and I quickly left him behind, a large dark mass in my mirror, then nothing. Although I found life on the road compelling, the idea that I would live like this "from now on" was hard to imagine. No permanent home, no enduring ties to other people, always a new place, different faces, constant motion like a shark that would die if it ceased swimming—a monotony of variety. Even now, a mere three months into a life on the road, I was looking forward to home, Jodi, the opportunity to *not* move on virtually every day. This for me was a journey, not a way of life. What had Fred lived through or lived without that now he chose this solitary wandering existence? He was a type, and I'd seen his type before, in the desert, too, on a trip to Arizona years before.

That day I climbed gently with a light tailwind and dropped into the expansive basin beyond. To the north stood the Bristol Mountains and Lava Hills, to the south, the Bullion Mountains and the Twenty Nine Palms Marine Corps Air/Ground Combat Center. Thoughts of the wars in Afghanistan and Iraq flooded my mind. As if on cue, a deep explosive boom rolled down the valley, a towering cloud of dust rising in the distance. Target practice. The rounds were infrequent and finally trailed off altogether. My main companions were the faint rush of my tires on the road and mind-boggling views to mountain ranges twenty, fifty, seventy-five miles or more in the distance. The air was so clear that everything was within reach.

I paralleled the Atchison Topeka and Sante Fe railroad, whose engineers when naming the sidings were not without a sense of irony. One of my detailed maps indicated names like Klondike and Siberia, further on a more expected Bagdad. Siberia, however, did somehow fit: harsh, remote, unpopulated, a place of exiles and misfits, wanderers and dreamers. To the mountains and the deserts go the prophets. Recumbent cyclists, too, smitten by solitude and silence. Before noon I reached Amboy, a dying town on the ragged edge of the frontier. I had last been through several years before, and at that time I found the place marginal at best. Now it truly was a village from the final zombie apocalypse. Roy's Café and Motel had closed, a big chunk of the café's sign having fallen out. The only spark of life was a car parked next to the post office across the street and a flag hung high indicating the office was open. The flag cord clanked forlornly against the pole. In the bright December sun on Route 66, no cars passed for twenty minutes. Rush hour in the low desert.

One needs to appreciate minimalist aesthetics to enjoy this desert. To some it is only good for bombing or storing nuclear waste, a setting for horror movies. I pedaled along, savoring the clean lines and naked honesty of a land that averages about three inches of rain a year. This is a tell-all topography, unashamed of its wrinkles and furrows, gullies, ridges and sand-blown bajadas. The climb out of Amboy was typical of the Mojave, long, steady ascents across huge mountains with immense fans of debris. Below I could see a vast playa, the flattest geologic features on earth. I reveled in a curving ascent to a rocky pass, the warm sun at my back. Then the desert offered up a gem, one of those encounters that can't be scripted but that rise unbidden into the lives of travelers.

Near the bottom of the second big descent of the day, I encountered a wondrous sight, a vagabond in the grand style. "Cowboy," as he liked to be called, was piloting a rig few could imagine. At first all I could see was a large, dark lump with a "slow vehicle" triangle affixed to the back and what appeared to be a bicycle wheel on the front. What strange conveyance was this? I eased to a stop: The front was conventional enough, a basic mountain bike with knobby tires. The trailer he towed, however, staggered the imagination. About fifteen feet long, built of plywood and heavy aluminum bar stock and two stout trailer wheels, it was piled high with an enormous load: three huge bags of crushed aluminum cans (each weighing 35 lbs.), a tall plastic garbage can on its way to being filled, a small mountain of personal gear and a radio/tape deck playing tunes. All this was connected to the trailer by heavy duty nylon straps with stout ratcheting mechanisms. The trailer was connected to the seat post of the bike with a custom ball mount and heavy welded steel hitch. The clincher: Cowboy said the whole rig fully loaded checked in at about *six hundred pounds*.

Cowboy grinned with pride as he described his vehicle. With mirrored sunglasses a CHP officer might wear, well-used black jeans, black "Corona" t-shirt, wild, thinning white hair and beard, Cowboy, perhaps in his early sixties, was living a strenuous, rugged outdoor life at an age when most of his contemporaries were warming up for the nursing home. He supported his nomadic lifestyle by picking up aluminum cans. When heavily loaded, he averaged about one to two miles per hour and covered less than ten miles a day. His routine was to walk up and back in quarter mile stretches of road, picking up any cans, and then move his rig along to the next section. And so, inching his way across the country, Cowboy filled his days. When he was fully loaded, he cranked for the nearest place to redeem the cans. A full load brought him about $140. The BLM, seeing the valuable service he was providing, made him an honorary ranger and dropped by with food and water every few days. Cowboy said the BLM gave him an official t-shirt that said, in essence, he said, "Don't fuckin' mess with me."

"Hey, I don't suppose, ridin' a bike like that, that you're one of those smokin' cyclists, are ya?" he asked. Thinking he was offering me a little illicit mind-altering herbal material—not an uncommon occurrence between wanderers on the edge—I politely declined.

"No thanks," I said. "I don't smoke."

"Oh, no," he replied, "I'm not offerin'. I'm beggin'! I'm just dyin' for a cigarette."

I had to disappoint him because I was indeed not "one of those 'smokin' cyclists." Cowboy told me a little of his life. He was a retired truck driver. In cycling and retirement he had found it impossible to leave his big rig behind and had been traveling from Colorado since October.

I shook my head, stood amazed and wide-mouthed, slapped him on the shoulder and said, "Fantastic! You're my hero!"

He inquired about my setup, the fancy disc brakes and micro-trailer, which could only handle one hundred pounds, although I confessed to pulling just forty. When I told him that for this day I was averaging about twelve mph, he howled, "Hooo! I'd KILL for twelve miles an hour!"

We stood there on the side of old Route 66, swapping tales, the lore of the road, information on conditions, destinations. The brilliant Mojave sun, a December blessing of warmth and light, washed over us, two souls hooked to the road. Creosote bushes and mountain ranges stretched for as far as we cared to see. The afternoon was getting on, however, and I still wanted to make some miles before dark. I bid Cowboy farewell, saddled up, and pulled away, yelling in my wake, "Tail winds!"

Cowboy yelled after me: "I hear we're gettin' head winds tomorrah!"

The Cowboy prophet was right, of course, but that was an adventure for the next day. For now I had the lengthening shadows of late afternoon and a desert highway under my wheels.

They had something right, these lone cranks of the open road. Free from mortgages, car payments and income taxes, they flew slow and low, occupying an obscure, ultra-low income fringe environment well below the radar of mainstream society. I could sympathize. Another edge-dwelling character, the rock climber-philosopher Eric Beck once said, "On either end of the social spectrum, there lies a leisure class." My own leisure consisted of a steady diet of more blacktop as I sliced across northern Arizona. Mike and his wife, Melissa, would host my last night in the state, but I had one more wild camp to go, a tent site beside a stream beneath blazing cottonwoods flanked by dark basalt ridges dotted with prickly pear and cholla, dried leaves carpeting the floor like crunchy potato chips. I settled in right next to the water and passed a fitful night. I listened to the creek, the wind in the trees, did battle with a lone mosquito. Thoughts of the end of the tour kept lurking about. In only two more days of riding, I would be in California.

In the morning I clawed my way out of the bag, only 47 deg. F., toasty. I rigged my pad into a chair and settled in, resolved to take my time. I didn't have far to go. The enjoyment of a hot drink, the purl of the shallow water at arm's length settled into my groggy consciousness, and by slow degrees the sun touched the dark rock ridge above and poured down the slope into camp. No rush, no hustle, slow contemplation, breathing, full immersion in sound, light, burnt umber of stone, hot sulfur yellow of incandescent cottonwoods and willows, blue above streaked by washes of diaphanous cirrus. Now I could begin packing. A hot shower and kindred souls were waiting in Kingman.

Known less for deep history than tourist traps like *The Road Kill Café* in Seligman—"You kill it, we grill it!" (yummy "Splatter Platter" and "Swirl of Squirrel") and the old black and white TV show, Route 66 is now part of Klassic Kitsch, but the story is deeper and more interesting than life-sized cutouts of James Dean smoking skillfully by the sidewalk. The first important figure of the route was a close friend and traveling partner of Kit Carson. He numbered among his associates Ulysses S. Grant, William Tecumseh Sherman, and President Cleveland. Before his death, he purchased an old Spanish land grant in California that would become the largest privately held parcel in the country, the Tejon Ranch, over 270,000 acres. And he loved camels.

Edward Fitzgerald Beale traveled around the world during his service to the U.S. Navy, living a life of high adventure, touching down in England, Mexico, Hawaii and Peru. With Kit Carson and a personal Delaware Indian servant, he crept through hostile Mexican troops during the Battle of Pasqual in 1846 to get reinforcements. The U.S. forces were doomed without immediate help. Later, during an exploratory trip in Death Valley, Beale suggested to a skeptical Carson that camels would be perfect for travels through the vast deserts of the Southwest. When Beale was appointed by President Buchanan in 1857 to lay out a wagon route through this arid land, Beale used camels as the principle pack animals, twenty-five surly beasts shipped over from Tunis. Beale had nothing but praise for the sturdy creatures, but the camels didn't play well with horses and mules, and the military cancelled the experiment. The route Beale and the camels traveled, however, turned out to be direct and fast with good water, the longest waterless stretch being only twenty miles. Route 66 and, later, Highway 40, would follow basically the same line, and if you know where to look near Kingman, it is still possible to see wagon tracks left from the original trail.

Perhaps the most dramatic event to occur along this stretch of Route 66 transpired during a blazing July day in 1973. Rail traffic has been key to the region for decades, and on this day, a huge tank containing over 33,000 gallons of liquid propane was stopped barely two hundred yards from the highway, two workers getting set to transfer the contents to new containers on the ground. The valve connecting the rail car to another tank was leaky and stuck. One of the workers then made a fatal mistake. Seeking to fix the connection, the man struck the metal valve with a heavy metal wrench. Only a single spark was required. A rocket blast of flame shot fifty, sixty, a hundred feet into the air, matched by another fiery tongue shooting out at an angle. Both workers tumbled back from the flames. One staggered for help. One would later die from his burns. Quickly, firefighters and onlookers began to gather, the fire crews seeking to cool the hot tank. Water could not douse a propane fire, but they hoped to keep the tank from blowing. Men scrambled to set up a heavy soaking hose, but they ran out of time. The design limits of the massive tank were pushed too far, the pressure too great. The tank ruptured. What the small desert community experienced that day was an accidental example of what ordnance engineers would call "fuel-air explosives," the ultimate expression of which is the MOAB—"massive ordnance air blast," what most observers termed the "mother of all bombs." At 21,000 lbs, it is the largest non-nuclear bomb in the world and functions by distributing a massive load of fuel into the air and then igniting it to create a fearsome blast capable of flattening six Super Bowl stadiums in an instant. The China Lake Naval Weapons Center points out that such bombs are especially good on "soft targets." Targets don't get softer than human beings, as the firefighters and citizens of Kingman discovered. The liquid propane, freed from the confining walls of the tank, exposed to low pressure and high temperatures, vaporized, expanded, and ignited. Firefighters call this kind of event a "boiling liquid expansion vapor explosion" or BLEVE. The fireball spread to 1,000 feet in diameter. The shock wave was felt five miles away. A three ton chunk of rail car was tossed a quarter of a mile away. Burning propane and splinters of tank shrapnel rained down. In addition to the one rail worker, eleven firefighters were killed, and over one hundred casualties, many of them observers standing along Route 66, poured into the local hospital. The tragedy marked the town forever and changed firefighting tactics across the country. Today a small park honors the fallen and commemorates that terrible day.

In 2007, I was content to follow a quiet camel path out of the mountains. Situated at over 3,000 ft. at the western end of a broad, dry basin, Kingman doesn't pull in the traveller like some sort of paradise. The expanses around the town are bleak, treeless, hot and dry, averaging about ten inches of rain each year. The most attractive feature is the pine-covered Hualapai Mountains to the south, a craggy granite uplift rising to 8,417 ft. For a half-baked desert rat like me, the scruffy nature of the place would do just fine.

Burros and Buffalo Burgers
Nov. 6th: 4263 miles

My hosts in Kingman fed me well and took me along for a little bicycle activism. A city council meeting was being held, and cyclists were agitating for better shoulders in the area, especially Route 66 as it comes into town. I could sympathize. It had been the worst sort of chip seal gravel, terrible for riding. I'd stayed mostly in the lane, crossing into the shoulder only when traffic forced the issue. One local cyclist had been killed when he was riding outside the rough zone. Helmet-wearing Kingmanites packed the meeting, making sure their voices were heard. As a brother in spokes and chain, the least I could do was add another body to the standing-room-only occasion. The council members were clearly impressed.

The next day, Mike and Mo led me through the gloom before sunrise. Mike turned off to head to work at the local jail while Mo acted as my guide to the far side of town and down a sweet curving canyon, cool banking, gravity assist. Mo and I parted ways when I crossed under Hwy 40 and picked up the Oatman Rd., California now firmly in my sights. Arizona had given me some of the worst riding on the tour, the narrow chaos through Showlow, the noisy mess into Prescott, but today it would give me one of the best days.

Oatman Rd. led geometrically straight across the gently sagging basin, the solitary track flanked by creosote bushes in the still and warming air. The miles without turns fell with hardly a thought, my speed in the high teens. My timing for hitting these low, hot deserts was perfect. Before and behind, not a car to be seen. As I began the long climb to Sitgreaves Pass at 3,550 ft., I took off my helmet and enjoyed wearing only a light cap to shade my eyes. To the north, the distinct tower of Thimble Mtn. pierced the clear sky, not a cloud in any direction. Shortly I tackled the circuitous ascent into the tortured folds of the pass, steep, slow, dry vertical cliffs and fearsome drops. No wind. Quiet solitude, steady effort, and an empty mind filled me completely.

From the top, I gazed in wonder at three states— Nevada, Arizona, and, at long last, the dusty barren shores of California rising like a rumbled beige blanket to the horizon. Thousands of feet below, I could see the depression cradling the Colorado River. I sat on the edge of the mountain crest and contemplated for long moments what this meant. Then my gut rumbled for lunch, and I remembered I had promised myself a meal in Oatman, so Mojo and I pushed off, gently, the plunging, twisting trail carrying us down and away. Before long, I could make out the corrugated tin, weathered planks and sun-bleached stucco of the living ghost town, burros wondering back and forth across the main street, Route 66.

Once a thriving mining town established in the early 1900's, Oatman's gold ran out by the beginning of WWII. Because it supported travelers on Route 66, it survived for a while longer until a gentler bypass was created, leaving the town to the burros and the hot desert wind. A modern enthusiasm for the old road and thriving gambling communities down by the Colorado River have resurrected Oatman, a place where feral burros roam the streets and tourists leave their dollars. The mining history of boom and bust is typical for the West, but the name of the town reflects a more interesting story.

Although she never lived in the town that now bears her name, Olive Oatman's life is hard to forget. A pretty, dark-haired Mormon girl, she traveled west with her family as part of the Mormon diaspora of the mid 1800's. Her family, however, was to follow a splinter group of Mormons called the "Brewsterites," named after James C. Brewster who was rejected by the main clan for claiming that he, too, at the age of ten, had seen the Angel Moroni. The church was only big enough for one "true" prophet, so leaving the

Midwest, the Brewsterites went in search of their own promised land, yet another Zion they called "Bashan." It wasn't long before the splinter group splintered. What did they argue about in the middle of the desert? Perhaps the oasis never appeared. Maybe someone else had decided he, too, had seen The Angel. Eventually all the followers split up, drifted off. Going their separate ways, Brewster finally made it to California, although he never did get his own church off the ground. The Oatmans, however, did not fare as well.

In the hard country along the Gila River in what would later become Arizona, the Oatmans were attacked by natives, likely Yavapai, and all but the children were killed. Olive's brother, Lorenzo, was knocked unconscious during the battle and left for dead. We can only imagine the fifteen-year-old's horror at coming to, his own head split and aching, and finding the bodies of his family bleeding around him, his two younger sisters gone. Mary Ann, the youngest, would live for three years until dying of starvation at the age of ten. Olive lived with the Yavapai for a time but was eventually taken in by the Mojave tribe, who looked after her and tattooed her chin in their customary way, a design of lines and arrow points vaguely resembling a striped goatee dribbling from her lower lip to the bottom of her chin. During this time, she lived along the Colorado in the area that would become present day Needles, not far from the town of Oatman. After five long years of captivity, authorities at Fort Yuma acted on stories they had been hearing about a white girl living with the natives. The military sent horses and blankets for a trade. After initially refusing the offer, the Mojave relented and traveled the twenty days to the fort to hand over the girl, now sixteen. There Olive learned that her brother, Lorenzo, was still alive and had been searching for her all these years. When the mining town was founded, residents named it in honor of the tough Mormon girl who had died just three years before at the age of sixty five.

Although I could not claim the renown of Clark Gable and Carole Lombard who spent their wedding night at the Oatman Hotel in 1938 after getting married that day in Kingman, I was the only elite recumbent cyclotourist in sight as I eased to a stop amongst the ambling burros and tourists, the waving flags of t-shirt racks and bobbing heads capped with cowboy gear. If the Oatman Hotel was good enough for Gable and Lombard, it was good enough for me. Advertised "World Famous Buffalo Burgers" sealed the deal. I tied up Mojo in front of the pale, two story adobe building, supposedly the first in the state when it was built in 1902, and moseyed through the front door, a lone traveller blowing in off the solitary trail. Stunned, I looked around at hundreds and hundreds of dollar bills stapled to walls, doorways, posts, the ceiling, every available inch papered with greenbacks.   My latent criminal impulses were instantly aflame—until I realized how much effort it would take to grab the dollars and how little reward they would offer. Besides, a recumbent bicycle is hardly the appropriate getaway rig for a 21st century desperado. No, today, I'd have to settle for a buffalo burger (they're *world famous!*), burro ear fries (should be world famous) and a window seat. No doubt Gable himself had looked out this very window. Baked tire tread could have satisfied my hunger, so the burger and monster fries didn't last long. I studied some of the money nearby on the wall.   Most had messages, slogans, notes written on them, many in foreign languages. One said, "God bless America," then, as an afterthought: "(and England)." I wedged the hot, savory food down my eager gullet and staggered out into the glaring light.

Outside, a folding table held a tape player and, inexplicably, a few Fez caps. In the street, several hombres strutted in full-on Western garb, chaps, boots, gun belts— with the guns—the big silly hats.   One was cracking a bullwhip, its exploding snap the result of the tip breaking the sound barrier—no lie. Great. They were going to reenact a gun battle on the street. I've never had a stomach for such theatrics, preferring to let the place itself do the talking. Time to get out of Dodge. I saddled up and rolled gently through the placid burros, their coats gray and brown, some with dark razorbacks of fur, beautiful desert survivors. I rolled and rolled and rolled, seemingly endless miles of effortless travel past a huge desert tower and down, down,

down to the Colorado River. I turned south towards Needles and picked up a spanking tailwind, warm bright sun. Welcome to the low desert in November.

California. Movie stars. Greedy politicians. Low-rent motels. A sign on the west bank of the river. Needles. Home? It's a rather desolate band of strip malls, fast food abattoirs, and molten pavement where summer highs routinely top 120 deg. F., where the summer *low* once bottomed out at 98 deg. F, a place where the 90's comedian Sam Kinison met his gruesome end on Highway 95 to the north, and the setting for the early post-apocalyptic roll playing video game *Wasteland*. The desert is a fine place, usually, until people get involved. Perhaps dust bowl travelers found some excitement here in that it was the first California town they encountered in their escape from a different sort of hell in the Midwest. If anything, the city limits contained the wasteland. The desert beyond held secrets and power and grandeur, the bristling name-sake towers to the south calling out in a voice lost to most who motor by in climate controlled glass and steel carriages.

That night, content after a shower and a meal, I hunkered down in the Imperial 400 Inn and watched the Weather Channel, and like all good cyclists, *willed* the weather to my liking. The Southwest was simmering under a mild, late season heat wave, Needles set for 89—90 deg. F. for the next day. I would have to start early. In Cleveland, Ohio, where I had been just the day before, a lifetime ago, snow was clogging the roads, my cycling friends and gracious hosts staring at the onslaught of winter. *Snow on the ground*, for crying out loud. In Needles, California, I slept to the intermittent growl of an air conditioning unit.

Back in the Big Lonesome
Nov. 7th – 8th: 4370 miles

Late afternoon, I slouched in my chair tucked into the shade thrown by Mojo's loaded bulk. The slender, waxy-leaved stems of the creosote bushes waved gently in the breeze. Dry, craggy mountains, burnt brown and weathered, cast deepening shadows into sharp ravines and canyons. Temperature: 87 deg. F. Humidity: 10%. Population for the surrounding ten square miles: One. Me. Two, counting Mojo. Up by 5AM, I'd battled the long gradual climb out of Needles at a comfortable, steady pace, eighteen miles, over 2,000 ft., the shoulder of I-40 providing ample space and a smooth surface for my labors. The truly outstanding quality of cycling the mountainous west is the fantastic payoff for each ascent—mile upon mile of effortless cruising after the bruising, sweet wages for sweat. For a long while, I unclipped my shoes, crossed my legs, and leaned back against the headrest and let the expansive Mojave Desert pull me in.

According to the gods who rule the roads, I was supposed to get off the interstate before Fenner, but that would force me into a circuitous route to backtrack. I needed the truck stop for water as my next camp would be quite literally in the middle of nowhere. A few miles downhill dodging construction cones? A small price to pay. Soon I was eating an ice cream bar and dozing in the shade, but I was not to find quiet, not here at the only stop for many miles along the freeway. A few trucks idled by the diesel pumps, and one particularly testosterone poisoned moron straddled his hot yellow super bike and burned screaming streaming clouds of rubber as if preparing for a do-or-die drag race. I slowly ate my lunch and did battle with steely-eyed black birds intent on pilfering my food. These avian thieves stood focused and resolute mere inches from my bag of chips, eyes intent, intelligences vast and cool, making plans, calculating. In the end, I was the winner, but even so one grabbed a chip corner and flew off. Hitchcock knew what he was talking about.

But tours don't ride themselves, and eventually, strung out miles and miles down a largely ignored length of the Mother Road, I found myself heavily loaded with water and pushing Mojo up a sandy line between the spindly desert vegetation. There is little that is "fat" in the desert. The plants, the sinuous snakes and bony lizards, the sere mountains naked and lean throw your senses into strange places. The land is about raw honesty. Nothing to hide behind here, no woods lovely dark and deep. The desert gave birth to Edward Abbey not Robert Frost. In this land of little rain, people, like the plants and animals, develop thorns and venom. Content with this contrarian landscape, I parked Mojo, the water bag bulging, and gazed out over the Clipper Mountains and the immense basin to the south, hundreds of square miles of perfect nothing.

This is not a dead land, however, regardless of place names like Death Valley, the Funeral Mountains, and the Devil's Racetrack. Unlike the exuberance found in the damp and humid East, this austere land displays little, but like a sharp poker player, the desert plays her hand close to the chest, reluctant to show her cards. The action of life is shifted, veiled by sand, rock and night. When darkness falls, the creatures emerge to make their living. Almost every shift is graveyard in the desert. Unlike humans who so often seem determined to make the worst of it, the animals here must be smooth operators, opportunists. And this night, I would have a visitor.

The sun set, the earth cooled, and I ate the last of my simple fare as the stars saturated the sky such that even the fetid glow of Las Vegas could not impugn their imperial shine. Wearing a headlamp, I scraped the last bits from the pot and glanced up and perceived a problem, a puzzle, a gift? Twin stars set down near the ground. They glowed bright and close, dimmed, set, vanished, reappeared. Eyes. Intelligence. *I'm being watched!* The eyes, like the Cheshire grin, implied the beast. Silently, they winked, shifted, advanced, retreated. Clearly, I was the object of some interest. At last I could take it no more, grabbed my bright bike headlight, and advanced on the eyes that now held me in a steady, unblinking gaze. What was this bold creature? With each step I expected the animal to bolt into the night, but our eyes held, each mesmerized by the other. Big ears...a rabbit? No, these were triangular, arrow-tipped. At last my light fell clearly on the visitor, a sly desert fox come to beguile me—the kit fox, *Vulpes macrotis arsipus.* I offered it no food but hoped its hunt was successful, perhaps a tasty kangaroo rat, the *Dipodomys*, a creature so adapted to the desert that it requires no liquid water whatsoever. It manufactures water from the dry seeds it consumes. Indeed, the *Dipodomys* will even refuse water if offered—a true abstainer that one. The fox, however, kept its eyes on me, and for all the time I was up, I could look out and catch a glimpse of my silent companion pacing the desert night.

For some long, quiet moments the next morning, I lay in the tent as turquoise and pink coral washed over the eastern sky. The dim spider web shadows of gently swaying creosote bushes shifted lazily in the growing light, and by the time I put tires to pavement, the heat was already coming on, a slice of summer in November. The sun at my back, the open empty way of old Route 66 ahead, life was simple, clean, pure. Then Mojo started giving me a little attitude, shifting awkwardly, not popping cleanly up and down as he'd been doing for thousands of miles. Finally, too annoyed at the misfiring index system, I swiveled a button and put the levers in friction mode, not my favorite. *Have to check that out later.*

I climbed towards a narrow, rocky slot in a sharp ridge, passing a wildly graffiti covered ruin on the way—huge white letters on orange background "DUCATI," the expected replica of the Route 66 sign, "Guire rules," and "Blade Chas

SUCKS," which I've heard is, in fact, true. I rolled quickly down from the rocky keyhole and out, out, out into the great empty beyond, vast salty playa, the Bullion and Bristol mountains, big bad basins and rangy ranges. I studied for a moment the view in my rearview mirror, contemplated where I'd been: In the foreground bulged my sweaty forearm, veins and arteries full and pumping, the thick surface vessels actually casting a tan "shadow" that I could see in the right light. I'm a phlebotomist's dreamboat. Above my crooked elbow flapped the bright yellow jersey. Behind, unfurling at 30 mph, the retreating horizon and a road stretching all the way to the coast of Maine. This, too, was a life giving blood vessel, an artery filling my heart, my senses, bringing me into this bright intense life.

Ahead, the town of Amboy marched steadily towards me. Then my shifting failed. Completely. Up and down went the lever for the rear derailleur, but the mechanism didn't get the message, gone AWOL. In too high a gear, I pushed on for the few miles to Amboy where I could deal with the problem—and deal I must. With only three fairly big gears to work with up front, I could easily explode my knees trying to muscle Mojo's fat piggy weight up and out of this valley. The road trended downhill almost all the way to Amboy, so I had no worries of making it to town. Likely I'd simply broken a shifter cable, the only reasonable explanation. Like a good boy scout, I had a spare. Shifter cable, brake cable, spare tires, tubes, and spokes—and the tools to replace them—are essential kit for the cycle tourist. Don't leave home without them. This problem I could handle, but without the simple, basic part, I'd be stuck almost a hundred miles from the nearest bike shop. With the tools and parts, I'd be on my way in the time it takes to say, "Zen and the art of elite recumbent bicycle maintenance."

Amboy of the Zombie Apocalypse was closing in. According to *Route 66 Roy's* website, the town was founded in 1858 to support the nearby salt mining operation but lingered in backcountry obscurity with no good road leading in or out. Route 66 changed that, and during its boom days in the 1950's over 700 people lived here, working in the salt works or providing for the needs of countless drivers coming through. Many were drawn to the Amboy Crater, a volcanic cone just west of town that geologists think may have erupted as late as 500 years ago. Roy opened Roy's Motel and Café in 1938, although the famous sign with the huge red arrowhead pointing down towards the motel was not erected until 1959. When Interstate 40 was completed in 1973, Amboy started to die. When I made my earlier passage on the ride from California to Arizona, the motel, café, and gas station had fallen into disrepair, cracking stucco, blistering paint, dust covering everything. A big chunk had fallen out of the café sign. Two dreamers purchased the town in 2000 for about $700,000. Rumors of using the town for "adult entertainment" film production likely resulted in what many folks claimed were unpleasant experiences when they passed through. Who knows? The town's population was down to seven when it was put up for auction on eBay in 2003. Asking price was $1.9 million, but the property went unsold, the highest bid reaching $990,000. The wife of the original owner repossessed the property in 2005, and, finally, Amboy was sold to Albert Okura, the Japanese-American owner of the Mexican restaurant chain Juan Pollo. He paid $425,000. Now there were some distinct signs of life, even if they were of the living-dead variety. Years before, Jodi and I had met and talked with a one-time resident of Amboy, one who got out alive, sort of.

He called himself Dan, Dan from Amboy, and he approached us with questions about rock climbing, which made sense as we had just descended from a big orange stone in Joshua Tree National Park. He sported a round, floppy hat on his middle-aged head and wore a loose fitting parka and jeans. When he told us where he was from, we yelled out in astonishment. "Oh my God, really?"

"Yes," he said, grinning, clearly delighted in our knowledge at how odd this was. "I lived there two years." Okay, so he wasn't really *from* Amboy. Who was? But we absolutely had to hear his story. It was beer o'clock, and, seeing the chilled beverages, Dan said: "Say, would you trade a beer for some of my art?" From a backpack he pulled several cardboard-matted ink paintings, all the same basic scheme: Swirling indigo and white sky, ghostly mountain skylines and black forests and foliage silhouettes in the foreground—not bad, surprisingly.

"Deal," we said, and I handed a cold one over to the thirsty artist.

"So how did you handle the heat?" asked Jodi.

"I slept in a hammock strung between two trees, put wet towels underneath and on top, and set a frozen gallon water jug on my stomach. By morning the ice was melted and the towels were dry. I got through."

"But what did you *do* there?"

"Worked security for a mine that didn't operate anymore. Owners didn't want it vandalized. So I spent all day in a room keepin' an eye out. That's where I did a lot of drawing. Didn't see a soul."

"What about the people there?" we asked.

"Oh, they're crazy. Everyone gossips about each other. We got a postal worker. We all hate her. Call her 'Shit Lips' on account of some terrible gum disease. It's really gross thinkin' about her lickin' stamps and envelopes. Nobody wants her touchin' their mail."

As he wandered into the evening, Jodi and I commented on how lonely he must be, living such a life. We questioned his relationship with adult beverages, too.

Dan from Amboy was no doubt long gone when I pulled to a stop in the shade of the café/gas station on a limping Mojo. Sure enough, snapped derailleur cable, the frayed ends of the wire dangling free. The good news: The café had a sound and fully nutritious menu: One pint bottles of "Amboy Water"—strange because the natural ground water in the area is poisonous, three kinds of Doritos chips, and Snickers bars, all stored conveniently in a refrigerated case. Hmmmmm, chilly chips on a hot day. What could be better? Yes, the Amboy Café—the *coldest* chips in town. No human brains on ice. Weird. I fixed the cable and soon moved on, pedaling quickly. Rule number one in Zombieland: Cardio.

Late in the afternoon, I topped a long gradual climb out of the Cadiz Valley and looked down on the I 40 corridor. I'd refuel in Ludlow, a typical truck stop, and drag my load out into the desert for the night. I cranked up the Eagles' "Hotel California" on the mp3 player and rolled down the long gentle miles into the valley, leaning back, feet up, cutting sweeping giant slalom turns into the late afternoon shadows..."On a dark desert highway, cool wind in my hair...." It was, in short, magnificent.

"How far have you gone on that thing?" he asked as I dismounted at the Ludlow Dairy Queen. I'd *earned* a milkshake, God damn it.

"About 4,300 miles," I replied. "I started in Maine."

he fellow's eyes bulged. "Man," he cried, "that's what they made these things for!" He gestured towards the cars and trucks in the lot.

"No way," I cried back, "that's what they made *these* for!" I pointed at my rippling thighs. He shook his head and walked way. Some weren't meant to get it this time around. I was reminded of another teacher at my campus who said, in all seriousness, that one couldn't engage in hard exercise after the age of forty. I pitied the man his self-limiting vision. As I took my order, an attractive woman and her male companion asked me about my trip. We engaged in the usual conversation. When she found out where I lived, she tried to set me up with a pretty blond woman she knew who lived in the mountains not far from my home. Milkshake and a date, talk about full service truck stops. I politely declined, explaining that my wife might not understand. "Okay, then," she said, "Carry on." Still, this couple *got* what I was about, although like most people, they pointed out how they "could never do that." I assured them it was all a question of desire. Outside, I guzzled the sweet shocking chocolate chill and rode, pushed and dragged Mojo down a soft sandy road as far as I could to get clear of the highway noise. In the last rays of the sun, I stopped.

Barstow Grotesque
Nov. 9th: 4,434 miles

I am Borg, Velo-man, half bicycle, half human, a 21st century Minotaur. After almost 4,400 miles, who can tell where the bicycle ends and the man begins? Do I exist for the bike or does the bike exist for me? We're an old couple these days, swapping fluids (sweat and chain lube), grinding away the hours in this steady continental crawl. The desert expands and swallows us whole, distance, sand, wind, the chocolate volcanic mountains sawing away on every horizon.

I pushed Mojo up onto the pavement and rode past a lot jammed with big rigs that had clearly been left idling all night, astonishing with gas at over $3.00 per gallon. Lunatics. This day, I would become the Rosa Parks of bicycle tourists. For a long stretch westward towards Barstow, I had two choices: one legal the other not so much. I had traveled the legal road once before, the old Route 66 that parallels I 40, which in every other instance had been the ideal path. Here, however, because of the nearby super highway, the maintenance of the old route had been severely neglected. The once smooth, proud surface had, through the ravages of time, transmogrified into anti-pavement, the Devil's blacktop, the worst of all possible surfaces: strange pressure ridges sticking up about two inches like ornery pack ice that ran across the full width of the road, pot holes to swallow fat children, cracks, splits, gouges, impact craters, grand canyons of erosion and bike riding misery. No, I'd been that way before and never again. I glared at the sign prohibiting bicycles on the interstate and ran down the onramp to my destiny. I paid for this road, and I was going to ride it.

A cool, grey sky kept temperatures mild, and the only officials I saw, a pair of border patrol officers parked in the median, had more important things to do. In less than two hours, I was able to swing back onto Route 66 at Newberry Springs and continue into Barstow, a raunchy clot of development wedged between I 15, I 40, and a heavily used rail line. Whatever you do, stay away from the local McDonalds. About every ten years, something terrible happens there. In 1986, some poor old fellow's car burst into flames in the drive-thru and practically burned the joint to the ground. In 1997, a murderous lunatic came in the back and started shooting, killing a nine-year-old girl before being killed himself by an off-duty cop. The place is overdue for another major catastrophe.

Interstate 15 is the main artery connecting Las Vegas and Los Angeles, so it roars with traffic, especially on weekends. Supported by the floods of travelers, a huge Marine logistics base, and an extensive solar power array to the east, the town at least has all the basics. I had five things to do: 1) Coffee, banana bread and newspaper at Starbucks 2) grocery shopping 3) fuel at an auto parts store 4) library for email and Internet 5) *get the hell out*. The coffee and jazz took some of the edge off the strip mall cacophony, but by the time I hit the library, I was eager to get moving. On my way out, I encountered a wondrous sight, something perhaps never seen by most Americans: A Unimog. These are outrageous four wheel drive trucks first built in post- WWII Germany for agricultural uses but now modeled for military and recreational uses as well. The key features include extraordinary ground clearance—about 18 inches in the case of the vehicle in Barstow, correspondingly huge tires, and blocky, imposing body style. An entire kids' soccer team could easily hide underneath "Wombat," as the owners had stenciled across the top. Unimogs seem to be imported most often by wealthy, adventuresome Europeans hell bent for serious desert travel. This rig sported a huge gray metal camper box that stood far above my 6' 4" head. Massive big rig style gas tanks hung from underneath both sides; a squat cab over the front wheels stood high and mighty. The attitude was pure military assault vehicle, and nothing could be more greatly contrasted against my little bike, also, in this case, of German origin. I took a photo of Mojo in front of this fantastical machine and hit the road. It was getting late.

Sun low, diving towards the horizon, glaring straight into my eyes, blinding me and the traffic closing in, wind pushing back—not good. Too much development, nowhere to camp, too little lunch, lightheaded. *Must stop but gotta keep going.* If I didn't eat something, I was going to bonk, lose it. Frustrated, I pulled into the sand and forced down a Clif Bar and a few fists full of peanuts. Chew, guzzle water, *go.* At last, I got beyond the significant development and began looking for a camp. There, a sandy track into some low hills, a slogging struggle up and away from the road—done. Dark pushed in against these sun and wind blasted slopes where even the creosote bushes seemed unhappy, and they *like* the bowels of hell. Still, it would work for me. I scrambled to get dinner cooking, called Jodi, watched the lights come on in the distant arid flats, listened to the train chug along below, and wandered around the hills and hollows to survey my temporary domain. Wind-blown flotsam and jetsam clung to the low vegetation; here and there empty DVD cases depicted extraordinarily graphic pornography, mano-a-mano, dude-on-bro, babe-on-dude, the usual mixing and matching of randy primates. I found it all rather sad and bizarre.

When the darkness was complete, my foxy friend returned, this time coming so close as to put a tentative paw on the tarp not four feet away. We could be genuine pals, he and I. The fox's curiosity made me think about the first dog and the first person to take up together, a relationship dating back at least 10,000 years. I did not choose the fox. The fox chose me. Clearly we were meant for each other, and I slept better knowing it was out there, keeping watch. The eyes of the desert studied me as I crawled into my nylon burrow and waited for the sun.

Crossing the Antelope
Nov. 10th—12th: 4,545 miles

At 3:23PM on November 10th, I topped the last hill for the day, and, for the first time in over three months, rested my eyes on the mountains of home, the massive Tehachapi range, the hook at the bottom of the Sierras that formed a stout forested wall jutting out of the desert. So close. Jodi was up there. I descended rapidly into the angular light, and on the eastern edge of the Antelope Valley, I camped in Saddleback Butte State Park after almost sixty five miles of effort across open country. I had to contend with windy conditions, but, thankfully, nothing brutal. I knew a weather system was coming, however, and my plan was to be resting on the day it did most of its mischief.

I had followed a long curving stretch of Route 66 past the bottle tree forest, a yard with metal trees, their branches capped by hundreds of bottles—red, green, brown, and clear jewels in the sun. Classic American weirdness. I rolled silently below a large cement plant, immense cranes, conveyor belts, and space dome holding back the pollution. From Victorville, my route headed due west across sections of rudely split pavement I termed "Mojave cobbles"—so quaint—and into gently climbing terrain. As I ascended, I entered the Joshua tree zone, a plant the "Pathfinder" John C. Freemont called, "The most repulsive tree in the vegetable kingdom!" I always liked their strange, contorted forms, the arms, supposedly, evocative of Joshua praying to the Lord.

And so the storm came to pass. On my rest day, as I was safely tucked in behind a wind shelter, the storm moved through. A rim of clouds in the western sky thickened and congealed, beat the sky black and blue-grey until the San Gabriel Mountains to the south were smothered in a fast moving wall. The winds sharpened, and I was grateful for my banging plywood barrier. Since every campsite had a windbreak facing the same direction, the prevailing conditions were clear enough. Clouds of dust filled the air and deposited a fine grit over everything. Twice that day I was visited by Craig from a nearby town. We talked bikes and life—what else? Another road angel, he even brought me a map to assist my navigation of the wilds of Lancaster, a crime-infested burg in the lawless border region of Los Angeles County, a city intent on spreading the love. People moved out of the city to escape the crime and expensive real estate. At least the housing prices were lower. Out-of-the-way places attract out-of-the-ordinary people. For Lancaster in 1971, this meant Charles K. Johnson, a man on a mission, a mission to stamp out once and for all the notion that the world is round. For thirty years, Chuck held high the beacon of truth and light for the Flat Earth Society, which, under his sure hand, grew to 3,000 members. Through their donations, he was able to publish *The Flat Earth News*, featuring ground-breaking articles like "Galileo Was a Liar," "Science Insults Your Intelligence," and "The Earth is Not a Ball; Gravity Does Not Exist." In one newsletter he wrote: "'Science' consists of a weird, way-out occult concoction of gibberish theory-theology...unrelated to the real world of facts, technology and inventions, tall buildings and fast cars, airplanes and other Real and Good things in life." That's a show stopper. When Johnson died, the society faded but was resurrected by Daniel Shenton, an American living in London, when he was inspired by the Thomas Dolby album *The Flat Earth*. Who can make up such stories?

My ride into Lancaster was more than I could have hoped—clear, quiet, a pleasant tailwind. I sailed the creosote seas at nearly 20 mph for many miles. All the while, I kept looking over at the Tehachapi Mountains, my home only a long day's ride away. Would I ride off the edge of this flat earth before I reached home? Lancaster is a typical example of the expanding desert communities all over the West. For all the fretting and hand-wringing about a housing slump, this placed seemed to be on full bore development—stucco and tile ticky-tacky ad infinitum. I feared for my sweet Leona Valley and what open space remained. With limited water, how could the development continue? A long stretch of steady riding took me at last to the wind-blown regions to the west. Plains of long dead grasses and low, scruffy vegetation dominated the landscape just beyond the final "Notice of Development" signs as I escaped the houses spreading across the land like a hot oil slick.

The clear dome of the sky met the mountains to the south, west and north, no trace of smoke or haze or bad attitudes to obscure the outlines or dull the details of color and form. My home peaks swept up almost 5,000 ft. from the valley floor. The long ridge to my south was not nearly as high, but I would climb over 1,000 ft. even so. Effort, strain, distance, every view worth having extracts its price. I camped in the embracing arms of the San Andreas Fault, the tectonic crease whereby California will at last be shed from the mainland. I slept below huge oaks and a smattering of grey pines, a spot familiar to me from previous rides.

I pushed on the next day through hills of startling steepness, but I was hardened to the mountains at this point, so no hill was too much. As I looked over at my home, I expected to be more annoyed or conflicted or *something* about being so close and not simply riding home, but this was a game, and games have rules—in this case to reach the Pacific, to conclude my quest. To go home before achieving that would dilute the experience, corrupt the narrative, for each journey has a natural arc or flow. In my story, a stop-over at home, besides requiring lots of extra miles, would amount to an unacceptable plot malfunction. Home, Jodi, all of that was for the absolute end of the trek. Now, the protagonist had to continue alone, see it through, however it might end.

In Frazier Park, a rough mountain town at 4,600 ft., I made a brief blog post and looked about for a place to camp. Everywhere I turned, everyone I talked to seemed to shut me down. I was in town early, however, hardly past lunch. Why stop? The sun was high, the mountains calling. *Keep riding and see what the road provides*. Climbing still, over 4,000 ft. for the day, I grunted out of town and towards the National Forest. Outside of Lake of the Woods (where's the lake?), I took the first promising dirt track and galloped Mojo up into the trees—success! My last wild camp would be wild, in the pines, my tent pitched beside Mojo.

My final camping meal consisted of hot chai and cold sandwiches—canned salmon, avocado, wheat bread, mustard. I needed to eat through the last of my food, so I sat in the dark forest and munched sandwiches. I was out of sight from the road but not the air. A Forest Service helicopter trailing a massive water bucket made some passes, and I instinctively whipped off my bright windbreaker. No rangers came calling, and as the night settled down, the chopper landed for good; the stars came out, and I faced the end of my journey—excited, anxious, happy. I lay there and thought about all the miles I'd covered, the days and weeks and months, now, of riding. How could I be so near the end? How could this be? The next day I would stand on a high pass almost a mile in the sky and look down on the sea. Would it be enough when I reached it?

The wind sighed in the tall pines that overhung my camp. An occasional car rumbled by, the drivers oblivious to my presence. Soon, the cars stopped coming, and only the stars were my companions.

When I reach the ocean, when at long last and finally I reach the ocean, will it be enough, when I reach the ocean?

Galumphing unto Zion
Nov. 13th—15th: 4,662 miles

The mountain wall of the coast range blocked any view to the west, rising as it did in a 1,500 ft. wave. Highway 33 snaked and twisted out of sight, up, always up until it wasn't always up. Then it would be down, always down—a Zen koan road. What had the cyclist in Gorman called it? "A terrible climb"? No, it was a beautiful climb. I didn't have the heart to tell him that I didn't find it that difficult, especially now, after crossing a continent. This was my second time around, and I wasn't worried. A good steady piece of work is all. Recent burns in the area detracted from the beauty, but much of the character remained. My end-of-the-tour high would not be dimmed. I geared down and winched my way into the sky.

The first, highest summit marked the penultimate climb. From my previous ride in this country, I knew one significant climb remained. Fittingly, I would not be free until I could see the ocean. Knowing it was there over the next ridge wouldn't do it. From Pine Mtn. Summit, almost a mile up, I flew in grinning joy down into sycamore-lined canyons, through narrows of glowering stone, under rock towers warm in the afternoon sun. My enchanted descent rivaled any on the continent.

Then I stood at the bottom of the last climb. I parked in the shade of a deep road cut and took a break, ate and drank, chewed on my thoughts and drank in my conflicting emotions, the stillness, the perfect autumn sky. The mountain wouldn't climb itself. I couldn't wait forever. This thing had to end. I clipped in and pedaled for the top. *This is my last climb, my last mountain pass, the final miles of a dream.*

I did not remember every turn, every corner. Was this it? This? *This? No. Still more. Good. Don't finish. Never finish. The ride goes on forever. Life is the ride, the ride is life.* Then a gap, only blue sky beyond, a break in the ridge, a turn in the road, a staggering drop down and down and down through convolutions of tilted earth and folded canyon out to a blinding mirror laid flat between the coast and the Channel Islands...the Pacific Ocean, the far side of the continental plate. I reined in Mojo at the very edge of the abyss and climbed off. *Damn it all to hell, Scotty! That's the Pacific-freakin'-ocean! Land's end! You've done it. You've done it...You've done it....*

I punched the air. I yelled. I cursed and sang and danced a cyclist's happy dance in the dirt at the edge of the world. *You've done it.* Anyone seeing me from afar would assume mental illness, a schizophrenic plugged into his voices again. And they would be right. I was mad, insane, possessed by voices of delight, relief, joy, a divine madness I wished on all of humanity. I sat down beside Mojo and ate lunch and looked out over the other side of my country, a view almost one hundred days from where I'd begun to ride.

Then I let gravity take over, an addiction, a high-grade narcotic, speed and corners, leaning out over the edge, pulling back, leaning out once more, the brakes whirring a song of restraint then letting go. *Let it go. Let it go. Everything? All of it. Let it go.* The sublime serpent of Highway 33 uncoiled beneath my tires, releasing me from the journey, the quest, the first half of my earthly life. The wind roared in my head and the road took me out into who I was to become. No regrets, no turning back. I rolled and rolled and rolled into the arms of Zion.

I stayed the night in Ojai with a fine host named Val. The last road angel of my epic, he opened his home and gave me refuge. We talked of my trip, his life, Ojai, but I was in a different place, a limbo of spirit, incredulous, stunned. How could this be the end? How could it ever end? Wasn't there another state, another mountain range? What's that next time zone? Keep pushing, keep pushing.

But when I climbed from bed after a fitful night, no struggle remained. I had no need to push. The ocean broke on the sand fifteen miles away—down slope. A quiet bike path separated me from the water, my wife, the life I'd left behind. Jodi was on her way. Django would be there. It was time to finish.

I took the final miles very slowly, hardly pedaling most of the time. I let the chill of the shadows ache in my fingers. I needed to feel everything. Slowly, slowly. The path curved gently between creek and road, trees and ridges that now and then blocked the sun. Cyclists passed with no idea where I had started my ride. I was just another lanky fool on a goofy bike. Perhaps they smiled, but I moved on, propelled by my private knowledge, a secret imperative. Each pedal stroke, every breath, kilometer after kilometer counted down, brought me closer. This was not Zeno's tour. I would reach the end. I rolled as if in a tunnel, a path that cradled me from coast to coast, images of the beginning playing across my mind. *The plane is just coming in from Boston. The clouds roil with my stomach. There is talk of not landing in Bar Harbor at all—but we do. Grey, damp, strange, in my foggy nausea, I stagger from the plane and search for my bags. Somewhere nearby the Atlantic waits for me. Good God, what have I done?! You can't do this, Scotty. But you've got to. You can't start. You can't finish. The dragon tightens around my gut and squeezes.* Then I turned, a palm tree, a highway underpass, a final strip of bike path, then sand, the ocean wind, surfers cutting turns. The Pacific in its salty glory curled and rumbled a hundred yards away.

I called Jodi on the cell phone. She was here! I pedaled the short distance down the beach and found her with Django and the car. Jodi's shock of tight black curls, her slim, muscular body—that was her all right. Django looked up when I rang my bell. His whole body wagged as he ran towards me. His dark fur glowed in the sun. I rubbed him all over with a ferocious joy. And when I stood up and at last held Jodi in my arms, I knew I was home and that my long ride across the country was over. It was indeed enough and more than I could have ever dreamed.

Appendix: Gearhead Prattle

Choosing a bike:

This has been a long and expensive path for me--lots of fun but lots of cash. Recumbents aren't cheap, and I have a penchant for nice gear. It's tough to select the right bike the first time, and then there's the issue of RBA, "recumbent bicycle addiction"--no known cure. One just has to let the disease run its course. I did a little touring on a conventional bike and found the experience deeply uncomfortable, lots of numb bits and the enduring joy of saddle sores. I recently came across two anecdotes that underscore these shortcomings of conventional touring bikes: One fellow developed a severe, deeply buried blister/saddle sore that required surgery to drain. Good grief. This ended his tour. Another rider successfully crossed the country but, twenty years later, STILL has nerve damage in his hands from the constant pressure and jarring he experienced. Clearly, something is wrong with the conventional diamond frame bike as a touring platform. To be fair, many riders "toughen up" to the point where they are reasonably comfortable, but many (most?) do a lot of complaining about discomfort even so. Time to chuck the old "wedgie," as recumbent riders call conventional bikes.

The recumbent platform makes a variety of steering layouts possible. The Phantom, my first recumbent, is controlled with over seat steering (OSS). However, one can also have under seat steering (USS). This second style is, for me, ergonomic nirvana. Totally relaxed and perfect for all-day riding. Absolutely no numbness possible. The wide, reclined seats eliminate sore spots on the butt. No saddle sores possible.

C'mon, there must be some drawbacks, yes? Nothing is perfect, is it? True, recumbents are not without their problems, but given the variety of configurations possible, there is a 'bent for everyone. In no particular order, here is a list of the main problems I've encountered:

1) Recumbent butt: This is a condition where the muscles of one's behind get quite painful during the course of a ride. In many cases, this is at first the result of poorly adapted muscles in the new riding position. Just riding more will solve the issue. In other cases, the relative position of the pedals (bottom bracket) to the seat can be the cause. I have discovered that, for me, low bottom brackets and upright seating, as found on the Tour Easy (see p. 343), leads to pretty painful R-butt. I just could not adapt to this riding position. I loved the bike, but it didn't work for my particular body. I need a higher pedal position and more reclined seat. Sometimes, a change in seat padding will solve the problem, too. For me, the question is more about body positioning.

2) Numb toes: Some riders find that they get numb toes after periods of riding, especially with higher bottom bracket configurations. I am one of these riders. This is not much of a problem for me, however, and takes some time to set in during a ride. Just a few moments off the bike, and my symptoms are gone. Hot weather makes this condition worse. For some, changing pedals, cleat position, insoles and the like can help or eliminate the problem. Looser fitting shoes do help.

3) Sore knees: Because a recumbent rider can apply more pressure to the pedals than on conventional bikes (leg press supported by seat) and because the pedal stroke is always the same (no standing on the pedals), recumbent riders can be subject to knee stress that they might not experience on conventional bikes. There are some important considerations here to avoid or deal with this problem. First, recumbent riders must use lower gears and put a lot of emphasis on "spinning," i.e. using high RPM, low pressure on the pedals. This translates into about 90 RPMs or so most of the time. Pushing too hard results in serious repetitive stress. Shift down, shift early. Keep the pressure light. Gears

are the key here. Most recumbents tend to come with gearing too high for comfortable riding in hilly or mountainous terrain. In general, most riders will want a low gear in front of about 24 teeth and a rear cassette of no less than 11 to 32 teeth--11/34 is better. In general, you won't be unhappy having lower gears, especially when the load is heavy and the climb never seems to end. Also, take time getting into bent shape. New muscles take time to adapt. We've only got one set of knees each. Take care.

4) Speed: In general, recumbents tend to be a little slower in hill climbing than conventional bikes, although super-light, fast recumbents are available. In touring, however, I've found my speeds tend to be, on average, average, i.e. 10—15 mph most days. Comfort and seeing the country are the main concerns. Speed is not. For those who want to travel quickly, the automotive, rail, and airline industries are happy to take your money.

5) Recumbent grin: This is another chronic issue without a cure. Once you've got the right bike perfectly adjusted, you ride around with this stupid grin on your face almost all the time.

Other recumbent considerations: Besides steering, one must consider a couple of other factors. Because recumbent tricycles are so wonderful (and growing in popularity), I had to look at those, too. They're great fun, super stable, and make excellent touring rigs. I enjoy touring on both platforms, but bikes are a good deal faster, which often times doesn't matter, but I can average 3 to 4 mph faster on a two wheeler. That kind of speed difference really adds up over the course of a day, a week, three months crossing a continent. So for this tour, it was two wheels for me. Another advantage of two wheels is the ability to slip the bike into obscure camping spots that might be inaccessible with a wider tricycle.

    With recumbent bicycles, another major factor is the wheel base, basically long and short. There is a mid-length size called a "compact long wheel base," but it's still long. How do these compare to conventional diamond frame bikes? In general, short wheel base (SWB) is identical or a little longer than standard bikes--between 39 (rare) and 47 inches. My SWB is about 42 inches. Long wheel base (LWB) can range up to 70+ inches, real Cadillacs. Besides my need for a higher bottom bracket (a few LWB's have fairly high pedals), I went with the SWB layout because of the ergonomics of the handle bars, the sporty feel of a shorter bike, and the fact that I can put my bike on conventional transit bus racks. This last concern is significant for me because I often ride a 44 mile one-way commute to my job. Coming home up the mountain is a huge undertaking and one I rarely have the time for, but I can ride down, get a good-but-not-extreme workout, and then take the bus home, a perfect arrangement. If taking public transit is one of your concerns, LWB's are out as well as any SWB's with a wheel base beyond 42 inches or so. A final point is that, in general, SWB's tend to climb a bit better than LWB's. The shorter wheel base means they handle better at low speeds, and the higher bottom bracket translates into better power. I climbed many big hills on my Tour Easy (LWB), but the steeper they get, the more I appreciate a SWB.

So, when I finally took the plunge and decided to ride the big ride, I came to the conclusion that a new bike was needed to properly honor the event. I'd always had a desire for a sleek, European recumbent, so HP Velotechnik was the obvious choice. The company optimizes its designs for utility, especially touring. The Street Machine is famous for durability and comfort. My Street Machine was purchased from Bent Up Cycles in North Hollywood, California. Dana, the owner, did a fantastic job and is a pleasure to work with. He's always eager to help customize and make that perfect bike. He's one of the biggest HPVelo dealers in the country.

I toured a little on a conventional bike some years ago. The experience was acceptable but for the usual discomfort of diamond frame bikes. I did not really become a cycle tourist until I started riding recumbents. I've toured on several different types of "bents" so far:

Tour Easy:

Haluzak Horizon with trailer:

Catrike Expedition:

Greenspeed tandem:

As you can see, the Greenspeed has a little of everything. We added the trailer for our faithful hound, Django, who trots alongside when the hills go up. This is a slow rig for a host of reasons, but it's a fine touring platform nonetheless.

Panniers vs. trailers:

My principle experience towing a trailer on a single bike comes from a tour I did across California and Arizona. As pictured on page 343, I pulled a Burley Nomad behind my Haluzak Horizon. The trailer performed flawlessly and offered a few nice advantages: First, it packed easily, and once you popped the cover, everything was easy to find, just like a suitcase; second, when I parked to go shopping, and I was nervous about leaving it unattended, I could easily unhook the unit and drag it with me into the store whilst I procured my kippers and beer; third, it seemed to encourage a bit wider berth on the part of passing motorists. The wider, strange stance might have had something to do with it. And, least of all, it is kind of cute.

So why am I a currently confirmed pannier man? Weight, drag, and complexity. The trailer has all three. There's no doubt. It is a load of hardware to drag around. It's a bit bulky; the wheels provide some resistance on the pavement, and the tires can go flat—though I've experienced only one flat on the Burley and that on a training run. Although the handling of the bike isn't really affected, there is a bit of noise and hassle moving it around at times. Think of driving a car with a trailer and scale back to bicycle size. Turnarounds in tight places can be a chore as well as fitting between tight objects, such as trees, barriers to paths, etc. Ultimately, however, I kept coming back to the weight issue. The trailer, without extra tubes, checks in at about 14 lbs. Now, regular racks and panniers do weigh something and offset the difference somewhat, but I've found the ultimate solution.

The recumbent bicycle offers some serious benefits for touring. In terms of load carrying, one can fit bags under the seat and between the wheels, lowering the center of gravity and leaving the handling of the bike virtually unchanged. See the Tour Easy photo on page 343. That beast, fully loaded for that winter tour in the desert, probably weighed about 80 or 90 lbs, especially with food and water (slosh, slosh). It handled perfectly. Now that I ride short wheel base recumbents, I've found the final solution: Radical Designs bags made in Holland. Although my Street Machine can handle an under seat rack, these bags make it unnecessary. The load is still carried fairly low and forward and in a very aerodynamic shape, fitting virtually in the shadow of my legs and torso. Don't underestimate the value of a slippery design. Wind is a drag, especially a stout headwind that saps the legs and spirit on a long day in the saddle. The power of the recumbent position with these bags was driven home to me on a tour down the California coast. I was leading a couple of European cyclists through the wilds south of Santa Cruz when we topped a short climb. I, just a little ahead, eased over the top and simply left them in the dust, vanishing specks in my rear view mirror. I did not pedal. All this talk of aerodynamics my sound silly to the uninitiated: *Dude, like, you're on a bike, dude, going, like, really slow.* Certainly, we travel more slowly than cars, motorcycles and fighter jets, but cyclists battle the elements in a more meaningful way. Every ounce of drag from a headwind is an ounce of power that must be supplied by the intrepid adventurer's legs. Chrysler and BMW do not provide the power plant. Mile after mile, hour after hour, little improvements can add up to a big difference. Another very nice feature of the Radical bags is that they require no hooks or tightening straps. One just drapes the bags over seat and rear rack and presto, tour ready are we. And the weight? I save more than **TEN POUNDS**.

I had the interesting pleasure of riding my Haluzak Horizon in both configurations: With trailer as featured on page 343 and with a medium-sized set of Radical panniers on the facing page. This is what nailed the choice for me. It's just a tight package that was a pleasure to ride.

Here's the 'Zak with panniers. These mediums were a little small, so I lashed my tent and pad to the sides of the seat:

Each rider will chose for himself what suits his personal style of riding and tastes. Just call me a Radical Pannier Man.

Mojo loaded for bear:

In this picture, the panniers are set too far back, a mistake I quickly corrected. Properly set, the front ends of the bags are about even with the bottom of the seat. This provides ready access to maps and other goodies in the mesh pockets clearly visible.

The tent:

Although it is possible to get by with only a waterproof tarp, the prevalence of mosquitoes and other insects in many areas make a good tent a very important piece of gear. There are many, many to choose from. For solo outings or when I want my own space with other riders, I prefer a single person tent. My choice for this tour was the Light Year by Sierra Designs. It checks in at less than four pounds, pitches with only three stakes, and provided excellent shelter. I'll have it for many years.

The sleeping bag:

Lightweight and compact are the key concerns. For much of the tour, I could have done well with a lighter bag, but this tour involved the hot Midwest and sub-freezing temperatures in the Rockies, so I needed a versatile bag. I went with a "Sub-kilo" down mummy bag by REI. As the title suggests, the weight is about two pounds, but with the high quality down, it was rated to 20 deg. F., a limit I flirted with several times on the tour. The only drawback to down, besides the added expense, is that it dries slowly when wet, so it's imperative to keep it dry. This model stuffed down to about the size of a football—an American football, that is.

The sleeping pad:

I'm a fanatic about sleeping as well as possible, so I don't skimp with the tent, bag or pad. I carried a deluxe two inch thick Thermarest self-inflating pad, which I placed in a special cover that converts into a chair using carbon fiber stays and straps—awesomely comfortable. This is a heavy arrangement, over two pounds, but worth it to me. I often see cyclists with very thin, non-inflating pads, and I wish I could tolerate such pads. After the age of nineteen, I could no longer sleep on a half-inch thick pad. There are many different brands and models of pads to choose from. I have been using a Big Agnes 2.5" thick air mattress, which is a chore to inflate but heaven to sleep on. Although it has the advantage of being lighter and more compact than the Thermarest, I've had three spring leaks along the seams, so I've abandoned this make. I'm currently exploring the Swiss Exped line of air mattresses with built-in pumps. All the inflatable pads can be punctured, so great care must be taken when you pitch camp.

The stove:

This is a vast and contentious topic as the variety out there is incredible. Basically, for backpacking and bike touring, there are three types: 1) Canister, compressed gas stoves usually running on a propane/butane blend 2) manually pressurized liquid gas stoves running on white gas, unleaded gasoline, and kerosene 3) unpressurized alcohol stoves such as the Swedish Trangia stoves and, what I used, the "Pepsi can" stove. As with everything, each has its good and bad points.

Canister stoves, such as Bluet, Jet Boil, and others, tend to be very compact, light instantly, and simmer beautifully, but the fuel is expensive, sometimes impossible to find, and for this reason these stoves tend to not work well for extended treks. For shorter trips up to a week or so, I've enjoyed this design.

Manually pressurized stoves, like the many in the MSR line such as the Whisperlite and XGK, are solid performers and usually work better in very cold conditions. Some models work well with unleaded gasoline, which is a huge benefit in long distance touring, and those models that burn kerosene can be very useful in remote, Third World countries. Some simmer better than others. When you have to cook for more than one person and want the heat and power of a serious stove, these are often the best way to go. Models that burn unleaded gasoline run on the cheapest fuel available.

Unpressurized alcohol stoves have a special place in the heart of lightweight fanatics around the world. These run on denatured or methyl alcohol and require no pumping or priming. They have virtually no moving parts and burn silently. When I read about the Pepsi can stove, I had to try and build one. On a training ride one day, I kept passing discarded cans along the road. I loaded up a few into my rack bag and took them home. A few minutes searching for instructions on the Internet turned up the necessary information. The stove worked brilliantly. It weighs hardly an ounce. When I go solo, this is usually my first choice.

The clothing:

Utility, lightweight, and durability are key functions here. Some cotton is okay, but it tends to dry very slowly, so for wet or very sweaty conditions, it should be avoided. Various synthetic blends are usually the best choices. I carried light cotton briefs that dried quickly, cotton t-shirt for off the bike, and a couple of cotton bandanas for cleaning chores. Everything else had a synthetic base—jerseys, long underwear, pants, rain gear, polar fleece sweater, gloves—everything.

The electronics:

What each tourist carries will be an idiosyncratic choice. It wasn't long ago that virtually no such gadgets were available, yet many people cycled across the country—no cell phones, no gps, no laptops, nothing. Because everything adds weight, each piece of kit selected must be carefully considered. Many a novice bike tourist has cancelled a tour or spent time and money shipping stuff home she wished she'd never carried in the first place. I carried three widgets:

tiny mp3 player (which runs on AAA batteries), a cell phone and charger, and a digital camera with charger. The camera was a Canon A540, which I picked because of its hand-filling size and the ability to run on AA batteries, just in case. When touring on paved roads in North America, having standard sized batteries is probably not necessary. I found many opportunities when I could have recharged a specialized battery for a more compact camera. The camera, however, functioned flawlessly, even—the horror!—after dropping into a urinal in Pueblo, Colorado. (Not much liquid.)

On future tours, I will consider—and probably reject—carrying a netbook. Although it would be nice to compose blogs and such on a computer, the weight and bulk penalties are significant, not to mention keeping it charged. Still, I know many who do carry such kit and do so happily. To each his own. Who knows what I'll carry next time?

Acknowledgements

The tour and this book would not have been possible without a lot of encouragement and support. The bike and related cycling gear were purchased from Dana Lieberman, owner of Bent Up Cycles in North Hollywood, California. Dana, you're a great drug—er—bike dealer, and I couldn't have done this without you. You keep my cycling addiction running strong. I owe massive thanks to my employer, colleagues, and supervisors at Bakersfield College who provide amazing professional support and the time to pursue my dreams, in cycling and writing. *Createspace.com* has made the formatting and publication of this book possible, even for a bumbler like me. I have to thank the American people for their generosity and kindness—and for not running me over. Lastly and most importantly, I have to thank my wife, Jodi. You hung in there, tolerated listening to all the rough drafts, and kicked me in the pants when I needed it. I couldn't do much of anything without you. Make no mistake: Any errors are all mine. Excerpt from *Abbey's Road* is reprinted with the permission of Don Congdon Associates, Inc. © 1979 by Edward Abbey. Excerpts from The Cantor Law Group News and Jack Becker web pages used with permission.

About the Author

Scott Wayland teaches English at Bakersfield College in Bakersfield, California. When he's not stalking the classroom like a crazed animal, he lives with his wife and their annoying animals in the mountains of Tehachapi. He's plotting another adventure even now....

For color photographs, some video, and the raw blog composed hot on the road:
> http://scott-findinghome.blogspot.com/

24808948R00197

Made in the USA
San Bernardino, CA
07 February 2019